JULIA KRISTEVA Interviews

D1604305

European Perspectives

EUROPEAN PERSPECTIVES

A Series in Social Thought and Cultural Criticism

Lawrence D. Kritzman, Editor

European Perspectives presents English translations of books by leading European thinkers. With both classic and outstanding contemporary works, the series aims to shape the major intellectual controversies of our day and to facilitate the tasks of historical understanding.

JULIA KRISTEVA Interviews

Edited by Ross Mitchell Guberman

Columbia University Press   NEW YORK

Columbia University Press

Publishers Since 1893

New York   Chichester, West Sussex

Copyright © 1996 Columbia University Press

All rights reserved

Library of Congress Cataloging-in-Publication Data

Kristeva, Julia, 1941–
  Julia Kristeva interviews / edited by Ross Mitchell Guberman.
    p.   cm.—(European perspectives)
  Includes bibliographical references and index.
  ISBN 0–231–10486–3 (cloth). — ISBN 0–231–10487–1 (paper)
  1. Kristeva, Julia, 1941– —Interviews. 2. Authors,
French—20th century—interviews.   I. Guberman, Ross Mitchell.
II. Title.
PQ2671.R547Z467   1996
801'.95'092—dc20   96–10589
                                                      CIP

Casebound editions of Columbia University Press books are printed on permanent and durable acid-free paper.

Designed by Linda Secondari

Printed in the United States of America

c 10 9 8 7 6 5 4 3 2 1

p 10 9 8 7 6 5 4 3 2 1

Contents

Perspectives

Acknowledgments

Grateful acknowledgment is made to the following for permission to reprint previously published material:

For "Julia Kristeva in Person," L'Institut National de l'Audiovisuel; for "Intellectual Roots," "Feminism and Psychoanalysis," and "Psychoanalysis and Politics," *Partisan Review*; for "A Conversation with Julia Kristeva," *Critical Texts*; for "Cultural Strangeness and the Subject in Crisis," *Discourse*; for "The Ethics and Practice of Love" and " 'unes femmes': The Woman Effect," *Les Cahiers du GRIF*; for "Melancholia and Creation," *Magazine littéraire*; for "On *New Maladies of the Soul*" and "On Céline: Music and the 'Blunder,' " *Art Press International*; for "Woman Is Never What We Say," "Interview: *The Old Man and the Wolves*," and "On *The Samurai*," *L'Infini*; for "Women and Literary Institutions" and the translation of "Interview: *The Old Man and the Wolves*," Columbia University Press; for "Memories of Sofia," *Le Nouvel observateur*; for "General Principles in Semiotics," *Etudes littéraires*; for "Intertextuality and Literary Interpretation," the Johns Hopkins University Press; for "Avant-Garde Practice," *Textual Practice*; and for "Proust: A Search for Our Time," *L'Humanité*.

I would also like to thank Jennifer Crewe, my editor at Columbia University Press, for graciously guiding me through two major book translations as well as the present undertaking.

Finally, I would like to express my deepest gratitude to Julia Kristeva, an unparalleled teacher, mentor, and thinker. She collaborated with me on the entire project and gave generously of her time and support.

If there is something original about me, I believe it lies in the totality of my existence: the existence of a female intellectual. Born in the Balkans during World War II, having learned French as a second language at a fairly young age, passionately interested in mathematics and astronomy, and then attracted to the human enigma—medicine and literature, choosing literature in the end, exiled in France to carry out this investigation, adopted by a universalist intelligentsia at the height of structuralism and poststructuralism, a lover, a wife, a mother, trying to think about the joy and distress that did not spare me during these states, trying to write about them. . . . Roland Barthes defined this adventure very early on as that of a 'foreigner,' and he was right.

—*"Julia Kristeva Speaks Out"*

Editor's Introduction

This book contains twenty-three of Julia Kristeva's most provocative interviews. The first of its kind to appear in any language, it is intended for three types of readers. First, for those who are unfamiliar with Kristeva's writings or who have been daunted by their difficulty, this collection provides a stimulating introduction to her complex and controversial views. The interviews included here will expose such readers to Kristeva's work on language, literature, feminism, and politics, to her novels and cultural criticism, and, perhaps most important, to her warmth, humor, and humanity. Readers will also be able to trace her work from her early theoretical studies through her two major "shifts" of focus (from linguistics to psychoanalysis and from psychoanalysis to fiction) and then on to her more recent ventures into sensation, neuroscience, and cultural criticism. For those who wish to continue their study of Kristeva's work, further readings are suggested in the notes and compiled in the bibliography.

Second, for scholars in such fields as linguistics, religion, aesthetics, women's studies, and psychoanalysis who find that Kristeva's is always a voice to be reckoned with, the interviews gathered here offer a rich resource for study and research. From semanalysis to *The Samurai* and from feminism to poetry and Proust, these conversations cover all areas of Kristeva's work and offer a medley of styles and approaches. They also present clear and lucid discussions of some of Kristeva's difficult and often misunderstood notions, including "crisis," "abjection," "intertextuality," the "semiotic" and the "symbolic," and the effect of aesthetic revolution on social change. Scholars will further appreciate Kristeva's candid remarks on her life and background and on timely political and philosophical issues.

Finally, for critics who have hastily labeled or categorized Kristeva, or have even dismissed her, this book offers a challenge. A careful reading of these interviews precludes any reduction of her work to facile maxims.[1] The portrait painted here is one that resists description; it depicts a thinker whose work seeks precisely to question notions of group identity as well as rigid systems of classification. It is my hope that these skeptical readers will put aside any preconceived ideas about Kristeva's political or ideological "suitability" and read her as she deserves to be read—on her own terms. Kristeva's ease with interview format and her well-reasoned and enlightening explanations of her beliefs should help clear up certain mischaracterizations of her work.

I chose the twenty-three interviews in this book from the more than fifty that Kristeva has given. Thirteen of the interviews were translated by me, and the others were translated either by the interviewer or by a third party. I have corrected typographical errors when necessary and have made some other minor changes. Although many of the interviews defy categorization, they have been placed into general thematic groups for the reader's convenience. Each interview is preceded by an introduction that provides, when available, the names of the interviewer or interviewers, the date, location, and publication history of the interview, the name of the translator, and some general expository remarks. The bibliography provides complete publication information for all previously published interviews as well as for other works mentioned. In the body of the interviews, I have often added notes that provide additional information, and I have reprinted the notes supplied by the interviewers themselves.

Kristeva describes herself in these pages as "polyvalent" and "intertextual," and the responses she gives to her interviewers often function as a true "text," as a "mosaic of citations" combining philosophy, literature, autobiography, history, and social commentary. At the same time, Kristeva's major writings and theories provide a constant point of reference, and I have tried to include interviews that complement and build upon her best known works. The basis for "semanalysis," the psychosemiological approach Kristeva outlines in *Séméiotiké* and *Polylogue*,[2] is addressed in an interview entitled "General Principles in Semiotics." The theory of avant-garde practice she develops in *Revolution in Poetic Language*, moreover, is discussed at length in interviews with Vassiliki Kolocotroni and with Andrea Loselle and Ina

Lipkowitz. Kristeva's "trio" of psychoanalytic books written in the 1980s is also well accounted for: *Tales of Love* by an extensive interview with Françoise Collin, *Powers of Horror* by an interview on Céline and by a discussion of "abjection" in the interview with Elaine Hoffman Baruch, and *Black Sun* by an interview on melancholia and creation and by an interview with Margaret Waller. As for the sociopolitical books of the early 1990s, Kristeva discusses *Strangers to Ourselves* in an interview with Suzanne Clark and Kathleen Hulley and takes up some issues raised in *Nations Without Nationalism* in an interview with Edith Kurzweil. I have also included interviews based on Kristeva's first two novels, *The Samurai* and *The Old Man and the Wolves*, as well as interviews that outline the major premises of her two most recent theoretical and psychoanalytic studies, *New Maladies of the Soul* and *Time and Sense: Proust and the Experience of Literature*. Many of these interviews contain ideas and material not found in Kristeva's books, and her explanations display pedagogical gifts that are often obscured in her formal writings.

Also of broad appeal are Kristeva's autobiographical notes—childhood memories of Bulgaria, revealing accounts of the Tel Quel group in the 1960s and 1970s and of time spent in the United States, and reflections on what psychoanalysis and fiction writing have meant for her. Similarly, Kristeva offers incisive commentaries on some of the major intellectual currents of our time, including existentialism, formalism, structuralism, deconstruction, and, more generally, "poststructuralism," which she discusses in a closing interview with me. Scholars in the United States will also be interested in Kristeva's provocative remarks on the American literary academy.

Readers already familiar with Kristeva's writings will not be surprised to find two other recurring themes. The first, of course, is *psychoanalysis*, which Kristeva describes at different points in these pages as a discourse of meaning, a transformative force, a source of subjective freedom, a form of political commitment in its own right, a "lover's discourse," a "fusion of practice and theory," and a model for "desirable dependency." An important subtext of Kristeva's remarks on psychoanalysis is her discussion of motherhood and the "maternal function," which she juxtaposes with Freud's and Lacan's emphasis on the paternal function. On that note, many readers will be pleased to read Kristeva's ample commentary on the theory and practice of *feminism*. Kristeva's remarks on the subject are far more nuanced than many accounts would indicate. Briefly, Kristeva contends that feminism has raised essential questions concerning the role of the mother, language acquisition, and women's writing and art and has served as a radical and indispensable element of the avant-garde; but she is concerned that feminist politics often prefers the collective to the singular and neglects the possibility for a mutual understanding between the sexes. The interviews develop these points in more detail.

The twenty-three exchanges included here vary as much in tone as they do in scope. Conducted on both sides of the Atlantic and in fashionable Parisian bars as well as sparse university offices, these conversations depict a multifaceted Kristeva—often warm, open, and pedagogical, but occasionally pessimistic or even hostile, especially in the later interviews. Some of the most revealing and accessible interviews were conducted by American professors who establish a congenial and productive rapport with Kristeva. Other interviews, particularly some of those conducted in Paris with Kristeva's French colleagues, adopt a guarded and scholarly tone and a more distant voice. Still others combine the two styles.

Yet as diverse as these interviews may be, they share a common thread that reflects and enhances Kristeva's theoretical project. Alongside their ever-present celebration of the individual, the particular, and the unique and their constant questioning of generalized categories of thought and of social identity, these interviews might be seen as a sustained footnote to one of Kristeva's favorite quotations from Proust: "Ideas come to us as the successors to griefs."[3] Kristeva shows us here that forgoing a rationalist conception of a unified subject laying claim to a particular group or "clan" and turning our attention instead to such "borderline states" as abjection, children's language, "foreignness," and avant-garde practice can help us confront the grief-ridden crises of the contemporary world and create gratifying ideas of our own. Even in more recent times, where Kristeva has become increasingly critical of our media-driven "society of the spectacle" and of the excesses of our technocratic culture, she holds on to the hope that "a genuine 'revolution' in mentalities and interpretive methods is taking place."[4] Forever oscillating between the instability of psychic crises and the promise of what she calls a "new humanity," Kristeva's subject is, quite literally, "in process." That is the dynamic, challenging movement that best defines these interviews.

In an interview with Serge Gavronsky included in this book, Kristeva pays homage to the role of dialogue in eighteenth-century France, noting that "conversation assumes that even hatred is mentionable [. . .] what better antidote to depression!" By embodying the daring spirit of the great Enlightenment salons and the brilliance of one of the most influential thinkers of our time, these conversations delve into grief and hatred to provide an antidote to depression—and to ensure that ideas will ultimately prevail. I hope readers will enjoy this extremely personal vision of Kristeva's unique and painful journey.

JULIA KRISTEVA Interviews

PROFILES

Julia Kristeva in Person

France-Culture broadcast this interview in 1988 as part of an hour-long radio show on Julia Kristeva entitled "The Pleasure of Julia Kristeva." The translation is by Ross Guberman. Several of Kristeva's former students and colleagues, including Alain Rey, Alice Jardine, Marc Taylor, and Pierre Fédida, posed the questions. The interview touches on Kristeva's personal and intellectual biographies and contains exceptionally open and succinct remarks about feminism, psychoanalysis, and motherhood. Kristeva expresses some of her concerns about structuralism and acknowledges her debt to Bakhtin and the Tel Quel group. She also describes her "conversion" from linguistics to psychoanalysis, rooting it in her work on the limits of language and the psyche and claiming that her experience with psychoanalysis has transformed her "personal style, lifestyle, and writing style." Regarding feminism, she emphasizes that she has a marked interest in the questions feminists ask, including the role of the mother and the process of language acquisition, but is disturbed that some feminist groups adhere to the very dogmas they oppose.

Under what circumstances did you begin working in Paris?

I was born in Bulgaria in 1941, and I arrived in France on Christmas Eve of 1965. I have since done all my intellectual work in French, that is, in a foreign language that evokes a culture that is not my own but has been a part of my life for a long time. My parents had the foresight to enroll me in a French kindergarten, so I learned the French language and was exposed to French civilization at a young age.

When I arrived in France, I felt liberated by my new political, familial, personal, and especially intellectual situation. I was pushed to the limits of my abilities and encouraged to expand my horizons—not only my own but those of society, language, and culture. This new context encouraged me to reflect on the many ways "foreignness" is manifested in our world—culturally and psychologically as well as poetically and pathologically.

Foreigners must confront a ghost from the past that remains hidden in a secret part of themselves. Although I consider myself to be well assimilated into French culture, I think that the French people themselves do not find me to be so. They communicate this to me indirectly, yet I am constantly reminded that I come from somewhere else. Even so, I do not always find their reactions painful. In my book on foreigners,[1] I describe the foreigner's situation not only as a source of hopelessness and confusion but as an opportunity to overcome such feelings of estrangement and to experience exaltation and enthusiasm. If we take advantage of this opportunity, we can realize our own potential, the potential of those around us, and the "foreignness" inherent in each of us. This can indeed be a source of joy.

We never lose the memories we have of the past, especially those having to do with our family. Our recollections of childhood are naturally linked with the geography of our homeland—its colors, its sounds, and its smells. Bulgaria is a spectacular country, both geographically and historically. I have never forgotten the Valley of Roses, the Black Sea, the hot sands, and the Greek sites studded with magnificent churches that I explored during our family vacations.[2] My analysis was conducted in French, which enabled me to "translate" my childhood impressions of the colors, tastes, and sounds of my country into French and to transpose them onto my new French culture. Because my work focuses specifically on language and culture, I found this process to be invaluable. Without such an experience, a foreign language would be merely a second skin, artificial and mechanical. If we want to understand literature or our psychoanalytic patients, we must translate childhood memories into a foreign language. For me, the analytic process is what enabled this translation to occur.

Yet how can we detach ourselves from the past? I have just mentioned one way: through psychoanalysis. In my case, however, there were specific historical considerations.

I left my country in part because Charles de Gaulle dreamed of a Europe that would stretch from the Atlantic Ocean to the Ural Mountains. His idea suited me perfectly because the French government was awarding scholarships for young Eastern European students to study in the West. So I set off for France with five dollars in my pocket and a scholarship I had to wait two months to receive. I had a few problems with the Bulgarian officials, but everything worked out in the end.

I must add that these were good times for intellectuals. The years between 1965 and 1968 were a period of intellectual turmoil and excitement. You had of course the *nouveau roman* and the Tel Quel group, who influenced and encouraged me, as well as the structuralist currents developed by Lévi-Strauss and Barthes. What is more, political changes in the French social fabric encouraged the French to pay attention to foreigners and to empathize with their plight. The French became more receptive to other people. That was no longer true in May 1968, but before then there was a certain harmony and tolerance that provided a professional work space to people like me.

My itinerary began at the Ecole des Hautes Etudes with Lucien Goldmann, continued with Roland Barthes, and then went on to Lévi-Strauss's laboratory of social anthropology, which had a department of semiolinguistics that sponsored me for a few years. I remember when Barthes asked me to give my first oral presentation on the "postformalists" just as people were beginning to explore the limits of formalism. I spoke about a postformalist named Mikhail Bakhtin who tried to explain that the basic linguistic structure of a text is influenced by historical and societal structures.[3]

When I gave my presentation, the audience was international in scope because people came to Roland's seminar from all over the world. I specifically remember a professor named René Girard who invited me right away to teach in the United States. I suppose that in his eyes I symbolized multinationalism. This was during the Vietnam War, and because I was even more political then than I am now, I had problems with the idea of going to America. So my international career was over, but I had already gained a multilingual perspective that took me from Moscow to Sofia and then on to American universities.

*When you came to Paris, you had no intention of staying. You came to write
a thesis on the nouveau roman, as you have said. Yet I believe your first book
was on a fifteenth-century novel.*

You are right; I did change my topic. I had planned originally to write a
thesis on the *nouveau roman* because I found the subject interesting, but
I lost interest once I was in France. Rather than investigate the way the
nouveau roman decomposed the form of the novel, I wanted to pose a different question: how did the novel establish itself as a genre? So I shifted
my focus from the end to the beginning, and I studied the structure of
the Renaissance novel. I chose a little-known novella: Antoine de la Sale's
Le Petit Jehan de Saintré. This fascinating work shows how the novel was
drawn from theater, from the carnivalesque genre, and from didactic,
scholastic discourse. De la Sale's novel offers a fresh conception of human
life and displays an acute awareness of language and narration.[4]

So why did you decide to stay in France?

Because of the intellectual environment provided by Goldmann, Barthes,
and, indirectly, Lévi-Strauss, who opened his laboratory to me. I had the
financial support I needed and a stimulating intellectual base. Yet what
really persuaded me to stay was my first meeting with Tel Quel and
Philippe Sollers, who later became my husband and who gave me a
stronger foothold in French intellectual life as a member of the Tel Quel
group. We would have deep discussions until all hours of the night at 55
Rue de Rennes, where many people would come to discuss philosophy
and literature. This animated intellectual world convinced me that I
could live abroad.

What role has structuralism played in your career?

I have always had reservations about structuralism. As I mentioned, I
was more interested in the postformalists, particularly Bakhtin.
Bakhtin, who has since become a well-known figure,[5] sought to go
beyond linguistic structures by introducing historical questions. The
members of the Tel Quel group encouraged us to go even further and
to consider something the postformalists had neglected: sexuality.
The Tel Quel group studied sexuality in the context of the French
Enlightenment and the surrealist movement. Artaud and Bataille
were very interested in rhetorical and literary manifestations of sexual
experience, which is a defining feature of French literature. They were

also greatly interested in Freud, who had been conspicuously absent from my intellectual training.

My Eastern European culture was German-Russian or British, but not Freudian. By German-Russian, I mean Kant and Hegel but not psychoanalysis. I discovered Freud through Tel Quel, which also introduced me to Lacan. Sollers was extremely interested in Bataille and Freud, who inspired the intensity of his own writings. All these elements eased my "conversion" from linguistics to psychoanalysis.

You have emphasized how much influence the Tel Quel group had on the future of French intellectual life, but you have also suggested that the group was plagued by internal friction and power struggles.

Absolutely. People have no idea how violent its criticisms, rejections, diatribes, and invectives were. It was all a bit surreal, and I realize that we were contemptuous of those who were not members of the group. Yet those of us who experienced these inner struggles felt very overwhelmed by it all. People do not realize this, and we (I should say "I") kept a stiff upper lip. I felt quite vulnerable during my years with Tel Quel because I found myself caught between all those angry men. I had a hard time of it.

What was your relationship to the feminist movement?

I have many problems with the feminist movement because I am uncomfortable with all militant movements. I made an institutional and personal criticism of leftist movements after my trip to China,[6] for I had begun to feel alienated from leftist ideology. French feminist thought exploded during this period, and I saw it as simply another form of dogmatism. So I was never willing to devote much time to any of these movements. I will not elaborate on the details of my discussions with different feminist groups, because that is all in the past now. Let's just say that I found that these groups often adhered to the very dogmas they opposed. As I result, I never joined any of the feminist groups.

At the same time, I was very interested in the basic questions they were asking: the specificity of the feminine, the mother's influence on her child's development into an independent being, language acquisition, the child's dependency on the mother, the mother's role in language and symbolic processing, the nature of women's writing and women's art, and so forth.

I wanted to approach these questions in my own way. Let me give an example: I did an interview with a Belgian feminist journal that we entitled "unes femmes."[7] This was obviously a bit awkward, but we did it for a reason: to celebrate women's singularity and uniqueness without reducing them to a generic category of "women" comparable to "the proletariat" or to "men."

You eventually became an analyst. I believe it was Benveniste who pointed you in that direction.

Benveniste and Lacan, but first Sollers. As I have said, I didn't know much about Freud when I arrived in France. Benveniste has meant a great deal to me. He was an extraordinary linguist who was also very interested in philosophy and psychoanalysis. He is one of the few linguists to have incorporated Freud's discoveries into his work. He published an article that I believe Lacan asked him to write on the role of language in Freud. This article is included in Benveniste's collected essays, and it gave me an authoritative introduction to Freud and his world.[8]

In the 1970s you had of course Lacan, who was quite appealing to young people. When I arrived in Paris, everyone went to his seminar at the Rue d'Ulm and later at the Law School of the Sorbonne. It was extremely stimulating because we felt that Lacan was analyzing each of us individually. At the same time, an atmosphere of group psychology characterized his seminar. Lacan was able to link psychoanalysis with such domains as linguistics, intellectual history, and philosophy.

Did you have any contact with Lacan outside his seminar? Did you have a personal relationship with him?

Yes, I did. In retrospect, my personal contact with Lacan was more important than my infatuation with his seminar. I suppose it all comes down to the same thing. I first met Lacan when I asked him to write an article for a journal I edited called *Semiotica*. The journal was affiliated with the *International Journal of Semiotics*. The article never came to fruition, but we were at least able to meet each other and to chat a bit. We later saw each other regularly to plan the trip to China. We spoke a great deal about the message we wanted to bring to China, what we wanted to see there, and so forth.[9] I saw him under more intimate circumstances when I decided to enter into analysis myself.

How did he respond?

I am reluctant to speak about such things publicly. Let's just say that he made it clear that I should not enter into analysis at his institution. I got the message and went elsewhere. I didn't want to go to his institution anyway: I was interested in his opinion, but I already had something else in mind.

Why did you enter into analysis? You shifted your focus from theoretical discourse to a highly personal experience involving language, the body, and a renewed perspective.

Well, I had some definite reasons that I will share with you. I later discovered other, more personal reasons that I will not share with you. Let's just say that the explicit reasons stem from my work on the limits of language, on language acquisition in children, and on the experience of poetry, or, more dramatically, on psychotic discourse. Because I was very involved in research on these limits of language, I decided I could no longer describe such discourses in neutral terms. I had to implicate myself, which meant participating in the experience of transference. I thus found it impossible to have this perspective of transference with other people without having first experienced it myself.

For me, psychoanalysis was not just an epistemological quest but a discovery of a private space that is off-stage, off-camera, and highly intimate. Unlike some people who make a big fuss about their analysis and their analyst, speaking about them at a restaurant table if not in public, I believe that analysis is extremely personal. It is my secret garden and I want to keep it that way.

So psychoanalysis has had immeasurable benefits for my work, my sensibilities, my relationships with other people, and my intellectual life. To put it simply, analysis has transformed my personal style, lifestyle, and writing style.

Didn't the end of your analysis coincide with your becoming a mother?

It was during my analysis that I discovered the maternal function as well as the pleasures, responsibilities, and difficulties of that extraordinary thing we call motherhood. I am referring to my personal experience with motherhood, but also to my relationship to my own mother. Yet the analysis itself ended for another reason, although motherhood may have played a role in it. My analysis ended because I believed I had something to say about other people's suffering. Discovering autonomy and authority allows you to work with your own suffering and to grant it a discourse—not in an autoerotic or self-enclosed way, but in a way that enables you to connect with other people.

I believe that we should trust mothers and listen to them. We should recognize the "civilizing" role that mothers play, not only in psychoanalysis but in general. Feminists have not stressed this enough, and neither have the media, who usually portray mothers as housekeepers. Mothers are the ones who pass along the native tongue, but they also perform an important psychological role that we are still discovering. They perform a sort of miracle by separating themselves from their children while loving them and teaching them to speak. This gives them a corporeal and sensory pleasure as well as an intellectual one.[10]

You have spoken recently about today's "new patients." What do you mean by that?

Today's patients are different from the ones Freud saw. They do not correspond to the traditional classification systems consisting of three or four categories (hysterical, obsessional, paranoid, and so forth). Two recent phenomena have prompted us to question the usefulness of these categories.

First, people have changed. Today's world is marked by many more conflicts, a great deal more violence, and new forms of repression stemming from a certain permissiveness and a certain acknowledgment of what we used to call "sexual freedom" (although it is somewhat curbed today because of AIDS). Second, today's analysts have modified and refined the way they listen to their patients. They now know that someone who appears ordinary, "neurotic," and normal can display psychological symptoms of self-disintegration and negative narcissism. Because of these two changes, we have expanded our definitions of psychological structures and introduced such new categories as the "borderline" personality or the "false self." In any case, we now place greater emphasis on the pre-oedipal stage and on the relationship between the psyche and soma.[11]

You have said that we are faced with an unprecedented situation. Society lacks transcendence, and we no longer feel connected to one another. You also speak of religion and psychoanalysis, claiming that religion furnished such a link at one time and that psychoanalysis can replace it. Are we not faced with an extremely dangerous positioning of the subject?

Absolutely. The media call it a "values crisis," and I believe it must be taken seriously. Although I have said that religion no longer fulfills its promises, I realize that churches still operate and that many people believe in God. Yet we still have a crisis of religious discourse, and people such as me (I don't know exactly how many of us there are) talk about the history of a philosophy that decomposes religious discourse and enables us to approach it coherently through atheism. I tend to subscribe to this line of thought, because I believe it enables us to analyze religious discourse. Yet once these analyses take place, they restrict the impact of religious discourse. So what will replace religious discourse? I believe that the link offered by psychoanalysis subsumes the illusion of religion. I wrote an essay entitled "In the Beginning Was Love: Psychoanalysis and Faith" that examines the interaction between psychoanalysis and religious discourse. It is often said that psychoanalysis can replace religion: first people confess and then you give them hope. That may be right, but it really isn't, for this hope is concomitant with the dissolution of the analytic contract. Believers belong to the name of the father, the community, the church, and an identifiable morality.

Ideally, those who have been analyzed should be able to connect with others and create communities. At the same time, they should always keep in mind that such connections are contingent on certain desires or pleasures.

Connections and illusions—of course they exist. We live in a society, and we will continue to live with illusions. Still, I am not fooled by them. I am going to analyze them. Why? Because I want to create new connections, not to isolate myself but to explore with other people. This requires another relationship to social bonds, another morality that is different from religious morality.

2

Intellectual Roots

Perry Meisel conducted this interview in 1980. It was translated by Margaret Waller and published in a 1984 issue of *Partisan Review* along with an interview by Elaine Hoffman Baruch (included in this volume under the title "Feminism and Psychoanalysis"). In this brief conversation, Kristeva presents some of the most important tenets of her theoretical project. She first situates her project historically, opposing Sartrean existentialism, which she characterizes as a "regressive" return to religious transcendence and reason, to the Marxism (through Hegel), structuralism (through Lévi-Strauss), and Freudianism (through Lacan) that, along with Benveniste's discursive approach to linguistics, form the basis of her own work. Kristeva argues that Sartrean thought, unlike the more "acute" and "lucid" currents that interest her, fails to acknowledge the unconscious and ignores "the great revolution of the avant-garde." She then discusses her own aesthetic philosophy, claiming to avoid the two extremes of the decadent "art for art's sake" approach and the notion of art as a pure political commitment. In the end, she downplays the question of the political component of art and declares moral or religious questions to be more "relevant" to the artist's positioning in "monumental history."

At what moment in contemporary French intellectual history would you say you arrived in Paris?

It was a very interesting moment. Politically, it was one of the highest moments of Gaullism, that period when Charles de Gaulle said that he wanted to create a sphere of influence stretching from the Atlantic to the Urals. Intellectually, there was the very interesting coexistence of the discovery of Russian formalism through Levi-Strauss; a certain revival of Marxism, also on the background of structuralism (I mean a rereading of Hegel), and a third very important current, the renewal of psychoanalysis through Lacan. All these movements were, for me, the real background of the 1968 events. Because if you look at the people who were involved in the 1968 revolution—students—most of them were involved beforehand in very advanced theoretical writings. *Les Cahiers pour l'analyse*, for instance, at the Ecole Normale were done by people who became Maoists after 1968. So it was a kind of intellectual turmoil, a sort of real theoretical fever. Where can you speak of Marxism, structuralism, Freudianism? Not in the Eastern countries, it's not possible. American society is too technocratic and too dominated by positivist ideologies, whereas that's not the case in French society. It was a very, very rare conjunction.

At what point did existentialism give way to this new wave and why?

On the one hand, existentialism was, in my view, a regression with regard to the great philosophical and aesthetic formal movements, to take only my own fields. The whole development of linguistics, of formal logic, was fundamentally ignored by Sartrean existentialism. If you're interested, on the other hand, in art, the great revolution of the avant-garde, Mallarmé, Lautréamont, and after them the surrealists—the entrance of psychosis into the life of the city, which modern art represents—these were also ignored by existentialism. Thus it was a reaction to all that. Structuralism, Marxism, Freudianism, joined together, are a reaction.

And yet Lacan was, with the surrealists, already at work in the late 1920s. Why did it take so long, indeed, twenty years, maybe more than that, for this to break out? Levi-Strauss had already begun his work before the war as well.

Because of political reasons: you had the war. At that moment there was a sociological way of thinking, more rooted in the everyday life and looking for immediate and simple causalities, that prevailed.

Existentialism lasted after the war, for historical reasons and because of economic difficulties.

So that a movement that claimed to interpret history was itself part of the determination?

Precisely. It couldn't distance itself.

It has been said that Sartre was unable to conceptualize the unconscious.

Absolutely. I think that Sartrean thought has no means to deal with the unconscious and, similarly, with everything that is material and formal—in other words, with the whole problem of the modern arts, of poetry, of plastic art. The unconscious as a logic, as a language, which is the essence of the Freudian discovery, is entirely foreign to Sartrean thought.

And yet in Marxism, even in orthodox Marxism, there is, implicitly at any rate, even before Lacan tells us so, a notion of the unconscious.

It's not the same unconscious. I think that what seduced us in Marxism was rather a materialist way of reading Hegel and a concept of negativity. It was and still is a matter of finding the agent, the agent of process, the agent of history, the agent of unconsciousness.

So to summarize, there were some lacunae that had been pointed out in each—Marxism, structuralism, Freudianism—and at the same time, some positive elements that had been brought in by the others. For example, Marxism had undergone a grafting of the theory of structuralism, but structuralism had undergone a grafting of the theory of subjectivity. In structuralism the subject was missing, so the subject was brought in the form of different technical considerations: in linguistics, for example, the subject of enunciation, the speaking subject in literary texts, and so on. There was a sort of exchange that enriched the three disciplines.

In a sense, then, structuralism provided the link between Marxism and Freudianism that had never been accomplished before.

At the moment we're in the middle of a regression that is present in the form of a return to the religious, a return to a concept of transcendence, a rehabilitation of spiritualism. It's a vast problem that can be interpreted in various ways. It is not uninteresting. There are now in France all sorts of spiritualist movements: pro-Christian, pro-Jewish, pro-this and pro-that. Here the Sartrean problem returns. I think that there's a religion of reason in Sartrean thought, just as in the new spiritualists there's a religion of transcendence. But both of them obliterate those forms in which the fact of signification is produced, the form in which meaning is produced.

So from this point of view, a religious notion of transcendence, a fetishizing of reason à la Sartre, are structurally the same.

I think so, and both are regressions with regard to the current of thought that is most acute, most lucid in the twentieth century, and that involves, as well as the discovery of the determining role of language in human life, the whole adventure of contemporary art. There's a blindness in Sartrean thought in that regard which gives it extremely charming ethical and humanistic positions, just as it gives extremely precursive ethical and humanistic positions to all the new spiritualists today, who are often in the foreground of the cultural, ideological battle in Paris.

It would be better to take up again the basic presuppositions, start from the small things, the small notions. I had a professor who bequeathed to me great wisdom in this area: Emile Benveniste, professor of linguistics at the College de France. He used to say to me, "You know, Madame, I concern myself with small things, the verb 'to be,' for example." Well, I think one must have this ambitious modesty, leave the meaning of history, production, leave all that and take up instead the minimal components that constitute the speaking being. The little elements that make me speak, the little elements that make me desire. It's still too difficult to be able to separate them. I mean that it would be necessary to start from a minimalism, to simplify things, and to be satisfied with more rigorous thinking rather than stir up emptiness with grand theories.

So could we say that Lacan and Benveniste together in some sense provided this next step, and that at this point one could situate the beginning of your work?

Exactly. Benveniste's work is important because it sees the necessity of introducing the notion of the subject into linguistics. Chomskyan linguistics, even though it recognizes the place of the speaking subject (although in its Cartesian form), has finally stayed very far behind the great semantic and intersubjective filed within discourse that Benveniste's perspective has opened up. What Benveniste wanted to found was not a grammar that generates normative sentences in limited situations. He wanted to constitute, and this is what is happening now, a linguistics of discourse. In other words, the object, language, has completely changed. Language is no longer a system of signs as Saussure thought of it; nor is language an object in the sense of generative grammar, that is, sentences generated by a subject presupposed to be Cartesian.

What is the difference, then, from our traditional assumption of the artist as subject—that it is the artist who speaks in the work?

I think that when you say that the artist speaks in the work, you suppose an entity that exists before the work. Yet we all know artists, and we know that very often their individuality is in total discordance or enormously different from what they've produced. In other words, the work of art, the production, the practice in which they are implicated extends beyond and reshapes subjectivity. There is, on the other hand, a kind of psychological ego, and on the other, there's the subject of a signifying practice. One mustn't imagine that there exists an author in itself, or that there is no relation between the two. I'm convinced that personal experience is very important for the materiality, the formal features, of the work of art, but there's no equivalence between the two. The work of art is a kind of matrix that makes its subject.

In other words, our traditional understanding of modernism as the assertion of the free will of the subject over inherited forms is a misapprehension of what the twentieth century has given us?

Precisely. Even more so because the problem of art in the twentieth century is a continual confrontation with psychosis. It's necessary to see how all the great works of art—one thinks of Mallarmé, of Joyce, of Artaud, to mention only literature—are, to be brief, masterful sublimations of those crises of subjectivity which are known, in another connection, as psychotic crises. That has nothing to do with the freedom of expression of some vague kind of subjectivity that would have been there beforehand. It is, very simply, through the work and the play of signs, a crisis of subjectivity that is the basis for all creation, one that takes as its very precondition the possibility of survival. I would even say that signs are what produce a body, that—and the artist knows it well—if he doesn't work, if he doesn't produce his music or his page or his sculpture, he would be, quite simply, ill or not alive. Symbolic production's power to constitute soma and to give an identity is completely visible in modern texts. And moreover, all this experience, literary as well as critical, is preoccupied with this problem.

So there is, then, to your mind, no way of one's role as artist and one's role as political activist ever being entirely coincidental?

I think that the artist, since we were just talking about form that is "content," is never more *engagé* than in his work. To ask an artist to *s'engager* in order to justify himself is an imposture into which many artists fall for reasons I have just mentioned: the work presupposes a lot of solitude and a lot of risks. You need to justify yourself; you need to identify yourself. But you have to know that, and if you know that, you can carry out *engagement* with humor; when you can, you take your distance. If not, *engagement* is the antidote to art. There's nothing more murderous for art than *engagement*. This is not to say that I am for art for art's sake. Art for art's sake is the reverse of *l'art engagé*. It presumes that there is such a thing as pure form, and contents that would be abject. I think, on the contrary, that contents are formal and forms are contents. Again, if you understand modern art as an experience in psychosis, to work with forms is the most radical way to seize the moments of crisis.

So there is a political component to artistic activity, and it cannot be direct.

It's not direct and it's not immediate, because I think you know that you always ask yourself what the political component is, although that's a very recent question. Why not ask what the moral or religious component of aesthetic activity is? I think it's a more relevant question. Remember Nietzsche's famous distinction between cursory history and monumental history. I think that the artist is in monumental history, his relationship to history is through what one used to call morality or religion.[1]

3

A Conversation with Julia Kristeva

This interview was conducted by Ina Lipkowitz and Andrea Loselle in November 1985. It was published with a brief and lucid introduction by Martha Buskirk in *Critical Texts: A Review of Theory and Criticism.* The questions and answers are comprehensive in scope, touching on semiotics, avant-garde practice, psychoanalysis, ethics, violence and perversion, and literary interpretation, particularly of Mallarmé. Kristeva traces her work from a structural and linguistic conception to a conception based on a study of "borderline states" in psychosis and language acquisition and of such "intersection topics" as abjection and melancholia. She then defines her notion of the "semiotic" and the "symbolic" and compares it with Freud's notion of psychic representation and with Lacan's registers of the Real, the Symbolic, and the Imaginary. Kristeva also accuses the American academy of being caught between "abstract deconstructivism" and "political commitment and political activity" and of criticizing French theory without producing a theory of its own. Commenting on her appropriation of a nonrepressive ethics that considers the violent currents of desire, she states that "the subject-in-process is always in a state of contesting the law, either with the force of violence, of aggressivity, of the death drive, or with the other side of this force: pleasure and jouissance." This supports her idea that the human being is not a theoretical unity but an "open system."

To begin on a rather general note, I wonder if you would reflect on the development of your work, which began with a rigorous, almost scientific examination of various signifying phenomena, and then moved into a study of the object and of love. Do you see a change of focus in your more recent work, or is there an underlying continuity that you would like to stress?

Both, I think. My work began in the context of French structuralism and, inspired by linguistic theories—linguistic models, actually—sought to set forth the most objective approach possible to literary texts. Ever since the early stages of my work, however, I have realized that this approach—which in your question you call "rigorous" or "scientific"—is based on a misapprehension, because it is impossible to have the same type of "scientificity," the same type of rigor in the domain of interpretation and in the humanities in general as in the domain of the exact sciences, since the position of the observer and of the theoretician is not at all neutral. A complex dynamic is at play in the relation between text and the observer: a dynamic that can be described in psychoanalytic terms as countertransference. So ever since the early stages of my work I have realized that it was not necessary to mechanically apply models to the literary text, but that it was necessary to consider the literary text as another language, another type of discourse. From this theoretical conception of the literary text as another type of discourse, I had to change the models of my approach and eventually make use of linguistic models, but after modifying them, taking into account that the text is not the language of ordinary communication. I was very influenced at this time by the works of Bakhtin, who, with respect to the formulations of the Russian formalist critics, also tried to seize upon something specific in the literary text that did not necessarily appear on the level of language, even if it involved deep laws of communication that could also be attributed to this same level of language. These laws are not dominant in language; they are in the text. This led me to speak of the dialogic, of carnival, of intertextuality, and so on.[1]

At the same time, from my studies in modern literature, I became interested in the borderline situation of language, the situation where language reaches its limits. It seemed to me that avant-garde texts explore this situation as much from the point of view of form as from that of subjective experience. When I speak of the avant-garde, I am thinking of the texts of Mallarmé and Lautréamont, for example, up to the present day by way of Joyce, Surrealism, Artaud, and so on. To try to understand more fully the borderline of language and of subjectivity functions, I began to study, on the one hand, the child's acquisition of language and, on the other, psychosis: two borderline states where language either does not yet exist or has ceased to exist. This led me to psychoanalysis and an attempt to understand the borderline situation not only from a formal point of view but also while trying to understand the subjective dynamic that is manifested in avant-garde texts. It seemed to me that this understanding was not possible without implicating myself as an interpreter who is no longer neutral but is entirely caught up in the attempt to come to some sort of momentary identification with these speakers in borderline situations, so as to learn to distance myself, to try to describe what it is that happens on the borderline. This back-and-forth movement, this identification-interpretation is not possible from a neutral "scientific" position, from outside the text. It assumes another rationality: the psychoanalytic rationality that poses many questions to Western epistemology. Is it a science? Is it a fiction? I think it is both at the same time. In any case, it is a different type of "scientific" discourse. It is a different understanding, and for the humanities I think that this understanding involves the consideration of a number of different theories.

From this point of view, I then became interested in "topics" that seem, perhaps, more psychological but are in fact intersections of various problems and can be examined by means of linguistics, philosophy, history, and religion. In any case, these topics require a recasting of separate discourses and assume that critical discourse is not simply a mosaic of this or that established science but an attempt to restructure, an attempt to form a new synthesis. And I think that the mainstay of this new synthesis can be the psychoanalytic position.

From there I became more and more interested in "intersection topics"—abjection, the love relationship, melancholia—that can be analyzed using certain elements in linguistics, in philosophy, perhaps in history and religion as well, and that demand a coherent position, which is, I believe, the psychoanalytic position.[2]

One of the main features of your work is your distinction between the semiotic and the symbolic and, similarly the genotext and the phenotext. By semiotic, however, you do not mean what other semioticians understand: namely, the interplay of signs. I wonder if you could redefine for us exactly what you mean by these terms and in what ways, if any, they parallel Freud's primary and secondary processes or Lacan's three registers: the Real, the Imaginary, and the Symbolic.

My distinction between the symbolic and the semiotic is explained in more detail in my *La Révolution du langage poétique*, which has just appeared in English. I think it would be more helpful to look there for a detailed explanation, which is naturally more complete than any I could set forth here. But to be schematic, I would say that for me signification is a process that I call *signifiance*, and to recognize the dynamics of this process, I distinguish two registers: the register of the symbolic and the register of the semiotic. By symbolic, I mean the tributary signification of language, all the effects of meaning that appear from the moment linguistic signs are articulated into grammar, not only chronologically but logically as well. In other words, the symbolic is both diachronic and synchronic; it concerns both the acquisition of language and the present syntactic structure. By semiotic, on the other hand, I mean the effects of meaning that are not reducible to language or that can operate outside language, even if language is necessary as an immediate context or as a final referent. By semiotic, I mean, for example, the child's echolalia before the appearance of language, but also the play of colors in an abstract painting or a piece of music that lacks signification but has a meaning. These are just a few examples.

More specifically, what I mean by these terms is that within the signifying process there is a level of arrangement corresponding to a certain order, a certain disposition of chromatic or vocal difference or of musical tones, but one that can't refer to a referent or have a precise denotative meaning in the way that signs have referents and signifieds.

The question to be answered, then, is whether this level exists independently of the study of language. I think not. I think that even the child's echolalias presuppose that the possibility of language exists either as a genetic program that allows the child to speak one day, so that the echolalias are stages before this possibility of speech, or as a social environment—the child is already in an environment where the parents speak, his desire to speak exists in the discourse of the parents, and so the echolalias appear in this environment. In short, there is an already-there of language. I think it is important, however, that our theoretical models represent the existence of a translinguistic level, which may perhaps appear as linguistic but is in fact translinguistic.

Why is it important to establish this level? So as to recognize the phenomena that are so common in the daily life of subjective experience, as well as in aesthetic practice, where we have passages to the zero degree of meaning, or where signification disintegrates, arriving at lower thresholds of meaning that do not coincide with normal communication, if not at a total eclipse of signification.

Can you give an example?

Very often we find examples in contemporary literature and in poetry, particularly in the poetry of Mallarmé or in the modern "cut-up" techniques, where meaning is very elliptical. In these cases, the reading of the poem implies that we either project our own ideas onto the place of meaning's rhythm or that we let ourselves be carried by the rhythm, by the intonation, by an almost vocal gesturing. This is a semiotic weft having no symbolic meaning but that constitutes, in fact, an extremely important level in aesthetic communication.

This brings me to the registers of representation that Freud perceived; but we would have to elaborate them more precisely because they don't coincide with the model of the Saussurian sign.[3] The model of the Saussurian sign is drawn from the level of consciousness and comprises the signifier, the signified, and, finally, the referent, whereas Freud speaks of the representation of things, the representation of words, the representation of affects that don't have the same status in the psychic apparatus.

What interested me was, by way of the semiotic, to further elaborate a level of psychic representation that for Freud remains extremely primitive and imprecise, which is the representation of affects that are psychic inscriptions, hence very primitive and very fragile: drives and affects that are in fact already psychic. Not only are they energies; they are extremely fragile psychic traces that respond to the primary process—to condensation and displacement. Thus I think that this level of representation was suggested by Freud, but I also think that it hasn't been sufficiently elaborated and that it hasn't been linked sufficiently to the problem of linguistic representation. This is what I try to do by means of this concept of the semiotic.

As far as Lacan's ideas go—the Real, the Imaginary, and the Symbolic—I think it extremely difficult, if not impossible, to translate one theory into another theory, because if one does, one ends in confusion and loses the specificity of each author and each approach. So I would not like to perform this reduction. But it does seem to me that the semiotic—if one really wants to find correspondences with Lacanian ideas—corresponds to phenomena that for Lacan are in both the real and the imaginary. For him the real is a hole, a void, but I think that in a number of experiences with which psychoanalysis is concerned—most notably, the narcissistic structure, the experience of melancholia or of catastrophic suffering, and so on—the appearance of the real is not necessarily a void. It is accompanied by a number of psychic inscriptions that are of the order of the semiotic. Thus perhaps the notion of the semiotic allows us to speak of the real without simply saying that it's an emptiness or a blank; it allows us to try to further elaborate it. In any case, it's on the level of the imaginary that the semiotic functions best—that is, the fictional construction.

In regard to what you said earlier about the connection between the semiotic and Freud's primary processes, would you say that the same mechanisms that work in the dream—condensation, displacement, and so on—are also at work in Mallarmé's poetry?

Yes. Exactly. Only I think it is important to point out that the primary process doesn't necessarily work on signs but can also extend to traces, to psychic inscriptions that aren't of the same order of the sign, but are instead colors, sounds, frequencies—that is, intonations and rhythms.

And this, then, would make it just as difficult to interpret Mallarmé as to interpret a dream? You would need much of the same work?

I think in a certain way interpreting Mallarmé is even more difficult, because in the dream there is already an established narrative: we are never in the fragmentation of the dream. When we analyze the dream, we already have this narrative; we can say that the dreamer has already performed the transposition. Whereas Mallarmé's text presents, if you will, a "dream" in an unfinished or unpolished state, as if we were in the dreamer's place, where the elements are extremely fragmented. Furthermore, we don't have the image; we have only the sound and a number of semantic or lexical relationships. We ourselves are called on to assume the place of the dreamer, to project ourselves into this place, and to pass between the fragmentation and the narrative. Thus it is a task that asks for an even greater regression than just listening to the dream, listening to the narration of the dream. We are constantly confronted with the narrative of the dream. In other situations closer to psychosis, the dream narrative approaches a Mallarmé poem, requiring the analyst to give more of himself or herself to the interpretation. This is why psychoanalytic reality has changed in a certain way: we have to work with discourses that are much more fragmentary and closer to the semiotic than to the symbolic. This explains why I feel that we have even greater need of models that insist on the semiotic, because in the discourse of today's patient, this level is more apparent than ever before. What is more, disidentification, the crisis of identity, appears much more explicitly today in the patient's discourse than it ever did in Freud's patients.

Your work, from the time of Séméiotiké *to the recent* Histoires d'amour, *has become increasingly informed by psychoanalysis. Since you are so concerned with revealing the ideological basis of any given theory, how would you respond to Gayatri Chakravorty Spivack's statement that you "lack a political, historical or cultural perspective on psychoanalysis as a movement"?*[4]

I think that one can't speak of psychoanalysis, as Gayatri does, from the outside, opposing it to what I would call a political theology. Gayatri's position is characteristic of a number of American intellectuals who find themselves wedged between, on the one hand, a completely abstract deconstructionism, detached from any psychic or political concerns, from any speakers or spheres of study, and, on the other hand, an attempt to compensate for this deconstructionist abstraction with political commitment and political activity. They insist on extraordinary divisions and esoteric refinements on the textual level and on a summons to take part in political activity. But deconstructionist analysis itself has no such concerns and responds to no such necessities and to no concrete societal malaise.

What I find interesting is the position I described in answering your first question: through an interdisciplinary approach centered on psychoanalysis, I am trying to provide a discourse concerned with "topics" that belong to the anxieties of people today. Love, as well as melancholia and abjection—these are subjects that fundamentally concern present trouble or anxieties. And this is not a problem that is outside politics. But I don't think we can approach political questions with a general discourse. I think the experience of the humanities has taught us that we have to specify the problem and have a precise discourse about precise objects, and that political concerns are not concerns of belonging to a party or of taking a stand on a political event. Finding a subject for reflection that involves individuals in their daily anxiety is a political concern; and seen as such, political concerns should, I think, be both more modest and more effective.

I was struck, for example, when I bought the *New York Times* yesterday, as I do every day, and there on the front page was a huge article about teenage melancholia—hence, a social problem. All sorts of friends, parents, and teachers don't know what to make of this problem, which is at once psychological, social, and political.

Faced with this, I'd rather concern myself with melancholia as a concrete problem and with trying to understand what the language of these individuals is, what the desires inside them are that push them to death, and at the same time to pose large and useful questions about the "cultural and political perspectives of the psychoanalytic movement." In general, though, these large questions are for the American academic who wants a job at a university as a specialist in the "psychoanalytic movement." This doesn't interest me.

Another apparently constant feature in your work is what you call the ethical imperative. In your article "L'Ethique de la linguistique" (Polylogue),[5] you mention that Marx, Nietzsche, and Freud represent the formulation of a new ethics for the twentieth century, an ethics that is not a coercive or repressive force. What do you mean by this new ethics, and what does it imply about your idea of the subject-in-process?

This is a large problem and therefore very difficult to answer in a few words. The question of ethics has generally been understood as a question of morals and of submission to the law. The upheavals that Nietzsche, Freud, and in part Marx caused in contemporary thought consist of the belief that we have to understand the violence beneath desire as an imperative of psychic life as well as an imperative of social life. This is a reformulation of the moral imperative, and this reformulation can lead to an ethics that would not be one of repression. Other philosophers have arrived at this position: we can see Spinoza's idea of happiness and of joy as related to this concern. Is it possible to find a common ground for the understanding and communication of a certain type of order—social life or discourse—that is not simply an order of restriction but instead an almost marginal individual unveiling of pleasure and of violence? We should consider that these are the imperatives of the speaking being and are necessary to psychic life, to the condition of the speaking being as a condition of innovation.

The notion of the subject-in-process[6] seems to me to correspond to this concern because it assumes that we recognize, on the one hand, the unity of the subject who submits to a law—the law of communication, among others; yet who, on the other hand, does not entirely submit, cannot entirely submit, does not want to submit entirely. The subject-in-process is always in a state of contesting the law, either with the force of violence, of aggressivity, of the death drive, or with the other side of this force: pleasure and jouissance.

The subject-in-process, then, gives us a vision of the human venture as a venture of innovation, of creation, of opening, of renewal. I'm reminded of what the biologists call "open systems." They think that a living being is not merely a structure but a structure open to its surroundings and other structures; and that interactions occur in this opening that are of the order of procreation and rejection, and that permit a living being to live, to grow, to renew itself, eventually destroying something outside itself, but at the same time giving something to the outside.

The metaphor that I have just used corresponds exactly to the Freudian idea of psychic life as founded on the death drive and on Eros. I think it is absolutely important to recognize these parameters.

On a social level and on the level of discourse, the question that arises from your inquiry is whether contemporary society can give a place to perversion and in what way. Because if we say that the speaking being is a being moved by violence and by Eros, then this assumes that one has in oneself an unending dynamic of transgression. Can this dynamic of transgression be understood by the social code? Certain societies come to mind, such as the late eighteenth century, which, through its Don Juan/Casanova figure, offered or tried to offer a certain possibility of encoding perversion.[7] Certain forms of baroque art offer this possibility as well.

In the modern world, the media culture tries to answer these needs in a rather basic fashion, perhaps, but one that is necessary to understand—for example, the role of the adolescent in modern movies, the role of violence, of the bully, of Mad Max, Rambo, or Schwarzenegger. These are debatable, provisional forms, which nevertheless arise from a deep psychological necessity, and which consist basically in asking for the recognition of narcissism, a recognition of the need for violence, for transgression, for pleasure, for identification. They are secular forms of the sacred: earlier in our civilization, this type of need was subsumed within, and channeled into, a religious discourse—representations of hell or representations of various fringes of society were condemned, but represented all the same. To represent hell with all its horrors and abjection is a way of representing and at the same time allowing the represented to be repressed. These are the primitive solutions. But we can't have this same primitive solution of representation, of repressing beneath a form of condemnation. Our solution is the polyvalent, polymorphous, essentially imagistic aesthetic discourse: the mass media.

The risk, therefore, is a certain complacency before these attacks of inherent perversity and the psychotic regression inherent in our psychic life. But in response to the psychoanalyst who is disturbed by the media's complacency concerning this phenomenon, we could argue that, happily, Western society is a polyvalent society, and that alongside the media's answer to these necessities, there are other discourses; there is a certain discourse of understanding—such as psychoanalysis—there is our interview; there are theoretical and philosophical questions about the meaning of nonmeaning, and so on. Thus if we recognize this multiplicity of discourses, we can see that there is an examination within contemporary culture that tries to respond to this ethical concern in a way that is at once polyvalent, dispersed, and postreligious, and that, at bottom, takes into account both the ethical imperative and the need for jouissance.

Interestingly, in the case of Rambo, we have a most violent character who's violent for the sake of the good. They've taken the two extremes and put them together; they're glorifying violence even though he's killing people. Then he affects people in real life. In the Times, there was an article about a man who was arrested dressed up in a Rambo costume and who had shot someone. He said, "Rambo could do it, so can I." This seems to be an interesting parallel.

Yes. What is interesting there is that the fictional discourse should be the mediator of the discourses, and that they must be accompanied by explication and interpretation to demonstrate that this is a fiction, not a reality, and to prevent the psychotic individual from mistaking signs for reality. But this presupposes an entire process of education that the university or television itself will have to make on the level of interpretation. What is a movie? What is an image? And, in fact, sometimes we must prevent an individual who confuses himself with the image from acting on his confusion. And this presupposes once again a plurality of discourses; the cathartic discourse and media discourse are all very good, but they must be accompanied by a process of explication, of understanding, without which we have these fragile psyches, like that of the man you mention, who identifies with an image and then acts on it, who instead of excluding aggressivity ends with it. And for this, we have clinics.

Jonathan Culler, in Structuralist Poetics, *has posed the familiar objection that your interpretations of specific texts are made more or less at "random."*[8] *This raises the old question of the relationship between theory and practical criticism. How do you perceive this relation in your work?*

There are various aspects to this question. One of the first is the reaction of English criticism to the theoretical work produced in France these past years. This reaction is a very ambivalent one and, at the same time, rather aggressive and inevitably necessary for epigones. When one has not produced a theory, one is not compelled to place oneself in relation to a theory, and in this situation there is a moment when one accepts the theory, and yet at the same time one feels the need to bring to it something new, other, different; consequently, there is the necessity to formulate criticism. I believe such a state of mind can be understood very well. I wish, on the contrary, that my American or English colleagues would simply offer a different way of reading, another type of theory, and get themselves out of this obligation to situate themselves in relation to the "French stuff."

But for what it's worth . . . First of all, I am not so sure that in the case of Mallarmé I tried to apply a one-sided theory while leaving out some of the fundamental aspects of Mallarmé's work. It is obvious that a literary work is in a certain way inexhaustible; this is why it outlasts the centuries and suggests endless interpretations. One talked about Mallarmé at the end of the nineteenth century, we talk about him now, and we will undoubtedly speak differently of him in twenty years or in fifty years. In other words, interpretation is always fragmentary; it implies a choice and does not constitute the totality of the work.

Of what does this choice consist? It is in a certain way inherent in the author's logic and is not purely arbitrary or simply a projection of the theoretician's fantasies. I do not think this is the case in my reading of Mallarmé, because the necessity of the paragram as a possible reading of Mallarmé, the play of signification, of permanent musicality, the composition of words in syllables, are overdetermined by belonging to a text by Mallarmé or to other texts. This is a technique of reading that Mallarmé himself indicated as necessary in his theoretical texts like "Crise de vers" or "La Musique dans les lettres," so there is a correspondence between the theoretical approach I am proposing and the approach Mallarmé himself wished to see applied to his poems and to his own conception of the poetic text as a profound musicality.

Yet although I consider it essential, I tried not to keep myself only at this level. I became, for example, very interested in phenomena that Mallarmé barely accentuated while nevertheless accentuating them, but that have all the same been developed by his interpreters. Examples are his relationship to femininity, to religion, to the family, to the different deities of the Indo-European pantheon. These are ideological and, ultimately, sociopolitical questions, and they are not at all dependent upon a Saussurian reading. From this a method became apparent to me.

I wondered also about another one of your articles in Séméiotiké *in which you say that for semiotics literature as literature does not exist, that it is another semiotic practice.[9] That is, when we say "literature" (and especially at the same time I formulated this position), we have the idea that we are speaking of a very nebulous object, and that we have not specified it as an object. We say "literature" without any discipline or adherence to theoretical presuppositions. We try to make literature into something that intersects philosophy, theology, psychology, aesthetics, and so on. It is true that the literary object is polyvalent as well, and so, at a certain point in the analysis, we are bound to take this polyvalence into consideration; but what occurred to me at that time is that if you remain with this perspective of generality and polyvalence toward literature, you will not be able to perform a thorough study of these different aspects; and, in the first place, it is necessary to arrange the problem, to say that literature is like a universe that extends over the complexity of human life—I do not deal with it as such, but within this immense X, I carve out a piece that is literature as a system of signs, as a "semiotic practice"; and I am going to try to speak about it from this basis, which gives me a little better grasp or a greater possibility of saying something concrete, or perhaps of saying something valid about the literary text as a specific practice; and this practice is not religion or psychology or aesthetics in general. So from this basis, I can return later on and ask myself what the philosophical implications are, what the psychological implications are, as opposed to beginning by dissolving the notion of literature in human experience right off the bat. The point is to try to find a specific springboard (what is specific to literary signs?) and from there perhaps regain that complexity the second time around.*

In A Midsummer Night's Dream, *Shakespeare wrote: "The lunatic, the lover and the poet are of imagination all compact." Would this make an appropriate epigraph to your work? We are interested in your decision to study the signifying processes not so much of the normal speaking subject but of the child, the neurotic or borderline individual, the artist, and now, considering your* Histoires d'amour, *of the lover. Does your choice imply that you agree with Freud's idea that the difference between the normal and the abnormal mind is one of degree and not of kind?*

I shall begin with the second part of your question. What interests me are borderline situations of subjectivity. It is not that I think the profound logic of the functioning of the symbolic is reflected in these borderline situations but does not usually appear in the situation you called "normal." Yet in order to take into consideration—and this in effect adheres well to the Freudian science—in order to try to give consideration to the deep laws of psychic work, I believe it is necessary to take an interest in the language of children or in poetic language, the situation of abjection, of being in love, of melancholia, and so on. This kind of interest in borderline topics, which are at the same time borderline topics for all individuals, in "normal" and pathological ones, since, if these phenomena are pathological, we are all involved in pathology; for at a given time we are all the child, the dreamer, or the lover, or we pass through abjection or melancholy.

So from this position, can one apply the quotation from Shakespeare to my work? Yes, if we are speaking of the object, of the "topic" that interests me. No, perhaps, if we are talking about my own approach, because I try it while in a position of osmosis and in a position of the greatest degree of identification with my topics. I believe that this is the only way to penetrate the dynamic in question. I try at the same time to have a point of retreat, a stepping-back, which is inherited from a certain tradition of metaphysical knowledge, and which is the possibility of understanding and the possibility of constructing stable objects that are distinguishable and analyzable. And, therefore, at this stage I do not simply apply a fictional discourse in order to give consideration to fiction. I try to keep myself in a position of understanding and of knowledge and not in a purely mimetic relationship to my objects of study. This is, therefore, a very difficult position to maintain because it assumes a back-and-forth movement between fiction and knowledge. But I think it is indispensable in the humanities, and especially in the interpretation of the signifying function, the interpretation of literature in particular; and it enlarges the sphere of what can be known.

It is, in fact, a grand wager on the possibility of the model of knowledge handed down from metaphysics. I think we are in a position where, through different apocalyptic and economic processes, the West has developed a feeling of guilt about this cultural legacy, and particularly about metaphysics and the science that came out of metaphysics, as well as interpretive discourse and the present developments, which fall either on the side of analytic philosophy or on that of psychoanalysis. I think this heritage is alive and susceptible to further development because what also belongs to this heritage is the possibility of fiction, the possibility of merging with the object of fiction—a discourse that is mimetic—and, on the other hand, of constructing a discourse of knowledge; but these two discourses are not necessarily separate. In the Western tradition, knowledge and mimesis are not separate. And in the relationship we have to the text I believe that we can try to maintain this bipolarity and not simply read fiction on top of fiction as criticism; it is not that I write another literary text that is the only response to the real literary text I am reading. The position can be proposed, but it is not my position. I think we can support the position that says that as part of this moment of mimetic identification, I create a text on top of the text, but at the same time I have access to this possibility of knowledge, and I bring forward a certain number of models that allow me to set a distance between the text and myself, so as to see it as "meta" or to the side and to see the possibility of this "meta."

And how do you perceive literary criticism in the United States in relation to this concept of mimesis and culture?

I have a feeling that there are some current trends participating in a return to our metaphysical heritage in order to try to analyze it with present-day perspectives. Examples can be found in the interest in history, in ethics, in moral objectives, and these are obviously the great themes that belong to this heritage. Yet it is a very fragile movement, one that entails a few regressions as well. We are returning to a religious or a historical perspective but forgetting the structuralist and formalist work. What would be very difficult and important to do would be to create a sort of *Aufhebung*, if you will, in order to take into account this formal breakthrough, but also in order to require it to give consideration to literary texts by going through a mimetic identification with these texts, and to take into account the truth of this attitude, while at the same time taking seriously "issues" such as moral, historical, and ethical objectives. It would be a kind of bridge, which would let the reality of criticism appear.

You have written that your work could perhaps have been accomplished only by a woman. How does this speculation relate to another comment you once made that "a woman's practice can only be negative, in opposition to what exists" (Polylogue, *"La femme, ce n'est jamais ça")?*[10]

Yes, what I was trying to say is that the position of the feminine in discourse is a very difficult position to specify. As soon as one specifies it, one loses it, seeing that, perhaps, the feminine is precisely what escapes nomination and representation. But if we are going to talk about this definition of the feminine, I suppose the practical and ethical question would be, What type of practice for women? Should this simply be, as certain feminists have said, a position of the "not-said," a discourse of lacunae, or just the discourse of a fictional construct? This can be an opposition, but not, I believe, a binding one. I think that one of the consequences of this definition of what is feminine—of this nondefinition—is that women are led to behave in a critical manner, so that this noncorrespondence between the feminine and the codes of representation manifests itself not as a re-creation of women in the scene of representation but as an attempt to enlarge and modify the scene.

When it is a question of literary theory, one should try to construct a discourse that confronts its legacies, its classical positions, and tries to bring in other solutions that take into account the experience of women, of the theoreticians, and that, in its own way, manages these things as, eventually, the literature of this personal projection on the text, a projection that would perhaps be different for men. Yet one should try not only to recognize these things but to formulate them, and to formulate them through theoretical discourse—whence this formulation, which is a little combative, and which I made concerning the position of the discourse of the feminine as setting itself up in opposition.

From this point of view, then, I think that the discourse of the feminine does not escape the general rule of all reformulations, and that, if a man, in whatever field he may be, proposed a change in model or discourse, he would be accountable to the same position; but then this would also assume that he were listening in on something that escapes representation and thus could perhaps be called "feminine"—which does not necessarily mean that it is "feminizing," but that it is closer to what I call the semiotics of personality.

Concerning your style, there is a big difference between, for example, La Révolution du langage poétique *and* Pouvoirs de l'horreur. *The style of the later book is much more literary. What is the reason for this change? Did the topic of abjection suggest to you or necessitate this change in style? And I also have a couple of related questions: are you thinking of writing a novel? And on what are you working right now?*

I was not able to respond to this question when I was talking about my interest in psychoanalysis and how the analytic position modifies the choice of one's objects of study or of one's discourse. I do not think that I chose abjection after I modified my style because it is a question of a more global, more synthetic perspective that consists in situating oneself differently in relation to things; rather, it is bilateral: the choice of object and the position of one's discourse go together, and such a choice assumes that the discourses of knowledge are, at the same time, knowledgeable and mimetic. And I believe this is precisely what happens in the case of analytic interpretation, but only when one follows it to its fullest in one's discourse and exhausts one's fantasies and narratives, and speaks one's language, which is at the same time not completely one's own language; in this case, there is an attempt to displace language, which starts from the knowledge we provisionally make of what language tells us without telling us. This style is, therefore, controlled in a way by the position of interpretation and by an interpretive discourse in the process of analysis.

Does this then lead me to write novels? For the moment, I think not, because first of all I have a feeling for analytic interpretation, and second, this way of writing literary criticism—which is perhaps a little more fictional while at the same time being knowledgeable—is enough for me; it engrosses my immediate needs, needs that are normally presupposed for the writing of fiction. But in the end, who knows? Maybe someday. For the moment, though, I do not see it happening. I am currently doing research on melancholia, which is in the same style of subject matter that we have been talking about, and which I am also trying to approach out of an excess of desire for distance—that is, from this abyss that is melancholia—but I am, at the same time, trying to get as close to it as possible. This once again implies an attempt to create a style that is perhaps a little more fictional and communicable.

I noticed that in Pouvoirs de l'horreur *you sometimes used the first person.*

Yes, sometimes. I think it is a way of showing that the person who is speaking is not in a neutral position, and that I do not talk about the knowledge of horror or of melancholy from a position up above. I am unable to do it without trying to put myself in the position of the suffering in question; that obviously implies certain avowals of personal experience and, above all, a possibility of identifying similar to the novelist's method of identifying with his characters. Again, I do not wish to give you the impression that what I write is literature; but there is a desire for knowledge, distance, an interpretation that makes it so that it is a matter of a less bivalent, less mimetic and knowledgeable discourse. I am convinced that one of the lessons of the work done recently in the humanities in France—but perhaps there is a tradition of French work in this sphere—is the lesson that one cannot speak, interpret, or talk about what is human without being side by side with art—or without a certain compensation in the discourse of fiction—and yet, at the same time, detaching oneself from it. From Baudelaire's *Salons* to Lévi-Strauss, from one to the other, their main features differ greatly, but in the details one can always find this space between fiction and knowledge. You can either accentuate fiction, or you can accentuate knowledge; but I believe that this is how the space is laid out.

4

Cultural Strangeness and the Subject in Crisis

Suzanne Clark and Kathleen Hulley conducted this interview in Kristeva's Jussieu office in Paris in 1989 and asked some follow-up questions by telephone in 1990. The text was translated by Clark and Hulley and published with a substantial and informative introduction in *Discourse: Journal for Theoretical Studies in Media and Culture*. This interview has an exceptionally broad scope, focusing on the notion of "crisis" as it pertains to history, modernity, psychoanalysis, pedagogy, foreignness, alterity, and creativity. Major texts discussed are *Strangers to Ourselves*, *Black Sun*, and *The Samurai*. In particular, Kristeva discusses her remarks on Io and the Danaïdes in *Strangers to Ourselves* and her chapter on Marguerite Duras in *Black Sun*. Touching on one of the main themes of *Strangers to Ourselves*, Kristeva contends that psychoanalysis offers a way to approach foreignness and alterity because "the Freudian message, to simplify things, consists in saying that the other is in me. It is my unconscious. And instead of searching for a scapegoat in the foreigner, I must try to tame the demons that are in me." She also speaks about her experience accompanying President Mitterand on an official trip to Bulgaria. Throughout the conversation, Kristeva celebrates singularity, suggests that marginality is not inherently adverse, and warns against communitarian ideologies.

Your recent analysis of psychoanalysis and theology is situated within a sense of historical crisis. Can you tell us more about this idea of crisis and how it is related to the question of modernity?

Yes, this problem of crisis is an enormous one. We formed a "groupe de recherche," a seminar, here at Paris VII, addressing this crisis. We tried to organize an interdisciplinary reflection across history, because the crisis has multiple aspects. It does not appear in the same form every century. But on the other hand, we can speak of a global notion of crisis nonetheless, and understand by that the rupture of a structure, the rupture of an equilibrium. Considered from this point of view, the fundamental crisis in which the contemporary world is living—and consequently the arts that interest us—began to unfold at the time of the French Revolution, and the results of this crisis are what we are living through, a crisis at once of royal sovereignty and of religion, but also of discourses in their communicative value. At the level of sovereignty, we are in the process of living new forms of democracy that are imposed by multinational states and societies, among other things. This concerns the problem of foreigners, but also the other forms of difference that a democracy is capable of harmonizing: the differences of women, of children, difference in sexual practices, and so forth. At the level of religion, this crisis poses moral questions that are very important today. In particular at the level of the reproduction of the species—genetic manipulations, the codes defining responsibilities and identities with respect to children—must we live with the former criteria? Or are the criteria in the process of changing? This is an important problem.

And at the level of discourses: as early as the eighteenth century (one cannot say this enough) a ludic discourse was developing, an erotic discourse, and a discourse of insanity. Examples can be found in Diderot as well as in Sade, or in the literature of pamphleteers, both of the right and of the left, which surrounded the French Revolution. You have the royalist press, but also the populist press, which was extremely sexualized, extremely virulent, and which expressed a sort of desire for pleasure, often by procurance. "We're not the *salauds*, the others are." There was this violence of discourses that in a certain way was expressed by the guillotines, but in another way was blocked and forbidden by the guillotines. We sense that the sexual liberation of the twentieth-century avant-gardes—surrealism, *après-guerre*, the discourse of homosexuals, May 1968, and so forth, the whole effort to find new forms of expression in language, for the libido, by changing the style—are perhaps conclusions of that crisis.

I would say, together with certain historians, that the French Revolution is now coming to an end. This can be seen clearly by taking account of the phenomena of the problems of authority, of democracy, of religion, and of language in its relationship to sexual identity. I think that the crisis has opened and there will be a succession of crises.

Are these crises fundamental to every culture then, or unique to our own modernist historical moment?

I think that modernity, in particular this radical break made by the French Revolution, has rendered the crisis explicit, and minimized the moments of equilibrium. We can think of it this way: previous social forms counted on a certain calm, and crisis came periodically; but now an epoch has opened when we live in permanent crisis. What is provisional now are the moments of status quo.

Then would you say that the subject of this crisis, the sujet-en-procès,[1] *is an anarchic subject?*

Yes. Anarchy generally has a negative connotation. But for me, from this perspective of a permanent crisis, anarchy is the nonrepressed state of subjectivity. So it is a permanent state of functioning. At this moment, the problem arises of two alternatives: is the crisis a suffering, is it a pathology? Or is it a creation, a renewal? And it is at this moment that recourse to a provisional and stabilizing apparatus is important.

This provisional and stabilizing apparatus—but it is important to insist on the *provisional*—is the role that a new form of power can play in society. This is the power of the therapist, the power of the educator, the power of a certain familial authority, a power that is, however, relative and flexible. We are in the process of seeking new forms of power in the city, in the state. But I think that this has nothing to do with the idea of an anarchy that is nihilism of power, nor with the idea of an absolute power.

Is it a dispersed power?

Dispersed and flexible at the same time, capable of flexibility. Relational. Taking as a starting point—I myself would imagine—the image of the analyst's power, provided we do not see the analyst as a "shrink" who reduces imaginative capacities or as a suggestive figure who exercises an indoctrination on his patients, but as an intermediary who becomes a fixed point of support and confidence and who permits the individual to find his capacities for play and for construction.

Let us find this kind of power—try to find it, again—in the therapist, the teacher, the social worker; that is, these different, flexible forms representing social authority that societies are in the process of inventing.

Can the profession of teaching play a role in this?

If the profession does not play such a role, it teaches nothing at all. Above all in the human sciences and in literature.

As for pedagogy, do you think it is possible to pay attention to differences, to individuals?

It is necessary. This will require a great deal of money, first. Because there must be many more professors. We must ask for it, not be ashamed to ask for it. But this also requires a certain personal devotion, a certain moral, pedagogical attention on the part of teachers, who are not necessarily prepared by their studies to do this.

But this work with differences is something that we should probe more deeply, perhaps not only to develop a favorable attitude but also more competence in the role of analytic listening. I myself am trying to do this in our university. We are opening our doctoral studies to secondary and postsecondary teachers who want to do further work in psychopathology, for example, to understand the phenomena they encounter, because students have trouble learning, certain psychological problems, and so forth. And the teacher is not necessarily adept in responding to these problems.

So we need to be retrained, in a sense, in psychoanalysis ourselves?

That can be done perhaps by self-analysis, by the psychoanalysis that the teachers can do on their own behalf. But I find that what one can do as an institution at the university level is to give them a kind of cultural baggage, to tell them what inhibition is, what autism is, what troubled thought is. Courses at this level that are taught by psychiatrists, psychologists, philosophers. And where the teachers can participate with doctors, discuss these problems, so they can be armed when they encounter these problems in the classroom.

We have created a diploma, as it happens, which follows the DEA [Diplôme d'études approfondies]. First we have an aide-DEA, which is preparation for the writing of the thesis, and now we have just created another diploma that is going to come after it. It is interdisciplinary—psychopathology, psychiatry, semiology—and it is going to permit teachers to acquire this competence. That is what we hope in any case.

How does this new program function?

This new diploma is called DRAPS, Diplôme de recherches approfondies en psychopathologie et sémiologie [Diploma of Advanced Research in Psychopathology and Semiology]. It's a very high level of research. And most of the people who are working on this diploma are doctors or teachers who are interested in very specific pathologies for which they have not received enough information in the usual course of events. For example, a high school teacher might find students who have inhibitions at the level of writing, at the level of speech, or various inhibitions in relationships, which range from depression to schizophrenia, passing through different other disorders. There is nothing in the regular instruction for high school teachers in France, for example, that prepares them for this kind of problem. And we thought that they could benefit from this research seminar. For example, this year we took up the theme of autism, which is, of course, a very serious pathology, and one does not encounter it in the schools, but it sends us back to difficulties with symbolization. We know that the autistic child is someone who does not have access to speech. And we ascertained that many psychiatrists and teachers were fascinated by this problematic, because we encounter very slight forms distantly related to autism and do not have the conceptual means to deal with this analogous phenomenon, which we are currently encountering.

But is it only a question of children who are autistic, or is it also a question of resistance to learning in normal children?

In the strict sense, autism concerns children who cannot speak, and who have a very developed sensorial system but no language. But no one can encounter holes in symbolization, incapacities in symbolization, which are suddenly manifested in, let's say, a neurotic person, or if you wish, normal persons like you and me. And consequently, one can find it in students as well. At the present time, there is an extension of this term, autism, which goes beyond a handicapped childhood.

You have extended psychoanalytic analysis into the subject of society and of the foreigner, in Etrangers à nous-mêmes, *at a moment when the problem is much discussed here in France. And in the United States, though in a different way I think. Is there a certain optimism in your view of the ethic that psychoanalysis would allow, an ethic of solidarity?*

Yes. The question that arises now is knowing on what moral basis one can regulate the problem of foreigners. Because it is evident that even if the jurists and politicians decided, for example, to let all foreigners live in France, or even to give them a right to vote—which is far from being done of course, but suppose that that happened one day—the problem arises of knowing whether morally and ethically the national populations are ready to take that step. And the answer is *no*. So where does one start to open up this very phobic notion of national identity, to permit the mixture of races and to welcome others, in order to proceed to what I call "puzzle" states, that is, states that are constituted from several types of citizens—immigrants, people who are part of the European community, people who come from Africa and Asia in addition to those in France—and then perhaps one day to proceed toward the disappearance of the notion of the foreigner? Montesquieu and the French revolutionaries had such an idea, but it is far from being realized.

We cannot look for the answer in religion, not even if certain religions—for example, present-day Catholicism—take steps toward the understanding of others. Why? In France, for example, we have an important Catholic assistance movement that is enormously interested in the immigrants, which gives them educational, moral, and material aid. But in spite of these current movements in religious institutions, these are discourses that welcome the other only on condition of delegitimating or annulling him. "You are accepted if you accept our moral code as Christian or Jew. The moment you do this, there is no problem. You are like us. We accept you." Still, they are moving toward more flexible forms of ecumenity, recognizing the right of the other to exist; they are not waging a religious war against heretics. This is true for Christianity, for example. But the great monotheistic religions like Islam are extremely reactionary and persecutory—look at the Rushdie affair. Orthodox Judaism also poses very grave problems—what is happening in the occupied territories demonstrates that.

Therefore we lack a moral code that would permit us to think about the question of the other. And I speak of religions because the question of the other is fundamentally, I think, a religious question. But with the religions in crisis, we must search for other means of approaching the question. I consider psychoanalysis to be a means of approaching the other because the Freudian message, to simplify things, consists in saying that the other is in me. It is my unconscious. And instead of searching for a scapegoat in the foreigner, I must try to tame the demons that are in me. "Hell," said Sartre, "is other people." Perhaps, but because hell is my unconscious and I do not recognize it. Therefore recognizing what is not doing well in myself—my death drives, my eroticism, my bizarrenesses, my particularity, my femininity, all these uncoded marginalities that are not recognized by consensus—I would tend less to constitute enemies from those phenomena, which I now project to the exterior, making scapegoats of others.

Beginning with such a conception of things, I think that one can proceed toward what I call in *Etrangers à nous-mêmes* a "paradoxical community," which responds to your idea of solidarity. Because that supposes, in effect, a community. We try to help one another, all. But not a community that unifies and banalizes. We recognize one another, as foreigners, strangers. That is to say, as weak, that is to say, as potentially sick. And it is by being able to hear the other as tracked by some pathology, by some anomaly, as I myself am, that I refuse to see in the other an enemy. And this would be a basis for a form of morality.

When you said earlier that the crisis of both history and the individual may be seen as a kind of suffering, a pathology, or as an opening for creation, do you mean to emphasize the creative possibilities of crisis?

I try to see the most optimistic aspects of the crisis. Of course, when you see a bottle that is half empty you can find it half empty or half full. I tend toward the direction that it is half full. A moment of crisis is a moment when something has crumbled, something is rejected, but it is also the moment when new sources appear, and in postmodernity I myself see this aspect of renewal, which interests me.

And this possibility of renewal is the same for the individual?

Absolutely . . . it's like the analytic process. There are many people who are afraid to undertake an analysis because they are going to dissolve many defenses, and it's a crisis, and they are going to find themselves at a certain moment of crisis of analysis extremely unhappy and disarmed. But when they have touched bottom, precisely, they are going to construct other possibilities for living, and so one cannot construct without destroying the old defenses.

In Etrangers à nous-mêmes, *you make the link between psychoanalysis and what you call "solidarity" among different individuals. What adjustments in the realm of culture might follow from what you propose in this book?*

I don't know. Really, I don't know. I think at the present stage we must keep ourselves from presenting great syntheses. We must try to be as concrete—I would even say microscopic—as we can be. To work at the level of individuals. At the level of individuals, pathologies, the concrete cases of foreigners, to take care of civil society and the problems that are not being solved. But we must not try to propose global models. I think that we risk, then, making politics into a sort of religion, while it seems to me that concrete interventions are more important. For example, I consider that my work as an analyst is political work, to take it in a microscopic and individual sense. I think that the outcome of the Rights of Man is the veneration of the individual and of his difference. And that we should try to preserve these singularities. How can we make a politics that takes account of the singularities? Obviously not by talking about the political, but by trying to maximize singularities. Of the political there is already too much, of political men and women. Perhaps they will finally listen to us, try to apply this. But our role, my role, as an intellectual, is to see the most exceptional things possible, what individuals have that is exceptional. And to emphasize irreducible things.

So literature is a way of getting to a politics of singularity, of keeping étrangeté *within discourse. Can you address the way fiction relates to the construction of gender? Nancy Armstrong, an American critic, argues that the discourses producing the idea of the middle-class woman, especially domestic fiction, are responsible for gendering difference and for creating the modern idea of the individual. How do you see women and gender in this question of individual difference?*

First, the idea of the individual as connected, as having been discovered from the feminine: I am not sure that that can be supported if one takes account of history. Because if you look, for example, at the emergence of the notion of individuality in the Renaissance, it is connected as much to the recognition of insanity in carnival as to the recognition of bizarre sexual practices. So . . . all forms of strangeness. It is true that the feminine, in particular in the eighteenth-century novel, comes to crystallize marginality, psychology, discomfort, and melancholy all at once. And the feminine heroine of Richardson, Sterne, Diderot, even Sade becomes the paragon of this individuation. But I don't think we should generalize and see in the woman the only can-opener [*le seul ouvre-boîte*], so to speak, that could permit a homogenous society to generate the notion of the individual. I think that we must also consider other currents.

Why do I say this? Because in the present state of things, I am afraid that if we insist on the fact that the feminine differentiates the individual, we may arrive at a new form of homogeneity. Because I see many women—at the university as well as on the couch—and what interests me in order to think about what a woman is, is the difference between these women. In other words, I would emphasize not the notion of gender, but the notion of singularity. Of the irreducibility of individuals—whether they be men or women. Perhaps there is a woman who has the sexuality of a baby, of a child, of a little girl, of a little boy, and each can be found within this notion of "woman."

But I would also like to multiply differences. I have the impression that the idea of the feminine as difference was good to begin with, but it risks fixing difference too much and making us think only of two, while there are more. And perhaps what interests me is a democracy of the multiple, and in this perspective, it is seeing individual differences, singularities. With the singularities of women included. On that point, let me recall something that we did several years ago in a Belgian feminist journal called *Les Cahiers du GRIF* (which is still in existence). The interview was called "unes femmes."[2] I put "unes" and "femmes" to show that, it is true, there are groups of women—we are communities—but that that makes no sense—these new groups of women have no meaning with respect to groups of men or of proletarians or this or that unless we take account of the singular differences of women. If not, if we put everything under the same common denominator, all the women the same, it is not so interesting. That would be to replace one providential force with another providential force.

Do you see a difference between Americans and the French on the idea of the individual, the domestic, and the woman?

Surely, but it is very difficult to generalize. The French are perhaps more individualistic, and at the same time more ironic about their individualism. Americans, it seems to me—in any case, Protestant Americans—have a sense of duty and of mutual help, of the necessity of devoting oneself to someone else, of being able to establish a bond of community, which does not exist with the French. I first became aware of this friendly side of the American university community when I arrived in the United States with my son, when he was a baby. In twenty-four hours I had everything needed to furnish a baby's room— diapers, bottles, pots, a little bed, a swing. People were altogether warm and helpful.

As for women, there also it's an individual matter, it's unwarranted to generalize. But I think the French tradition—in spite of its misogyny and antifeminism, which are widespread—nonetheless gives a certain valorization to feminine work, feminine spirit and wit, to a sort of social aura of women. Through the salons of the eighteenth and nineteenth centuries, there is something that endures, which it seems to me is still living. I myself sense that women in the French university are less subjected to harassment, to surveillance, than in the United States.

There is also the question of individualism and ideology. For example, the American ideal of an autonomous individual makes it difficult for my students to imagine a subject-in-process.

There are two aspects. There is, on the one hand, the sort of permanent exceeding of the individual, who is not an atom closed on herself, who is in fact a process—you are right to stress that. And then there is this problem that is posed more and more on the political level in French society: how to arrange it such that this aspect of singularity does not become isolation, but that there is nevertheless a kind of communication among singularities. Here we are trying to find new forms of society that are not constraining, but there are no societies that are not constraining that do not respect individuals. I think that it is one of the fantasies of feminism to think that one can make a collective without singular individuals. It's a caricature of communism into which certain feminists have fallen.

But the problem for some American feminists is that the idea of individualism is linked to a discourse that is liberal, positivist, middle-class, a class controlled by patriarchal discourse, and that serves the consumerist culture only too well.

They imagine that there is an alternative that exists in the East.[3] Because what is happening now, in Eastern countries, is that the collapse of the Marxist and socialist idea is showing something else. It shows that we can arrive at a better society not before bourgeois individualism but after. I think they ought to revise their ideas, seeing what is happening in the East now. Because many feminist ideas were unconsciously calculated and modeled on the image of communist and Marxist countries, as if a progressive and communitarian ideology could produce the economy of bourgeois society. Now one realizes that one cannot just make the system of a society from the model of ideology. It is necessary to transform it. But not on this side of it, but by passing to the other side.

In thinking about your new book and about the question of becoming a stranger to oneself, becoming uncanny, we wondered—given women's marginality in relation to power or to discourse, given women's foreignness— whether women could be anything but étrangères.

I am very attached to the idea of the woman as irrecuperable foreigner. But I know that certain American feminists do not think well of such an idea, because they want a positivist notion of woman. But one can be positive by starting with this permanent marginality, which is the motor of change. So I think that for me femininity is exactly this lunar form, in the way that the moon is the inverse of the sun of our identity. From this point of view, perhaps we women have it more than the men, but the men have it also. And to try to preserve this part as unreconcilable permits us perhaps always to be what Hegel called the eternal irony of the community. That is to say, a sort of separate vigilance that keeps groups from closing up, from becoming homogenous and so oppressive. That is, I see the role of women as a sort of vigilance, a strangeness, as always to be on guard and contestatory.

In fact, it's the role of the hysteric, a little; and why not? I accept that altogether. We can play our hysterias without necessarily making a psychodrama and exposing ourselves to being the victims of the male order, but with great lucidity, knowing what we do, and with great mastery and measure. That is, perverse hysterics. Very wise.

How does this work, to take this perversity, this hysteria on oneself as a strategy?

First, it is two things. It seems to me that the possibility is less distinct and strong with women than with men, because it is more difficult for a woman to break the law, to choose different, multiple erotic objects, like a Don Juan or a Casanova, for example.[4] This is due, probably, in part to her fusion with the maternal image, and in part to a great dependence with respect to paternal law. So in this context feminine perversion is a rather rare phenomenon, which explains why we encounter more depression than its opposite, which is perversion, in women. But in compensation, when the capacity for perversion succeeds in finding a place—notably, when a woman detaches herself from the maternal weight, or when she succeeds in arranging a lighter, freer relationship, more detached as well with respect to paternal authority—then, under those conditions, there can indeed be a perverse coloration of hysteria that permits her to play with the norm. I think that all creations go through that, and especially artistic creations, for women as well as for men. But it is very clear: when one encounters aesthetic successes in women, they are supported in individual experience on a sort of fringe that I will call "père-pervers d'hystérie," the perverse father of hysteria, without putting anything pejorative into this word, but simply the possibility of playing with the law.

So it is a choice that a woman can make to play this role.

It is difficult to say if it's a choice, because often they are so bound up by the maternal weight and the authority of the father that this choice is impossible. But I think that a successful analysis, for example, could lead a woman to this solution.[5]

Speaking of a perverse hysteria as a strategy leads me to think of another figure of the woman that you have delineated. I am very interested in this story of Io, which you tell in Etrangers à nous-mêmes.

Oh, yes, the sacred cow.

I wondered if you had thought of proposing it as an alternative to the Oedipus narrative for women?

I haven't worked much on this, but it should be done. There are psychoanalysts who have worked on Io. Paul Claude Racamier in France has published a text on Io and the Oedipus complex, as it happens. But in any case what fascinated me was that the first foreigners about which occidental history speaks were foreign *women*, because the initial Greek example of the foreigner is found in a fragment which remains of Aeschylus, in the play about the Danaïdes. Who are the Danaïdes? They are women who descend from the sacred cow, Io. What did she do, this sacred cow? She was a person who fell in love with Zeus, and who thus committed an illegitimate act because she seduced the husband of Hera. One has, consequently, a sort of authoritarian couple, Hera and Zeus, a parental couple, and here is this girl—one imagines a girl—coming to commit an act of lèse-maternité by making an enemy of Hera and taking the father. And Hera, obviously, is furious. She sends a sort of insect, a horsefly, which crazes Io, who is turned into a cow and chased from her native land. So she becomes foreign from that moment on; there are no more lands that can become her own because she is condemned to wander in the world, until the day when Zeus decides to touch her. But he cannot permit himself to do that in Greece, because Hera, who is the goddess of the foyer, prevents it. Indeed, the maternal authority is so strong that even Zeus cannot transgress it. He profits by the moment when Io finds herself in Egypt, he touches her, and she becomes calm. The madness of foreignness is eliminated, and Io can become the mother of children, who eventually have as descendants the fifty Egyptades and fifty Danaïdes. So Io is the ancestor of the Danaïdes, who are the first foreigners.

That is, we find the Danaïdes at an important moment that concerns both women and the problems of foreignness. They are fifty girls who are forced to marry their fifty cousins. They do not wish to do so; they are resistant to marriage, and in certain variants of the myth, on the day of the marriage ceremony, they kill the cousins. We have the impression that this is a memory that the Greek society preserved about the passage from an endogamous society where one married to the same clan, to an exogamous society where one must leave to marry someone else who is not a cousin. And that that passage was experienced in an extremely violent manner, so painful that the refusal was imagined as a murder. The women do not wish to marry their cousins, and at the extreme they would murder these cousins. So these women are viragos, against marriage. In other variants of the myth the Danaïdes are seen as very ambiguous characters. On the one hand, they serve the cult of Hera, who is the goddess of marriage; they carry the cask of the Danaïdes with which they pour the water symbolizing the domestic household. On the other hand, they participate in the cults of Demeter, which are very violent. Once a year the women gather together. They pour not water, as they do in their housekeeping tasks, but blood. As if this double myth of water and blood wished to show that marriage is an affair of extreme violence, and that if one makes water flow, one must not forget that there is the potential for making blood flow. And that this act of alliance between two persons is in fact based upon an extreme ferocity, a great aggressiveness, a great violence.

I give this example to show how violent, clear, and explicit the idea of the war of the sexes, of the difference of the sexes, was in this Greek mythical and postmythical consciousness, and why it was necessary to follow such rites to facilitate the catharsis of that consciousness. In our societies we try, instead, to repress this idea of violence. Feminism has had the advantage of putting the accent upon it, reemphasizing the incompatibility of the sexes. This is perhaps going too far—to declare an absolute war of the sexes seems to me an exaggeration—but such a declaration is the opposite of puritanism. I think that we can try to find an agreement: neither the discrete veil over the contradictions in order to see only the harmony, nor absolute war. But that we can recognize the difficulty of an alliance between two people and try to deploy all possible tact so that these foreigners—which men and women are to one another—can find a modus vivendi, which is not easy. The developed societies, which we call decadent, have the advantage of being confronted with this truth that I would call mythical and fundamental, because it is not in Islam that we can reflect on this difficulty. It is in our society—it's in New York, or Paris, where couples are becoming impossible. It is by starting with this impossibility that one can perhaps try to live with a man, with a woman, like one lives with foreigners.

Let's move, then, to the East/West question, which is also connected to étrangeté. Many people would like to know more about your own history and your own view of European history, given that you grew up under socialism and then moved to France. Can you tell us anything about your own experience—about the Bulgaria of your childhood, what it was like to grow up there?

I was raised in a francophone family which had the wonderful idea—it's rare that children recognize the wonderful ideas of their parents, but I can do so here—of putting me in a French *école maternelle*. So I learned French rather early. And I had a sort of double education, up to the moment of coming to France, because in the morning I went to a Bulgarian school and in the afternoon I went to a French school. But it was less harmonious than it appears, because my parents were not members of the communist party. I did not have the right to study as the children of the red bourgeoisie did—that is, to study in the foreign language schools. In the sixties there were English, French, and German high schools created and the children of the red bourgeoisie who were good students went directly into those schools. I myself did not have access to them, so I was somewhat segregated. But there were courses in foreign languages, which meant that I could catch up by doing two schools. The experience in Bulgaria permitted me at once to live in an extremely closed environment (which is called totalitarian for good reason, with enormous constrictions), to understand the weight of social life, and at the same time to try to find the small spaces of freedom, which include, for example, the arts, the interest in foreign languages, even religion. This does not necessarily appear in a very secular tradition like that in France, but it is an extremely important phenomenon there, which one can see, notably, in Poland today.

I came to France because of General de Gaulle. He had a megalomaniac idea that consisted of connecting Europe from the Atlantic to the Urals, and he gave fellowships to young nationals from the East whom the authorities would not send. They were afraid that the nationals would stay in the West, and they were right. But as it happens, in the days before Christmas of 1966, the director of my thesis—I had begun a thesis on the *nouveau roman*—took advantage of the absence of the director of the literary institute who had left for Moscow—and who was dogmatic—to send me to the French embassy and support my candidacy for scholarship. So I arrived at the beginning of 1966—or rather in the Christmas season of 1965—with five dollars. And my scholarship was to start two months later. I won't tell you all the peripeties of the plot. I fortunately happened upon people who welcomed me.

Above all, what was extremely important and decisive for my life here was that I happened upon a France in a total upheaval, because it was still very traumatized by the Algerian war and at the same time very interested in socialism, in the communist experience. There was a spirit of contestation, which meant that above all on the intellectual plane, people were very much interested in the East. Not so much, really, in order to apply the model of the East, not even at all, but partly as a political curiosity and above all on the intellectual plane. Don't forget that this was the period of the structuralism of Lévi-Strauss. Everything that we could bring which was connected to Russian formalism and all the predecessors of structuralism was extremely interesting. What interested me was to go beyond structuralism, because what was immediately apparent to me were the limitations of structuralism, while in Russia, as it happens, in the postformalist years we had had Bakhtin and the interest in what I called the intertext, history, and subjectivity.

I immediately spoke to Roland Barthes, who was an extremely welcoming person. He is the only professor I know who knew how to read his students. We read our students looking for our own ideas, and if we don't find them, we give them a bad grade, whereas he really read the unknown that the students brought him. And he was altogether welcoming, positive, and encouraging. He invited me to give a paper in his seminar about what I had told him. He had that paper published in the form of an article in *Critique*.[6] And that is how I began to work in France. In the same circumstances, I met the people in the Tel Quel group, who were, in fact, the basis of the acceptance of structuralism by the French intelligentsia, without which structuralism would have remained contained in the university. It would never have had the aura that it now has, because that was the moment that connected structuralism to literary experience itself. I met Sollers in the same group. I was married. So my life was somewhat brought together, thanks to the welcome that I had in the French intellectual milieu.

I had the luck, several months ago, to receive a telephone call from President Mitterand, who asked me to accompany him on his presidential trip to Bulgaria. And it was completely overwhelming. I went. And I was impressed by two things. First by the great freedom of the students. The outlook is a guess, because economic life has gotten worse; at the level of food, business, things are going less well than before. But beyond that, there are also some elements that lead to a positive hypothesis, knowing that the higher echelons of the communist party and the young are more and more inspired by democratic ideas, and they are not afraid. For example, Mitterand was greeted by a crowd of students at the university. This is already startling, because it proves that university authorities were allowing it. They did not choose three students, but they let *all* of them gather. People asked questions in French, declaring their identity in front of the police, who were there as well, I suppose, and in front of television cameras, and being extremely critical of the government. That would have been totally inconceivable several years ago.

And then there was another event. My father was a strong believer; he sang in the cathedral choir. Mitterand wanted to go to religious places to show that he is for a plurality of consciences and not for communist ideology, which totalizes. And so in the crypt of the Alexander Netzky church we saw this gentleman singing—it was not a mass; it was a concert of religious music—and I waved at him. Mitterand asked of me, "Who is that gentleman?"

I said, "He's my father."

"But I absolutely must see him." They met one another. And then they talked about the role of art, of faith for the freedom of individuals, of the power of art and of song in religious rites. That lasted only ten minutes, but everyone was delighted. And I was happy to give a gift like that to my parents. I have the sense of having abandoned them a little. This was extremely important to me because it was a way of giving homage to the humility and the exemplary ethic of my father, and also of protecting him from the authorities of the country, because he was having a great deal of trouble obtaining a passport to travel to France. So a certain proximity to the president of the French Republic would shelter him from persecutions to some extent. And above all, since he died [this past] September under completely barbarous conditions, this was my last meeting with him. It remains something very luminous.

Would you like to comment a little on the current situation in Bulgaria?

At present the general state of the Eastern countries is a great deal of confusion and a great deal of hope. There is a collapse of the former Stalinist rigidity, but there is not yet any competent democratic force. And in the interim, one has the sense that the old system is getting cosmetic changes. In other words, former communists of the old school disguise themselves as democrats and await events. And in the meanwhile, there is an enormous economic crisis that makes the situation very alarming. For example, I received catastrophic appeals about the children: there is no food for very young children; in the hospitals, there is no cotton for bandages. So this situation continues to get worse; to what extent the population is going to put up with this is a great question. And on the other hand, there is a great deal of desire of democracy and very little competence: they do not know what a democratic party is; they do not know how to organize an electoral campaign. Now that there are going to be elections in most of these countries, they appeal to us in France in particular to start broadcasting. I participated yesterday in a meeting at Radio France International to comment upon the broadcasts in Eastern bloc countries, to explain the organizational problems of electoral campaigns, for example. Or to talk about other questions, for example, the questions of nationalism that are reawakening in these countries, or the questions of religions—because after the death of Marx, there is nationalism and religion that return—how to cope with all those problems? They ask for much help from us on that level, on the level of ideology.

They have these serious economic problems, and then the questions of nationalism and religion that they do not succeed in thinking through—they are not at all prepared. I had some Eastern people ask us for psychoanalytic and structuralist literature, to know how to analyze a discourse, how to become lucid about these phenomena. So I think that there will be a sort of intellectual contact that is going to continue, but we are in it for years. It will be long, very, very long.

Let's now return to the question of psychoanalysis and its implications for literature. Your book Black Sun: Depression and Melancholia *has now appeared in translation in the United States. In it you trace the way melancholy appears in both psychoanalytic patients and literature. Here, we're especially interested in the final chapter, where you look at the work of Marguerite Duras. Can you talk about how, in Duras, history and the depressive psyche interact? How do you read Roland Barthes's* Fragments of a Lover's Discourse—*in particular, the idea that the lover's discourse is isolated from history—in light of the way Duras is obsessed with the way history infects both the lover's discourse and desire?*

I have already tried to answer this aporia posed by Barthes with the idea of intertextuality.[7] Because I think, on the one hand, that we must maintain the autonomy of discourse with respect to the social level, because it is a level of autonomy that guarantees freedom. We can speak in a different manner from our familial and social determination. There is an undecidable part that comes perhaps out of our biology, a certain number of determinations that escape us, but in any case that are not reducible to what we know of society. And if one does not keep this autonomy of discourse, one falls very quickly into a reductionism and a sociological conception where all aesthetic or personal performances are explained by the social milieu or a similar fate: from the fact that you were born red, black, white, or poor. This said, there is an incontestable interaction between discourse and society, and I myself would consider that the fact of taking society as a generalized text permits us to see how, for example, a literary text does not live in an autistic fashion, closed on the interior of itself, but borrows always from the discourses of the press, from oral discourses, from political discourses, and from other texts that preceded it, that provide vehicles in turn for these cultural and political texts of history.

To take the example of Duras, I believe that one cannot understand the depression of the women she describes if one does not take the Second World War into account. That is what I try to show. She made this explicit throughout a text called *La Douleur*, and it was already present in *Hiroshima*. So it is a political context that individuals lived through, of immense physical and moral pain, of death and destruction. But it is also a metaphysical context, which is the context of a generalized doubt about values. God does not exist, and nothing can replace the good and the beautiful. And, finally, the good and the beautiful do not exist. Even my own text, Duras seems to say, is neither beautiful nor good; it is nondescript; it is something unmade, a woman without makeup. It resembles a depressed woman. Thus the extremely contagious role, and the contagious effect—I say even, at moments, noncathartic—of this text, which obliges us to live through the pain without proposing a way out. Not even its own beauty. Because it does not present itself as a seduction that is going to pull us from the abyss. It shows us the importance of the abyss. But this can only be understood not only from the interior of Duras's text, which one could analyze to show how much it resonates with a problematic of depression, but from the interior of the context of war and of the crisis of values of which I have just spoken.

Given the interior crisis of the war that Duras explores, then, how is any catharsis possible in art? She is one of the living writers who explores that crisis, the heart of that void, and shows it to us. It's true that her work is not cathartic, but once we have passed through Hiroshima and Auschwitz . . .

There are those who cannot pass through. I have been surprised to hear many students, for example, say to me, "We cannot read Duras because it is so close to us that it plunges us back into the sickness." And so when one feels a little fragile, there is such a force of attraction that one does not have the means to get through. This is why I said she has the force of a sorceress perhaps more than an artist.

We wanted to know if you think melancholy in Duras is a personal pathology or a symptom that is global, widespread. Is it private, something in her family, or history that created this melancholy?

I do not know her well enough, but I suppose in looking at her writing that she is capable of great depressive moments. That said, it would not be of much interest if she had not succeeded in making this problem, which is perhaps personal, into something general that joins a universal symptom of our generation, I think. That is why her books speak to many people. Her work is personal, but it also joins with the depression that we know. But I consider that it is not cathartic but, let's say, an echo, a connivance with depression. Catharsis supposes that we leave depression, while I have the sense that these books plunge us into depression and do not give us a way to get out of it.

Do you think we should try to get out of this historical depression? Because when we look at history, perhaps we ought to press the things that are unthinkable—Auschwitz, Hiroshima.

I tend to think, as a therapist, that it is better to come out of depression, because if not, you die.

Speaking of the same chapter from Soleil noir, *at the end you compare Duras and Sollers, modernity and postmodernity—melancholy and parody. Readers have interpreted this ending of the book in completely opposing ways. Some see it as a valorization of the parodic and the postmodern, and others accuse you of maintaining the melancholy of modernity, of valorizing the tragic vision.*

I think that I tried to give perhaps a more direct response through my novel *Les Samouraïs*. The young generation has a desire to cross this postwar period, the existentialist periods, the Duras-Blanchot period when one was perhaps too close to anguish and death. They want to pass into a less burdened world, more playful. But that is a bit naive. And what I tried to do in *Les Samouraïs* was start with the color black, but also go toward the sun—to a sort of balance between pain and solace. I think that the postmodern crosses this black experience and, with a full knowledge of the facts, allows itself a certain abandon. But abandon simply like that—the game for its own sake—that does not interest anyone.

Let us go on, then, to the question of your writing and your own work as a novelist. You have advocated looking at the subject as le sujet-en-procès. *How is that connected to the question of style? I would like to know how you see your own style, which in fact performs this procès by displacing any fixed position for the subject. How do you see your style in relation to will, to the possibility for choice and agency?*

I think that questions of style cannot be raised on the level of conscious choice. Style is one possibility of being in contact with our unconscious and, I would say, even our sensations. I am increasingly interested in the importance of memory and sensation in language. And I think that the role of analysis, and also of writing, is to put the neutral surface of abstract words into contact with a whole dynamic of recollection that leads us at once to recall our traumas, the pains or the pleasures, and the most archaic sensations. And it is when we are capable of translating these sensations and perceptions and traumas or joys into the language of cognition that one obtains a style. For example: Proust.

Most of your writing, except in the parallel texts of, say, "Stabat Mater,"[8] has had a framework that is not literary yet is deeply informed by a "style." How would you say, even in a style that one might call "rational," that the unconscious can play a part?

We must make a distinction that is connected to my personal history and then to the nature of theoretical discourse. I think that there is a discourse of knowledge in the [West] that mobilizes or disciplines stylistic experimentation. When one wishes to appropriate this discourse of knowledge, one imposes a certain asceticism on oneself at the level of style. From this perspective, when I began to work, it seemed very important to me, as a person and as a woman, to show that I could take hold of that discourse. In the course of its development, this rational discourse has begun to interrogate its own mechanisms of asceticism, of neutrality; it has come to introduce more and more the personal side, the unconscious rapport. We have only to see philosophical discourse in France—Barthes, Derrida, Serres—which was influenced by Heidegger in a certain sense, but even more by Freud. This philosophical and theoretical discourse has become increasingly a very stylized, very fictional discourse. But I believe there is a defiance in it, a critique of certain restrictions on the discourse of knowledge and its pretensions to neutrality. As for me, my pathway through psychoanalysis has perhaps reconciled me with my memory and my body, and that has had a considerable importance for the change in my style.

Does this mean that we must abandon the discourse of knowledge and what I spoke of earlier as its discipline, its ascetic side? Personally, I do not think so. It is a way of clarifying certain texts or certain films or certain undeveloped societies, to take several different examples from the human sciences. Even if the understanding were schematic and neutral, it is a way of throwing light on the phenomenon. So we must not deprive ourselves of the discourse of knowledge.

Often students are pushed too quickly to write literature about literary objects, or about objects taken from human social practices. And the result is a sort of swamp of fuzzy intuitions that inhibits students' intellectual capacities and their instruction in the techniques of cognition. I think one must carefully differentiate the capacity for cognition from the capacity to exceed it, and give students the models of knowledge, of a neutral distancing. Then afterward allow for a certain softening. This is for those who engage in a theoretical discourse. Those who wish to do literature right away—all right, let them. But in the domain of pedagogy and knowledge we get rid of discipline, judgment, argument, and thought a little too rapidly, and we often produce individuals who are incapable of reasoning.

Deconstruction was very harmful in this respect because it was misunderstood. One does not deconstruct before having constructed. Those who are not capable of a certain classicism should return to Cartesian ideas, to maxims like "Ce que l'on conçoit bien s'énonce clairement" ("What is clearly conceived is clearly expressed")—and afterward produce an effect of flux, of orchestration, and of polyphony. But as enrichment, not as confusion.

To finish up, many women have been hoping you would write about women writers and artists in particular; now you've done so in writing about Marguerite Duras. Do you think you will look at other women writers in your future work?

Perhaps I am becoming a "writer" myself, to do more fiction for a while, perhaps to return later to philosophy. Which does not keep me from being interested in other women writers. But it is an idea that attracts me for the moment, to try to speak about my experience in a more fictional way for a while, which is a form, perhaps, of finding the maximum of singularity and the maximum of communicability. Thus the political impact. I think that there is in fiction something that reconciles the fact of being very particular and the fact of carrying a message that is understood by the most people possible. It is a form of atomized politics, if I could say so, in the sense of the atomizer, "the spray."

So because I think literature has importance, I have written this novel, which has just come out. The title, *Les Samouraïs*, is a wink at Simone de Beauvoir and *Les Mandarins*. Very briefly, it is about intellectuals from 1968 to the present, an effort to describe the life of the passions. One recognizes Foucault, Barthes, Lacan, perhaps myself. There are other characters who are prototypes and who represent our generation without being stars. On the feminine plane—I am going to stop at that—the characters are three women. One is named Olga; she is a young linguist who comes from the East—one recognizes in her, of course, myself. There is another named Carol, a woman who undergoes all the crises that we lived through around May 1968, who is affected by depression—whom I consider at once as a prototype of our generation and as a nocturnal double of Olga. And then there is a third who is a psychoanalyst, who keeps her journal, and who sees all this French and Parisian society with distance and irony. The three can be considered aspects of the narrator. I think it will entertain you. There is also a chapter where Olga goes to the United States and has an affair with an American professor. That enables her to make a fresco of American society, which she knows a little from a distance. This gentleman who becomes her lover is named not Mrs Dalloway but Mr Dalloway, a dialogue with Virginia Woolf, a sort of intertext with

Woolf. I think it will make you laugh. I wanted to write a popular novel, very sensual and ironic.

Two other questions, on the subject of Bakhtin and the carnivalesque, and on the subject of the crossing of voices in your writing. We wondered if you still have the dialogic in mind.

The French critics have not noticed this for the moment, because I think it is more particular to Russian or English novels. Or course in Rabelais it is evident—but the modern French novel has become thin, a little univocal—they do not have this practice I think. I regret it.

PSYCHOANALYSIS

5

The Ethics and Practice of Love

Françoise Collin conducted this interview for a 1985 issue of the Belgian feminist journal *Les Cahiers du GRIF*. The translation is by Ross Guberman. The questions are based partly on Kristeva's *Histoires d'amour*, which appeared in 1983 and was translated into English in 1986 as *Tales of Love*. The interview begins by discussing dependency in the mother-child relationship, contrasting men's dependency on the erotic object and women's dependency on the maternal body. Kristeva also describes ways in which this dependency is manifested in women's writing and literature. She suggests, moreover, that perversion can offer men an alternative to their dependency. The next section offers a historical perspective on love, noting that "the greatest moments of Western civilizations have been revivals of love" and commenting on the status of the lover's discourse today. The interview then turns to the "contractual" nature of relationships between men and women in love as well as the psychoanalytic "contract" between analyst and analysand, which Kristeva believes can serve as an ethical model for "desirable dependency" and offer lovers a way to speak about their experiences. In so doing, she places love at the center of analysis: "If the analyst does not love his patients, he should give up his efforts to treat them." At the end of the interview, Kristeva links maternal dependency with creation, suggesting that the imaginary of a literary work is "the most extraordinary and most troubling vestige of the dependency between mother and child."

My thoughts on love in *Tales of Love* are based primarily on maternal love, which I believe is at the heart of all loving relationships. I believe that maternal love is also at the base of the nuclear relationship of dependency: a mother's relationship with her child entails not only an emotional, painful, suffering, and ecstatic identification similar to the identification that takes place in other kinds of love, but a state not far removed from hypnosis and submissiveness.

Are you referring to mothers' relationships with their children or to children's relationships with their mothers?

I believe it is a reciprocal relationship, although we are more apt to see it from the child's point of view. It is easy to understand why a being who is needy and not fully developed would become dependent on his progenitor, on the mother that Winnicott calls a "transitional space,"[1] and then on the "object" of love and hate that she becomes. The situation becomes less clear, however, if we look at it from the other direction, in which case the mother relives her own childhood and finds herself dependent again on the ideal object, that is, on the narcissistic mirage of her child. Since she is willing to set aside all the tokens of her narcissism and masochism because she will be rewarded by this other's growth, accomplishments, and future, she can subordinate herself to the ideal whom she is trying to raise and who will soon exceed her bounds.

Are the notions of dependency and suffering inextricably linked?

Not necessarily. I distinguish between two strains of dependency: primary dependency and secondary dependency. I believe there can be no relationship to the other and no acceptance of alterity without a certain dependency, a certain debt, and a certain gift that presumes a subjectification to the other. When this goes too far, however, we run the risk of complete submission, a renunciation of the same for the other, and total enslavement. In that case, dependency becomes a slow death that can be quite painful.

It seems that the notion of complete submission would apply to a woman who has given up her autonomy for someone else's sake; but doesn't impassioned dependency have exactly the same effect as submission? Doesn't it, too, cause suffering?

A vestige of the mother can be found in every passionate relationship. When a woman is in a passionate relationship with a man, her dreams or fantasies often depict a ghost of her mother hovering over him. Her painful jubilation often suggests that she is reliving her infantile dependency on her mother's body, the jouissance that this body gave her, and the suffering that frustration or even an intrusion of the mother's body can provoke in the child.

You have described how this process occurs in women. Do you believe that dependency and submission are unique to women, or do they simply function in a particular way in women?

Men's dependency on the erotic object is extremely important, which one sees in analyses in which men talk about such things without feeling the need to cloak them in phallic glory or masculine dignity. Several of my male patients have brought such a dependency to my attention. I could give the example of the young man trapped in a state of imbalance and instability that turned into quasi-psychotic episodes when his girlfriend left him, cheated on him, or simply refused to play his game. For an older man, this could manifest itself as an allegiance to an ill wife who found herself taking on traits of an ill or abandoned mother.

Men's servitude to their erotic objects is thus complete and fundamental. Their servitude even includes an element that offers a way to become free of it: male perversion. Perversion also gives men an opportunity to change objects easily, to amass partners, or, on the other hand, to enter into sadomasochistic, exhibitionist, or masturbatory relationships with a particular object. Perverts find these relationships to be essential, even though they are socially unacceptable and dominated more by the repetition compulsion than by desire. Such relationships reveal a manipulation of the excitability of a perverse erotic object that is both dominating and dominated. So the man becomes a slave to the woman, although he still does not feel a need to carry out the erotic act through desire. This results in masculine erotic addictions that are not so different from drug addictions and that are dominated by manifestations of a maternal object experienced as omnipotent, phallic, and hypnotic.

It seems that women's relationship to dependency is different from men's; men seem to manipulate their dependency and to be somewhat free from it.

Female dependency has more to do with narcissism, which paradoxically makes it seem more psychological. A woman needs reassurance, acceptance, stability, security, and a future—she seeks all the elements that constitute a psychic identity and that prevent it from being fractured, inconsistent, and fluid. This economy may appear to be less corporeal, or even sexual, but it is central to the psychic apparatus because it guides us into archaic domains. Narcissism is a modality that precedes object relations, desire, and the ensuing oedipal struggle. Women's addiction to the core of this dependency is thus located in these narcissistic regions; it is more archaic and less erotic than men's. It is archaic in the sense of an archeology of one's own image, of many parts fused into a whole. Indeed, if I fail to fuse the parts of my dismembered body into a whole, I cannot exist, speak, or enter into relationships with other people.

So would female dependency be more radical and more dangerous than men's, which is more of a dependency on an object?

It is hard to define and compare these categories, for men's relationships with erotic objects can guide them into regions that made them question their own identity. Perversion is an attempt to stabilize a narcissism disturbed by the discovery that the mother has no penis. Afflicted in this way, a man might become so dependent on satisfying his excitability that if it ever remained unsatisfied, his entire image would be shattered and his identity would have no phallus, causing a direct relationship to form between the phallic realization of an object and narcissism.

Even so, what you say is true: male sexuality and the social process of sexualization clearly offer men a greater opportunity to amass fetishes and substitutes capable of replacing the fundamental lack and offering a hope of satisfaction—a satisfaction that may be only temporary but is satisfying both phallically and narcissistically. That is why men seem to be able to deal with this lack more easily, except perhaps when they are in such critical stages as adolescence or male menopause.

I am struck by the fragility of today's adolescents. Because we have celebrated the image of a young woman who is promised a great deal and who supports feminist and progressive causes, the problems of adolescent girls may be less apparent to us than those of boys, who have felt threatened in many ways, particularly by their confrontations with girls who seem to have it all: the opportunity to play competitive sports, to experience sexual freedom, to go on the pill, to train for professions traditionally reserved for men, and so forth.

Do you believe that sociohistorical factors affect sexual structure?

We could look at this relationship more closely, but it is not of the utmost importance. If a boy feels weakened by a given social context, for example, he probably has more profound reasons [than sociohistorical ones] to feel the way he does. Yet when someone's psychic structure corresponds to his social discourse, his psychic situation becomes more complicated. We would then be mistaken to ignore historical events.

As soon as we speak about dependency, we must face narcissism and acknowledge that our self-image is dependent on someone else. When this other fails to present us with a satisfactory image, our dependency becomes so great that we break down. Social discourse, then, is quite essential to the narcissistic structure. Narcissistic vulnerability entails an ambiguous relationship to language and an unstable, ambiguous symbolic bond.

Does that mean that those who have a relationship to the symbolic, such as artists, are less fragile?

Not necessarily. Some people with narcissistic personality structures fail to create secondary elaborations that reflect their affective or archaic experience. Their symbolic elaborations (as well as their imaginary ones) act as a second skin, as something superficial. Analysts often hear patients complain that what they say does not express how they feel. Such complaints are often interpreted as hysterical defenses against a complete narcissization of the body and of affect, but I believe they may point to a personality rupture that prevents what is obtained secondarily from penetrating into the deepest layers of the psyche.

Does this situation occur beyond language and in writing or literature?

Yes, it could also apply to artificial symbolic constructions that serve as defenses against a reality that I call "semiotic" because it is neither meaningless nor substantially and biologically amorphous but the beginnings of a primary psychic articulation. At the same time, such constructions adopt paralinguistic forms that are not symbolized through linguistic signs. This explains why some texts, though skillfully constructed, resemble a "false self," an "as-if personality," or a vitally important impostor.

This goes back to what I was saying before, that when we are faced with personalities with a strong narcissistic component, we must take into account the event and not rely merely on verbalization and on the individual's free associations. Yet it is also important to consider the traumatic event, the sublinguistic, vocal, tactile, and visual forms it may take, and all the other types of bodily movement (which, as I have said, are psychic inscriptions and not simply biological energies). If we take all these factors into account, we may eventually gain access to other, more secondary and symbolic, forms of elaboration.

I sometimes have the impression that the semiotic is more pronounced and more resistant to secondary and linguistic considerations in women than in men.

Even though works written by women often appear to tell their author's story?

I have the impression that when women tell a story, they often resort to mimetic acts and to repetitions of already developed narrative structures, even if fragments of an original and authentic discourse sometimes make their way into the gesture of such imitations. I also find that recent efforts to create a "women's writing" [*écriture de femmes*], however inconsistent they may be, have relied on the very transverbal or preverbal elements I discussed earlier.

These elements characterize Nathalie Sarraute's *Tropismes*, Virginia Woolf's *The Waves*, and Duras's somewhat pallid discourse. That does not mean that they cannot be found in male writers such as Blanchot or Mallarmé. Yet since this sort of rhetoric is a way of reaching the narcissistic continent, when women have the impression that they can no longer access language and when they say that language is phallic, they believe they are more closely identified with this archaic register.

Which means that it is a choice that women make. Is it also a limitation?

It means that they must choose a polemical view of culture, but it may also be a limitation for those who have a strongly narcissistic or phobic structure. Such a structure could not be otherwise, for it defines its reality by choosing this sort of discourse and then putting it on display as if it were a mirror—as well as a challenge to other people. Some women writers may deal with phobia by giving a semiotic expression to its breaking point, which protects them from the perverse solution of gravitating toward the erotic object or the object of knowledge.

Is this perverse solution impossible for women?

No, but I believe that female phobics have a harder time gaining access to it than do male phobics.

What stands in their way? Cultural conditions?

What stands in their way is the impact of the maternal relationship, which brings us back to the problem of dependency and to the little girl's relationship with her mother. Since her mother is an object of need, she is the ideal, though she is not an erotic object (except in homosexual inversion). So I cannot possess her, nor can I abandon her and hand her over to another man (to the father, to the man) or to another woman (to an object of homosexual desire). Even if a boy's mother is forbidden as an erotic object (the Oedipus complex), that possibility exists for him, if only because it is forbidden.

So you believe that the possibility of creating a literary work as a detachable object is contingent on the ability to play around with one's mother?

Yes, and that is why female creators need at least some degree of female homosexuality, whether it exists in reality or in fantasy. In order for my mother to become an erotic object that I can eventually master, abandon, and replace with other objects, I must somehow assume a phallic and manly pose that imitates a father or an authoritarian male figure. At that point, I can participate in another mimetic system and another identificatory game involving falseness and an identification that is impossible, yet manifested as an imitation, a supplement, and a fetish used as a substitute.

That makes me think of someone like Gertrude Stein, whose writing shuns the highly corporeal side we find in other women writers' work—and hers is the work of a female homosexual.

I am not a great fan of Gertrude Stein, but I do believe her work exhibits a phallic identification made tolerable through irony and through her poking fun at herself and at her relationship with Alice B. Toklas.

Do you really believe that the only choice we have is between the phallic position and the other? Can we ever get out of this dilemma? Are there any relationships among women or between women and writing that fall out of this register? Are you perhaps oversimplifying things a bit?

Escaping from this "dilemma," as you call it, entails playing a game between the two sides of this dilemma. This game is possible in the imaginary register, but both sides are needed everywhere else. Still, one could imagine protected social bonds in which entire lives could be constructed inside the imaginary register.

I would like to set aside for a moment the question of dependency in love and return to the question of love itself. Love, after all, is a historical reality, particularly in the way it has been formulated through time. The love that was the theme and leitmotif of an entire literary genre—in the nineteenth century, for instance—seems today to have fallen by the wayside in works of literature, especially in those written by men, whereas it can still be found in works written by women. At any rate, we still find this sort of love in what women read, even when they read for pleasure, whereas it is often absent from what men read these days. Are these purely superficial observations, or is there a valid historical approach to the theme of love and its formulation?

One can certainly speak of a history of love, of mutations in the lover's discourse, and of changes in the role this discourse has played in the aesthetic imaginary and in philosophical or religious discourse. It is striking to note, for example, how important the lover's discourse was for the construction of Christianity. Everyone knows that the Christian religion is a religion of love and that churches are filled with people who go there to hear that God loves them; but we don't give it much thought, because it has become commonplace. Perhaps we still to need to stress that the entire history of the patristic is a story of highly nuanced variations on different modes of love and forms of love, the importance of the body in love, the importance of the "self" and the "own," and so forth. I myself have tried to analyze two strains of this loving relationship: the importance of the body in the writings of Saint Bernard and the importance of self-love in Saint Thomas.

Yet it is also true that the greatest moments of Western civilizations have been revivals of love, such as those led by the troubadours in the eleventh and twelfth centuries and by the romantics in the nineteenth. The problem lies in knowing (and this is one of things that has intrigued me the most) if the lover's discourse is dead today, resurfacing only in Hollywoodesque folklore or in bored and archaic women who dream like Madame Bovarys, sitting in front of their television sets.

I believe we are experiencing a disintegration of "Our" civilization, and thus of the social bond in general and the lover's bond in particular. As a result, one of the characteristics of the crisis in the West is that we no longer have a homogeneous lover's discourse. There is no more religion, which once served as a lover's discourse but is currently breaking down. Nor is there a homogeneous aesthetic, which means that we no longer have a lover's code rooted in an aesthetic practice such as that of the troubadours or that of the romantics. All that remains are traces of prior lovers' codes, which tend to return in women's literature and to attract women readers. More than just archaic elements placed in society, such discourses can adhere rather harmoniously to the quieter areas of society—those in which women are away from their work and in which women are not members of the workforce.

Yet this literature is of great appeal to working women. I'm thinking, for example, of the Harlequin collection.

That is true when women leave work to create an imaginary haven in which they see themselves as Angélique, the marquise des Anges, or, through Régine Deforges, as an Angélique of the 1940s. These women become mirrors of a past or of a memory that can be put to rest only if they are given some space outside the contradictory processes of production, professional commitments, erotic troubles, reproductive issues, and other crises experienced by "working women," as you call them.

At the same time, we are experiencing a revival of philosophical or religious discourse on love that has not kept it from disintegrating.

Today's religious discourses are remnants or archeological excavations of a lover's discourse from the past that some individuals still use in our plural, nonhomogeneous history, an era in which each person lives in his own time. We may all *be* citizens of the twentieth century, but we do not all *live* in the twentieth century. Some of us live in the thirteenth century, others in the fifteenth, and still others are Buddhists, nihilists, and so on. Such shattered time brings individual archeologies into contact with amatory feelings and identifies with them by relying on a given religion or discourse from the past.

Yet there is something that I believe to be at the heart of today's cultural landscape—something that also happens to be rooted in love: psychoanalytic discourse. Psychoanalysis has given shape to a lover's discourse striving to be new; it is the only place laid out explicitly in the social contract that allows individuals to speak about their loves, to find a discourse appropriate to their amatory experiences, and to construct it through a relationship that is itself a loving relationship with their analyst. What is more, love serves as the catalyst through which this psychoanalytic discourse can reach the biological realm. This movement has led to an extremely courageous conception of the individual that challenges the metaphysical dichotomies between the body and the spirit. What is new about psychoanalytic discourse is that it questions these dichotomies, the dichotomy between theory and practice as well as the one between the body and the spirit. It also relies on the signifier to reach the realm of the somatic.

In the wake of these developments, philosophical discourse, influenced to some degree by psychoanalysis, has tried to question its own premises by considering the way it has formulated itself and the way it has taken shape, by diminishing the force of concepts by integrating narration and fiction into the philosophical statement itself, and by adopting a Heideggerian etymologism, which nowadays includes a Freudian element and resembles a dream analysis more than a linguistic one.

I believe that some important existential and theoretical breakthroughs have come from attempts to reformulate the lover's relationship and to find a discourse for it that does not correspond to archeologically known discourses but converges on a space that I believe to be at the center of Freudian theory.

Listening to you speak, one might think that "love" can be found only inside psychoanalytic space. In other areas of life, this sort of relationship is in decline. Women have the impression that they are the guardians of love, but they find it only inside themselves.

We may need to be slightly Marxist, or at least sociological, and place a renewed emphasis on events. I believe that the expansive freedoms that people now seek in sexual behavior (thanks to the pill, to artificial insemination, and so forth) as well as in economics makes their survival less dependent on other people. Since the couple, as a unity of production, is much less necessary now than it was in the past, we have become increasingly aware of the psychic autonomy and divergent psychic interests of the two sexes.

So how can there be a relationship between these two heterogeneous structures?

Through an amicable contract—a frightening prospect that requires adult individuals who are strong enough to tolerate another person's freedom. Each individual must find his or her own motifs, causes, and objects of gratification and satisfaction while establishing a modicum of consensus and communication with a steady partner. Yet this is only a minimum; it cannot be the absolute and the totality.

Are such relationships based partly on negotiation?

You could say that. The contractual element of the couple has become increasingly clear to me. A couple is a dependency in which we choose to participate. Kafka says, "temporarily and forever." He was referring to literary and metaphysical choices, but I believe it also holds true for love. The easiest part is the "temporary" aspect. When it becomes "forever," a negotiation must precede the temporary stage.

If what you have said about this negotiation between the permanent and the temporary is correct, women are the ones who carry out the negotiation even though they get the lesser part of the bargain, a bargain that seems better suited for male desire. Does this arrangement lead to suffering and abandonment for women and satisfaction for men? Is the contract not skewed from the beginning?

It may be more complicated than that. Women's sexual and material independence has helped them by creating an image of autonomy, performance, and social value that gives them a certain amount of pleasure. Women are increasingly finding this aspect of the contract to be accessible and attractive. Since the female structure has been partly subsumed by the male structure, the difference between the sexes may appear less clear-cut today. Yet the dependence on the mother we spoke of earlier has not disappeared. I have noted, moreover, a very striking split in the discourse of postfeminist women. We see a joyful liberation ("our life is our own," "our body is our own"), but at the same time we hear women express deep feelings of pain. Today, in the wake of the feminists' militancy, I am well attuned to the manifestation of this pain and this fundamental and forever unsatisfied narcissism. The media talk a great deal about staying home, but this home often seems empty once the husband and the children are gone. Regardless of any professional or other attractions that society may offer a woman (and that she accepts even though she doesn't really believe in them), we must acknowledge that women are suffering. Perhaps their pain is greater today because they are more acutely aware of the dichotomy between phallic aspirations and certain narcissistic gratifications.

I do not want to make too much of this, however, for we have more ways to deal with this than we used to. We live in an era marked by an extraordinary upheaval of humanity that is shaking up its psychic and biological foundation. A woman experiences this mutation with great intensity, for it is occurring inside her, in her body as well as her psyche. Although this upheaval also affects men, women are its greatest beneficiary. So the sudden importance of women, who were once believed to be interchangeable and who have obtained a power and an independence never seen before, is accompanied by a challenge to their own male jouissance and narcissism.

Do you think that such contemporary phenomena as the transformation of the familial structure and the displacement of the maternal role will modify, through the help of new scientific and cultural reproductive conditions, the psychic structure of individuals, men as well as women, who are born in such conditions? Will mothers play a very different role in the future?

These mutations are no doubt on a small scale, and mothers, because of pregnancy, the care they give their newborn infants, and the substantial role they play in their children's upbringing, still exert the primary influence over an individual's development—that is, either mothers or a maternal substitute, who is usually a woman. The redistribution of traditional familial roles (dad as "maternal" and mom as "masculine") has not always affected children's psychic life for the better.

If scientific and cultural developments won't lead to a new mode of human relationships, must we look to psychoanalysis?

We often forget that psychoanalysis is also a therapy that maps out a journey between language and the body. Analysis also introduces us to a type of social relationship that I find intriguing and perhaps original. We are all premature, fragile beings, and we seek to cling not to a real mother perhaps, but to something we can depend on and use to satisfy our needs. The end of the analysis teaches us to rely only on ourselves even as we try to form bonds with other people—"temporarily and forever." I may be dreaming here of an adult humanity, but even if all patients cannot go that far in their treatment and it remains merely an objective, it still is a worthy goal.

Are psychoanalysts able to detach themselves from this model that constrains them because they reinvigorate it and perpetuate it?

In my view, the crisis of psychoanalytic societies and the terror they can incite in analysands is a sign that analysts must break free from the group as well as from the religiosity that has dominated them for some time and that must now be put into question. If analysts remain faithful to what they have become accustomed to doing, they should question both their own discourse and the people who have remained loyal to the discourse of the past. Their task is to do so with a maximum degree of serenity and detachment.

You have discussed the analyst's relationship to the group and to its cohesiveness, but do analysts also need to examine the nature of the control they exert over their relationships with their analysands?

Freud laid out some basic notions, and the generations of analysts that have followed him have built on this foundation. Analysts try to implement their vision of symptoms and anxieties by relying on their imaginative abilities to identify with their patients, their rhetorical gift of naming what is unnamable, and their theoretician's distance.

So you believe that the social bond is rooted in the psychoanalytic bond?

Since analytic discourse occurs in private and enjoys the greatest degree of freedom, I believe that an individual who undergoes the experience of analysis and so becomes a social individual learns to carve out free spaces inside the social bond. But the analytic bond is a contract with another person requiring that I recognize his rights and thus forgo some of my own desires. This relationship could be said to be one of desirable dependency.

Yet in this sort of contract, aren't the two "contracting parties" in very different and unequal positions?

Only on the surface, although this surface is important. I say "only on the surface" because analytic work requires countertransference, that is, it requires that the analyst be needy and weak. The language-driven journey between the symbolic and the organic, which is the most important ingredient in a successful analysis, relies on the analyst's neediness. So the inequality between analyst and analysand that you mentioned appears only on the surface. Yet it is an important surface that brings to mind social hierarchies, since at one point in my dependency on the other I must accept his law and acknowledge that he is superior to me. In this sense, the analyst is the master of the situation, and the money he receives only reinforces his position. Yet this mastery is merely a pretense if it is not accompanied by an analyzed countertransference. Certain analysands proffer a discourse that makes us go as far as, if not further than, our own analysis does. Role reversals can also occur in which the analyst plays the role of an object for the analysand, who becomes the subject.

Are analysands aware of the effect they have on their analyst?

That depends to a large degree on the way the analyst chooses to conduct the treatment. It also depends on the analysand's sadism and on the analyst's relative ease at dealing with it. Without reveling in the analysand's aggression or resistance and without behaving like a student, the analyst could make the analysand aware, for instance, that the patient wants to see his analyst as a depressed mother who nevertheless does not die. We are constantly working with the imaginary, with what Freud called an "illusion." We find this imaginary displaced onto our own person—which represents the height of the illusion—in the name of an ethical goal: to return to the subject the complex panoply of his symbolic abilities.

I take it that for you, ethics entails making the other person aware of a relationship to something resistant, not simply a relationship to something already known.

It is both—a relationship to something resistant and a relationship to something already known. It entails revealing the possibility of tolerating someone else despite the constraints and the violence he may represent. I believe that ethics is intertwined with love in a highly Christian sense, which is why it is intertwined with the analytic relationship. If the analyst does not love his patients, he should give up his efforts to treat them. This love is an imaginary one, and that is where Lacan's genius comes into play. Freud had already discussed the role that the imaginary plays in treatment in *The Future of an Illusion*,[2] but Lacan is the one who has shown how the imaginary is indelibly linked to the symbolic and the real. I may be very well aware that the couch and the armchair are merely a device and that strictly speaking I don't really love this patient or that patient, but my adventure consists in participating in the imaginary of love, which exposes my discourse and my personality to the joys and sorrows of love. Therein lies the source of the effect my discourse has on the other person: transference.

If the dissymmetry always works in the same way, do we leave the ethical and enter the domain of the political?

In the analytic relationship, the power struggles between the two participants are all the more intense because one of them is asking the other to relieve his suffering. So the analyst's power is placed very high indeed, although it diminishes as the treatment progresses until it reaches the point at which the bond between the two of them can be broken. Still, this symbolically high position looms over the horizon. It is as if the analysand were saying, "I am capable of elevating someone to a high position, but I am entirely capable of bringing him down from his pedestal; I'll never see my analyst again, though I won't cry as if I had lost a person dear to me even if I do go through a mourning period at the end of my analysis . . ."

Is separation essential to the human condition?

Absolutely. Religion is rooted in our inherent separation. For the Indo-Europeans, "to have faith" means that I make a pledge and a gift to someone from whom I am separated and whom I expect to pay me back, which presumes that separation is a place of suffering. The analytic contract presumes that someone comes along who is suffering because he is separated. He enters into a new relationship to remedy this prior and traumatic separation and must be able to separate himself in a less painful way. In effect, he must learn how to separate.

What does this separation entail?

Not necessarily the repetition of breaks, since one could imagine a continuous series of potential departures. My knowledge that I can leave is what enables us to be together. Similarly, the reason I can have a partner may be precisely because I can leave him by reading Hegel, by going to Israel, or by realizing a scenario in which my erotic partner doesn't follow me at all.

Is it also because I accept that he will not be there when I return?

It may be true that the more I accept his leaving, the more he will leave with a desire to return to the woman who accepts his leaving.

Yet what do we return to under such conditions? Do we still want it? Is it worth the "pain" it might cause?

The "pain" can be the pleasure of "getting your hands on it." This pleasure-pain is a need for authority and for the mother's presence—a need that is altogether blissful. We may need it in a purely erotic way, in which case we lose our attraction to the freedom we were discussing earlier. Because of this "pain," which acts as a true narcissistic screen, independence may become very trying and intolerably lonely.

So this return is worthwhile no matter what it takes?

Dissemination can provide a jouissance, but so can a centrifugal force stemming from the need for a possible identification with a single magnet and a single authority that can give stability. Since we are open structures, we have our moments of stability—of dependency—that make us invisible. We also have our moments of instability and of opening up to others: to the sun, to the water or to dirt, to the risks that we take.

Your remarks suggest that the "maternal" point of reference, which is what demands continuity in male-female relationships, is of central importance. We cannot get away from it; we can only alter it. Yet will everything fall apart if this continuity slips away from our grasp?

I believe that in the imaginary, maternal continuity is what guarantees identity. One could imagine other social systems in which the situation might be otherwise. If we created children through surrogate mothers or "incubators," for example, the imaginary of the mother who guarantees identity might be replaced by the imaginary of the group or the hospital.

Even so, do you believe that the imaginary of a work of literature, among other things, can ensure this identity? Can this identity be constructed only through the maternal reference point you mentioned, one that is restricted to a reference to the mother herself?

You are right: the imaginary of a literary work is the most extraordinary and most troubling vestige of the dependency between mother and child. It is replaced and displaced onto a limit that is intriguing because it is inhuman. A work of literature represents an independence that has been conquered through the force of inhumanity. It breaks off natural relationships; it is patricide and matricide, and it is eminently alone. If you look beneath the surface, however, as analysts do, you will find a dependency and a secret mother that provide a bedrock for this sublimation.

6

Melancholia and Creation

This interview with Dominique Grisoni appeared in *Magazine littéraire* during the summer of 1987, following the publication of Kristeva's *Soleil noir: Dépression et mélancolie*, which appeared in English in 1989 as *Black Sun: Depression and Melancholia.* The interview was translated by Ross Guberman. It provides a useful introduction to Kristeva's complex work, outlining a clinical approach rooted primarily in Freud's *Mourning and Melancholia* and in his controversial remarks on the death drive in *Beyond the Pleasure Principle.* Kristeva also expresses her debt to Karl Abraham and Melanie Klein, warning that the use of psychiatric drugs to treat depression must be complemented by analytic work. She claims that both melancholia and depression are characterized by the "divestment of social bonds" and the "devaluation of language" and links them to the relationship to the mother. In the second part of the interview, Kristeva traces the history of the term from the ancient Greeks to the Renaissance, focusing on the way melancholia has been a theme of literature and art but also a source of creation itself: "Depression is at the threshold of creativity." The interview concludes with some provocative remarks on the writings of Marguerite Duras, lauding her "clinical and magical" genius but arguing that her novels are noncathartic and embody the "nihilism of contemporary thought."

Perhaps you could take a moment to explain what melancholia means today.

The term does connote a wide range of realities. One could say (and please excuse me if I go through this rather quickly) that three principal meanings are accorded to the word "melancholia." Psychiatrists view melancholia as a serious affliction characterized by a slowing-down of psychic and motor functioning; a lack of zest, desire, and speech; the ceasing of all activity; and the irresistible temptation of suicide. This despondency exists in a second, less serious form that often alternates (as does the psychiatric version) with states of excitement; it is a neurotic state known as depression. More often than not, psychoanalysts treat depression. Finally, in the broadest sense of the term, we speak of melancholia as a "distant soul," as "spleen," and as nostalgia depicted in literature and art. This third form of melancholia is still an illness, but it takes on an element of beauty that can be quite sublime. As I say in my book, beauty is born in the land of melancholia; it is a source of harmony that goes beyond despair.

Which of these three domains is your primary guide?

My starting point is clinical. Although I consider the observations made by psychiatry, I have been greatly influenced by the legacy of Freud, Karl Abraham, and Melanie Klein. In *Mourning and Melancholia* (1917),[1] Freud links melancholia with the experience of mourning, noting that both phenomena involve the irrevocable loss of the beloved object (which at the same time is secretly hated), a loss that is never worked through. By reflecting in this way on the subject of depression or death, Freud laid the foundation for the second portion of his research, which culminated in *Beyond the Pleasure Principle* (1920).[2] Although Freud continued to believe that psychic life was dominated by the pleasure principle, he became increasingly convinced that the death drive was the purest drive. Freud makes a revelation here that has been refuted by many analysts, but I find it to be extremely helpful when treating certain forms of psychosis, especially melancholia. While *Eros* means the creation of bonds, *Thanatos*, the death drive, signifies the disintegration of bonds and the ceasing of circulation, communication, and social relationships.

Disintegration of bonds? Isn't that the notion you use to describe the com-
posite you term "melancholic-depressive?"

Absolutely. After pointing out the differences between melancholia and
depression, I argue that it is still possible to speak of a "melancholic-
depressive composite." Why? Because even though important differences exist between melancholia and depression, they have at least two
things in common. First, they are both characterized by a *divestment of*
social bonds and the ceasing of all relationships. It is as though melancholic and depressed people were saying, "No, we're not interested in
your society, your activities, or your language. We are different from
that; we do not exist; we are dead." Second, they both entail a *devalu-*
ation of language. Depressed discourse can be monotonous or agitated,
but the speaker always gives the impression that he neither believes in
it nor inhabits it, that he is outside language and inside the secret crypt
of his silent pain. I believe that my work on the speech of depressed people is my principal contribution to the way psychoanalysts listen to
depression and treat it. I attempt to address the following problem: if
the depressed person rejects language and finds it to be meaningless or
false, how can we gain access to his pain *through speech,* since psychoanalysts work with speech? That is why I have emphasized the importance of the voice and of other signs that are not linguistic even though
they are communicated through language. Indeed, such signs may offer
the surest route toward understanding the depressed person. I also
believe it is important to show how much the depressed person, who
experiences a pain that often remains silent, is secretly emotional and
cunningly impassioned. In brief, one could describe melancholia as an
unnamable and empty perversion. Our job is to raise it to the level of
words—and of life.

These clinical observations raise a number of questions, as you
might imagine. For example, if melancholia is the latest form of
"world-weariness" and if the number of depressed people is growing, is
it because melancholia functions in a social context in which symbolic
bonds have been severed? We are currently experiencing a fragmentation of the social fabric that offers no way out from (and may even
intensify) the fragmentation of psychic identity that depressed people
experience in their own lives. What is more, Freud's emphasis on the
death drive, which has become known as his "pessimism," is far more
than a mere symptom that afflicted the Viennese doctor because of the

impending World War. Instead, it makes our conception of psychic identity correspond more closely to today's rough, violent, disturbed, and crime-ridden world. Indeed, "desire" may simply be a thin layer that is pleasant and entertaining though extremely fragile, a layer hovering over the world of the death drive. Culture would thus be a precious, yet highly volatile, resource. The melancholic who rejects life because he has lost touch with the *meaning of life* prompts us to search for ways to bring back meaning: for our sake, for his sake, but also for the sake of civilization itself. So a clinical matter—of grave proportions in depressed people, who link meaning and life—also affects the formerly religious roots of culture itself. I believe this notion touches on another question: is a civilization that has abandoned the meaning of the Absolute of Meaning a civilization that needs to confront depression? Here is another question: is atheism inherently depressed? And yet another: where might we find the optimistic immanence of an implicitly morose atheism? In Form? In Art?

You also mentioned that you are influenced by psychiatry.

A large part of my book is devoted to female depression, which is more common than male depression and in some respects more difficult to treat because a woman's attachment to her mother is often insurmountable. I have also observed that attachment to the mother plays a crucial role in all forms of melancholia. Even the panic experienced by the obsessional neurotic when he is faced with his own depression appears to be related to his depressed mother. His outbreak of melancholia makes him confront the intolerable idea that he himself is a depressed woman. What does all this have to do with the psychiatric practice of treating depression with antidepressants? It has recently been hypothesized that a "depression gene" is transmitted by the X-chromosome, that is, by the female chromosome. This is only a provisional hypothesis that still needs to be proved. In any case, it does not repudiate the psychoanalytic view of depression. Does analytic interpretation not attempt precisely to free the depressed person from his attachment to his loved-and-hated mother and to give him other words and desires?

We should avoid psychiatric dogma as much as psychoanalytic dogma. Progress in the development of antidepressants has given us powerful means to relieve serious cases of melancholia. Once antidepressants or lithium salts have reinstated a psychic fluidity, the patient often seems to possess a neutral, "mechanical" discourse. At that point, psychotherapy or psychoanalysis can intervene and attempt to change dramatically the patient's personality by linking his affect with language and other people.

The contemporary image of melancholia, as you describe it, seems to suggest that melancholia is solely a matter of the subject's relationship with other people and with the social realm. Yet what did it used to mean?

The first Greek melancholic was Bellerophon, a character in the *Illiad* who is in despair and who becomes overwhelmed by sadness. Abandoned by the gods, he mistakenly avoids all human beings. In Hippocrates' theory of the four humors, melancholia is attributed to black bile. In my view, the most important text on this subject is Pseudo-Aristotle's *Problemata* 30.1, which claims that melancholia is a pathological condition and a borderline state of human nature, a sort of "natural" crisis revealing the truth of being. The melancholic would thus be a man of genius. This ancient conception has clearly intrigued modern philosophers, for it appears that the ancient Greeks believed that the depressive state was a precondition for thought, philosophy, and genius. Indeed, would we ever have changed thought or artistic forms had we not first been obliged to acknowledge their banality and inanity? In summary, depression is at the threshold of creativity. When depression becomes creative, however, it has been given a name and has thus been overcome.

And then everything changed?

Yes, but only imperceptibly, through neo-Platonism and the link it established between melancholia and the cosmos by way of Saturn, the planet of depression. Dürer's "Melancholia" (1514) is an icon of this tenet. Then, and more radically, Christianity considered melancholia to be both a sin and a source of mystical experience, portraying melancholia as a path toward God, a process that medieval monks called *acedia*.

Was Christianity the only perceptible influence on the medieval conception of melancholia?

Certainly not. Esoteric influences also came into play, some of which I discuss indirectly in my interpretation of Nerval's sonnet *El Desdichado*. Think of tarot cards, the Dark Prince of Melancholia, the idea of blackness at the bottom of an alchemical vase, and so forth. These are all metaphors for different stages in the creation and destruction of matter. They could also be seen as metaphors for the creation and destruction of psychic life and social bonds.

Let's remain with history for a moment. What other ruptures and transformations have influenced our conception of melancholia since the Middle Ages?

A number of points should be developed at length, but I will limit my response to a few brief remarks. In fifteenth- and sixteenth-century Europe, the poets wrote about the Melancholic Lady, and the Protestants displayed a renewed interest in the theme of melancholia. This provides a stark contrast to the imagery depicting the Renaissance man as an exuberant and jovial character who moves toward the future with a divine bottle in hand. I am not saying that this imagery is false, but it is not the only one that existed. This jubilant imagery coexisted with the appropriation of an illness defined as the fundamental characteristic of humanity—we see this clearly, I believe, in the paintings of Hans Holbein the Younger. Despite this Melancholic Lady, however, the French Renaissance, and particularly the seventeenth and eighteenth centuries, were not melancholic. France, then, seems to have avoided the anguish of Europe. In general, I would suggest that throughout the history of French culture, France has gone beyond (or perhaps merely covered up) the melancholic movement through eroticism and rhetoric—and for that we must thank Sade and Bossuet.

Yet contemporary France has authors such as Marguerite Duras, whom you discuss at length in your book and whose writings display an unmistakable melancholic strain.

One individual does not constitute an entire culture. Still, you are right to point out that many melancholic figures exist in the works of Marguerite Duras—figures of women curled up beside one other, maternal figures, figures of hatred and internal devastation. Duras also describes the growth of an implicit and devastating female homosexuality. She is very adept at depicting the relationship between one woman and another, particularly between a woman and a maternal figure. Duras clearly exhibits a sort of genius that is both clinical and magical. But Duras's entire work calls for a fusion with the state of female malaise and melancholia and suggests a complacent fascination with destruction and despair. In my view, then, hers is a literature that is noncathartic, embodying what Nietzsche calls the nihilism of contemporary thought. With Duras, there is no afterlife, even for the beauty of a text. I will tell you how I feel about her writings: they are cleverly careless, written in the manner of clothes or makeup that are taken off to hint at a malady that can never be cured and must be preserved. Her texts are at once captivating and deadly. I have often discussed Duras's writings with my female students. Do you know how they respond to them? They respond with a sense of loyalty and a sense of fear. They dread reading her texts, especially when they feel weak, because they are afraid of being caught up in her world. They feel imprisoned by the truth that Duras reveals. Today, what upsets us and frightens us is not so much sex but the threat of permanent pain, of the potential cadaver that we have become. Who among us wants to confront this directly? Depression remains a secret force, perhaps even a form of modern sacredness.

7

New Maladies of the Soul

This interview with Catherine Francblin followed the 1993 publication of *Les Nouvelles maladies de l'âme* and appeared in *Art Press International* and *L'Infini*. The translation is by Ross Guberman. The interview follows the organization of the book, which was translated as *New Maladies of the Soul* in 1995. Kristeva responds to questions about the title of the book and about its theoretical underpinnings, defining what she means by "new maladies of the soul" and laying out the principles behind her renewed emphasis on drives, the body, and countertransference. Kristeva reiterates her view that the "inner life" esteemed by psychoanalysis can serve as an antidote to the banal images of our society, and she offers her opinion on the use of medication in psychoanalytic treatment. The remainder of the interview takes up themes from the second half of the book, including the dietary taboos in the Bible, Madame de Staël's notion of glory, and transubstantiation in the work of James Joyce.

The first thing I noticed about your book is that the title refers to the "soul." Hasn't psychoanalysis made this word defunct by challenging the ancient dualism between the body and the soul?

I try to address this question at the beginning of the book. Freud always maintained that psychic life was doubly determined—by the biological domain and by the symbolic domain. He even encouraged analysts to view this dualism as an opposition between the life drive and the death drive, although he never strayed from the notion that the object of psychoanalysis is the psychic apparatus. That is why I believe we must reinstate a notion of the psyche and the soul that avoids the two major detours the psychoanalytic movement has taken, the first of which seeks to thrust psychic space into biology (which makes it closer to psychiatry) and the second considers psychic space to be a product of language alone and disregards the signs emitted by the body. I myself try to use Freud's dualism as a way to envision the soul as a heterogeneous construction.

The title of your book raises other questions: are there "new" psychic maladies? If so, what has brought them about? Is it changes in our society or in our values? You say that modern man "has run out of imagination."

My remarks are grounded in what I hear from the analyst's couch. I have noticed that my patients have a hard time representing their emotions, joys, and sorrows. Modern men and women often appear to be impaired by two sorts of problems, the first having to do with the body and the second with a relentless desire for social or financial success. These troubles are so overwhelming that they prevent people from having an inner life—from having a darkroom that could provide a space for the representation of affects, drives, and even goals. Psychoanalysis has become one of the rare places where this intimacy can thrive. I do not know what the future holds in store for us, but I believe that the new maladies I discuss are maladies of civilization. Western society has always revered the richness of inner life. It has even inflated it, with positive results in art, philosophy, and theology and such negative ones as psychological apathy, soap operas, and the like. What will happen to Western society if this psychic space finds neither the time nor the space to grow? Perhaps we are approaching the ideal of a superman who would be satisfied with a pill and a television screen. . . . For now, at any rate, those who try to live without a psychic space are quickly exposed to exhaustion, relationship difficulties, and extreme frustration.

Yet we hear all the time that we live in a society of images . . .

I try to resolve this paradox by telling the story of one of my patients, an amateur painter who never bothered to ask himself what his images meant. I found that he acted in a quasi-hypnotic manner: his drives were expressed in gestures and colors, but he made no connection between these images and the workings of his drives. We looked at his artwork together (employing an admittedly unorthodox technique), and I had to interpret his paintings for him to make him aware of their extremely aggressive meaning. Our society creates many images, but they cannot foster our imaginary life if we remain unfamiliar with their meaning. In the example I just mentioned, the patient fabricated his own images, yet we usually behave like passive consumers for whom images act as a bludgeon. Images can absorb psychic life, but they can also keep it from growing in a personal way.

It seems you are saying that psychoanalysis, which has recently shown great interest in linguistic signification, must now return to the drive. Is this not a critique of Lacan? Are you bypassing Lacan and returning to Freud?

I am a member of the generation that was attracted to psychoanalysis because of Lacan's teachings, so I am very grateful to him. I find that the renewed emphasis he places on language and the symbolic is extremely important. Yet I believe that the Lacanians have neglected the role of the drive. The drive is clearly an imaginary construction (we can neither see it nor locate it), but it is an essential one that enables the analyst to remain at the crossroads between the symbolic and the somatic.

When reading your previous books, I was surprised to see that you, unlike many other more "linguistically" oriented analysts, appear to support the idea of treating patients with drugs. Since you broach this subject in your most recent book, could you tell us your opinion on pharmacological treatment?

Progress made in neuroscience presents psychoanalysis with opportunities as well as risks. Today, the question of "to be or not to be" has been replaced by "the pill or the couch." Under the influence of the media, many people are gravitating toward the pharmacological solution. Yet psychiatric drugs often have the drawback of decreasing the patient's responsibility: since the patient feels responsible only to his pills, he no longer feels curious about his illness.

On the one hand, my experience with depressed patients in particular has shown me that we must not snub chemistry, for it can reestablish conductivity among neurons and encourage verbalization. It also places a third party between the patient and the analyst, and this intermediary status endows it with a psychic power that enables it to be used as a temporary antidote to certain inhibitions. In one of my case studies, I discuss a patient who had dreams under the influence of psychiatric drugs, which was the only way she thought she could dream at all. Yet since the descriptions she gave of her dreams were unimaginative and artificial, I had to use chemical means to restore her confidence in a transferential relationship. At that point, we were able to set aside the drugs.

Speaking of transference, among the means available to the analyst, you grant an important role to countertransference, particularly in the treatment of hysteria. This is an innovative view.

I speak of "new" patients because society, as I said, has changed. At the same time, however, analysts have refined the way they listen. They are aware of things today that they never would have noticed before. This leads me to your question: I do believe that analytic practice often requires a countertransferential mode of listening—especially when we are treating obsessional neurotics, children, and others, including hysterics. With hysterics, who are seductive and whose seduction acts as a defense, it might seem that the analyst should adopt a distant approach. In reality, however, a more invested response, such as a manifested identification, can be a very effective way to curb the hysteric's defenses. Such responses allow the analyst to follow the patient into what I call his "sensory autism" (a state of hyperexcitability that ignores the existence of the other, a sort of "autoeroticism" verging on autism and psychosis), and they play a very significant role in the early stages of treatment. If we listen to hysterics by presenting ourselves as a potential mirror ("I understand you," "I know what you're saying," "You're saying it to me," etc.), we will have a deeper understanding of the relationship between their discourse, on the one hand, and the body and the drive, on the other.

At the same time, analysts must back away a bit so that their patients can find a psychic translation for the drives to which they are exposed. The treatment process relies on this constant oscillation, one that Helene Deutsch (to whom I pay tribute in my book) understood very well when she said that psychoanalysis should be an "open structure." This "open structure" could be likened to the psychic structure of the adolescent. I am not saying that analysts are adolescents, but when analysts experience countertransference and before they reach the law, they must confront the opening-up, fragility, and exuberance that characterize the adolescent. If they fail to do so, they run the risk of creating beings who are merely conventional and demanding and who lack creative abilities. These observations have come to me when treating hysterics, but also when treating children. Specifically, I tell the story in my book of a boy who was unable to talk and who prompted me to sing to him.

On that note, is there not a contradiction between psychoanalytic theory, which recommends that analysts "play dead," and psychoanalytic practice (particularly when children are involved), which has always endorsed the therapist's active participation?

There is a contradiction there, and every therapist knows it. Still, I do not reject completely the idea that the analyst must "play dead." It is simply a matter of timing: you do occasionally have to "play dead," but not with every patient. For example, if you do so with an obsessional neurotic, who already spends his time playing dead, you will force him to be in treatment forever. Regarding paranoiacs, Freud set us on the right path by saying, "I succeeded where the paranoiac fails." In other words, he accepted his identification with the paranoid person, but he did not stop there. The expression "to play dead" recalls the essential figure of the dead father that analysis tries to bring into our awareness. Yet Freud also refers to a living father when he speaks of the father of prehistory, the identificatory figure he discusses in *The Ego and the Id*.[1] This archaic paternal function is perhaps what is at stake when we are engaged in intense countertransference.

You speak about the shared fate of hysteria and interpretation, yet you write that analytic treatment protects itself from hysteria. It's quite complicated!

That is why I suggested that the analyst walks on a tightrope! The hysteric and the analyst share the same fate because Freud developed his model of the unconscious, the cornerstone of his theory, while listening to hysterics. The origin of psychoanalysis, then, can be traced to the treatment of hysterics. At the same time, the analyst must break his pact with hysterics to free them from his structure and his dependency—a dependency that they seek incessantly to deny it more forcefully, a dependency on their master, the law, and, in the end, the mother.

Your book is divided into two parts. We have been discussing the first part, which focuses on the clinic. The second part has to do with history and includes essays on the Bible as well as on Joyce and Madame de Staël. What does an analyst such as yourself read, for example, in the Bible?

What interests me in particular about the Bible are the Levitical abominations, which are dietary taboos related to the murder taboo and the taboo concerning the joining of two conflicting elements. The Bible states that joining differences is an abomination, which suggests to me that the Levitical abominations are rooted in the recognition of the difference between the sexes. The taboo refers to the maternal: "You shall not boil a kid in its mother's milk" [Exod. 23.19; Deut. 14.21]. This dietary taboo is a sort of incest taboo that could result in a rejection of the feminine, but it also has the advantage of inviting the speaking being to take some distance from the origin. I will take a moment to underscore the importance of the maternal space, which I believe that recent psychoanalytic currents, Lacanian ones in particular, have underestimated. I believe that the maternal function must be revived, along with the need to take some distance from it. The woman, moreover, is the one who should encourage this distancing from her child, who forms a part of herself. This gives an idea of the immense cultural role that mothers play—and we should not be surprised to see them fail to measure up to its demands.

As for your interest in Madame de Staël, I think everyone will see that what strikes you the most about her is that she is a female intellectual—the first member, you write, "of that awkward species." This notion frames your description of theory as a form of melancholic contemplation protecting us from depression. Does this not also apply to male theoreticians?

As I explained in my book *Black Sun,* I believe that women must grapple with depressive states more often than men. Reflecting on Madame de Staël's famous notion that "glory is the radiant mourning of happiness," I have realized that between the twin poles of glory and grief, which dominated de Staël's life and times, happiness travels through a maze of passions and disappointments. I myself would be more inclined to say that happiness is the mourning of unhappiness. . . . That is the only kind of glory that interests me, one that is rooted in nothing and that assumes we have overcome depression and suffering. Given the tragedies and xenophobia that surround us today, and given my status as a foreigner, I do not see how we can avoid unhappiness. But as Proust says, "Ideas come to us as the successors to griefs."[2]

To conclude, I would like to mention your fine essay on Joyce, in which you say that Joyce finds himself in the "same identificatory boat as the analyst." What do you mean by that?

In my view, the experience of Joyce is a transtheological experience of writing. His work displays a connivance with the themes of incarnation and transubstantiation. He embraces the notion that the Word can become flesh and that we can be reincarnated through writing. Joyce's approach to language presumes an ability to identify with the other, the world, sounds, smells, and the opposite sex, as shown by a narrator who becomes incarnate in female characters. This flexibility, which goes to the heart of the alchemy of Joyce's language, allows him to go from the idea to the being. The writer is in the being and not only in the signifier. I believe that this experience could serve as a model for psychoanalysts. Unlike other writers, Joyce was never hostile to Freudian psychoanalysis, although he looked at it with healthy skepticism. I find that an aesthetic experience as singular as Joyce's could be very enriching for analysts, who stand to gain a great deal from poring over his work, less to analyze it than to illuminate their own practice.

WOMEN

8

Woman Is Never What We Say

This interview was conducted by the Psychoanalysis and Politics group of the French Women's Liberation Movement. It was first published in a 1974 issue of *Tel Quel* and was reprinted in *Polylogue*. The translation is by Ross Guberman.[1] In "A Conversation with Julia Kristeva," also included in this book, Kristeva explains that the title of the interview emphasizes that "the position of the feminine in discourse is a very difficult position to specify. As soon as one specifies it, one loses it, seeing that, perhaps, the feminine is precisely what escapes nomination and representation." The four questions that frame the interview are unusually incisive, focusing on avant-garde practice and poetic language, the ontological status of "woman," China and gender roles, and the future of the women's movement. Kristeva claims that poetic language "breaks down and rebuilds restraints" and that the crisis it depicts requires that we "completely rethink the traditional critical and conceptual paradigm." Avant-garde art, moreover, is said to bypass notions of gender identity by incorporating both axes of sexual difference and thus challenging the "principle of unity." Kristeva also states that "woman" can never be defined because it is "precisely that which shuns being." She situates the women's movement within a "large-scale upheaval," praising its radicality and negativity and urging women to express the movement's connivance with other avant-garde phenomena.

In Revolution in Poetic Language, *you analyze the internal logical and historical function of texts by such authors as Lautréamont, Mallarmé, and Bataille. All these texts could be described as "dominated texts," particularly those of Artaud. You also subject traditional and even "earlier" modes of inquiry and criticism to an irreversible process that recasts old notions and forges new ideas. In your view, how can the study of these dominated, ruptured texts assimilate the dynamic production of the new analytic approach you have outlined?*

The texts to which you refer, which have become known as "avant-garde literature," have erupted in Western culture since the end of the nineteenth century and have paralleled the explosive crisis of the State, the family, and religion. I believe these texts are symptomatic of a large-scale upheaval of Western society that includes the women's struggle and can be compared to the metamorphosis that occurred during the Renaissance. Yet the crisis of the sixteenth century had to do with God, and not with the *principle* of *unity* or perhaps the principle of social, familial, or linguistic *cohesion*. During the age of Rabelais and Michelangelo, people were still able *to believe*—in Man, the State, the Family, Beauty, and the Masterpiece. Such beliefs were ideally revived in a secular form, but at any rate they were revived. A new phenomenon has arisen since the rise to power of the bourgeoisie, the onset of the free market, the inflation of capital permeating relationships of production and reproduction and dominating them, and the crisis of the patriarchal family, which fell apart in ancient Rome but was restored by Christianity. Capitalism has shown an extraordinary capacity for restructuring this explosion while using it to remake the State and the family and to create an ideological means to rein in the most violent of forces. At the same time, it is lodged in the neuralgic space where this restoration is the most difficult (if not impossible) to accomplish.

I want to discuss the speaking subject, focusing on its relationship to the constraints of social unity and to the jouissance that relies on it as long as it can surpass it. Religion was once the privileged vehicle for the speaking subject's expression. In modern capitalism, however, destructuring takes precedence over structure, and excess overrides restraint. As a result, religion has not been able to acknowledge the speaking subject. And when social groups or classes rely on instinctual forces no longer held in check by traditional moral constraints, they cloak them in totalitarianism, which is why capitalism has led to different forms of fascism. The space between the failure of traditional moral codes and the new paranoid paradigms paves the way for theorizing and freeing up the drama of our monotheistic capitalist society, but also of social life itself and of the symbolic being in its most basic sense. This makes me think of Freud's breakthrough in examining the logic of the unconscious as it pertains to social restrictions. It also brings to mind the theoretical practices before Freud (or perhaps apart from him) that have tried to formulate a new relationship between social restrictions and drive process along with the jouissance it entails. These are the very dominated practices considered to be "avant-garde"—the productions that we read as texts even though they have little in common with broad literary formalities, for they bring into play the speaking body's complex relationship with society.

Lautréamont, Mallarmé, Bataille, and Artaud make an explicit and violent critique of the State, the family, and religion. At the same time, however, their critique permeates the very economy of their language, which is often said to be esoteric, unreadable, and elitist. Since the linguistic rebellion that these authors carried out disturbs the very rules of ordinary soporific communication, it breaks down the structure of language itself. The cry and the gesture encode the system of language and inscribe it with what society represses or destroys when it defines itself. Not surprisingly, this society wants nothing to do with these cries, gestures, and encodings. One thing this century has taught us is that social life imposes a restraint just as language does. Poetic language breaks down this restraint, but it also reinforces it by providing it with a new apparatus. As I define it in my book, theoretical discourse seeks to show and to understand the way poetic language breaks down and rebuilds social restraints. This project requires that we completely rethink the traditional critical and conceptual paradigm, for the methods of classical thought favor those moments of signifying practice that point to stability and not to crisis.

Our [i.e., the psychoanalysis and politics group's] theoretical practice advocates a different relationship to a text, one that you yourself have embraced. Could you tell us in what way your work is the "work of a woman" and in what way being a woman affects this sort of work? To what extent has the women's struggle, which seems to have an increasing hold on your attention, changed your relationship to writing, to the text, and to theoretical or textual production?

The notion that "one is a woman" is almost as absurd and meaningless as the notion that "one is a man." I say "almost" because women still have important goals to attain: the right to abortion and contraception, state-provided day care, job recognition, and so forth. The idea that "we are women," then, can still be used to communicate women's political agenda. On a deeper level, however, a woman can never *be*, for woman is precisely that which shuns *being*. So women's practice can only be negative; it remains at odds with what exists. All it can say is, "That's not it" and "That's still not it." In my view, "woman" is something that cannot be represented or verbalized; "woman" remains outside the realm of classifications and ideologies. Some "men" are familiar with "woman," and the modern texts we were discussing earlier never stop signifying "woman."[2] As long as we avoid speaking about it, such texts allow us to experience the axis of language and the axis of social life—the law and its transgression, mastery and jouissance—without assigning one axis to "males" and the other to "females." In that sense, certain aspects of the feminist agenda have brought us back to a naive romanticism and a belief in identity (the opposite of phallocentrism), particularly if we compare them with the experience of *both* axes of sexual difference reflected in the discursive economy of Joyce and Artaud and of such modern composers as John Cage and Karlheinz Stockhausen.

What makes my work the work of a woman is that I pay close attention to the element of avant-garde practice that eradicates identity (including sexual identity), and I try to formulate a theoretical rebuttal to the metaphysical theories that censure what I just labeled "a woman." I should also add (although this in no way contradicts what I have said) that because of women's determinative role in reproduction and the importance of the father-daughter relationship, women are more apt to respect social restrictions, are less inclined to approve of anarchy, and are more concerned with ethics. This may explain why women's negativity is not a Nietzschean fury. Since my work strives to make society aware of the very aspects of avant-garde practice that it rejects, I believe my research is mindful of this ethical imperative. The problem is whether the women's struggle will separate this ethical penchant from negativity. If so, ethics will degenerate into conformity, and negativity will degenerate into esoteric perversions. The women's movement must now confront this problem, yet if the movement did not exist, women would not be able to accomplish anything today.

You have just returned from a trip to China.[3] *We would very much like to go to China, but we believe that our true China is here in France, where we are changing reality. What we would like to ask you is this: where in France does "your" China fit in? What we have learned from the work we are doing here, with women and among women, often overlaps with what we have learned about the life of Chinese men and women, including the metamorphosis, disappearance, or even nonexistence of phallic domination in political struggles and in celebration. How did you experience this "difference" during your journey?*

I just came back from China after spending three weeks traveling to Peking, Shanghai, Louyang, Xian, and then back to Peking. I met many women and men, including workers, peasants, schoolchildren, teachers, and artists. Yet even though I had these experiences and studied the Chinese language, you can never be sure that you have been to China and lived in its space and time. Going to China makes you think about recent challenges to sexual tradition and political tradition. For a Westerner, China joins sex with politics in its struggle for women's rights, its efforts to rectify social inequities, and its insertion of its own vast, repressed culture into world politics. But I am also (and perhaps especially) interested in the way this all relates to the impossible task of leaving behind our own society, an impossibility of which avant-garde art, the women's struggle, and the fight for socialism are merely graded symptoms. How will the West handle the awakening of the "third world," as the Chinese call it? Will we be able to participate in this awakening sensibly and actively even though the center of the planet is shifting toward the East?

If you do not care about women and do not like them, there is no point in going to China. You would get nothing out of the experience; you would be bored there; you might even become exhausted from thinking you have understood nothing (or everything). First, although ancient China may not have been the truly matriarchal society that Chinese historians since Engels have claimed it was, it was the most matrilinear society the world has ever known. And even during the time of Confucius, when women were considered to be "slaves" and "little men," wives played an indispensable role in family life and even in sacred representations of reproductive relationships. Particularly today, however, substantial efforts are being made to give women the primary role not only in family life but in all levels of political and social life. This is an important element in the current campaign against Lin Piao's and Confucius's ideas. Abortion rights, equal pay, the encouragement of artistic, political, and scientific pursuits and of all forms of education, first-rate medical care for mothers and their young children, and safe nursery schools and playgrounds are merely a taste of what I saw in the communities we visited in China. And none of the performances we saw (films, plays, and operas) had a man as its main character, who in each case was a woman.

It is very difficult to say just a few words about the relationship between this trend toward emancipation and the "phallic" principle or "power." I will treat this matter at length in my forthcoming book on Chinese women, which will be published by Editions des femmes.[4] The problems of Chinese women, who have fled a feudal and Confucian society, are clearly different from those faced by Western women, who are trying to flee from capitalism and monotheism. It is therefore absurd to criticize Chinese women for their alleged lack of sexual liberation, just as it is absurd to see their lifestyle and combative efforts as a manifestation of what some believe to be a universal revolutionary ideal.

Let me make a few empirical observations. Even though women play an indispensable role in the current campaign and men dominate the Confucian patriarchal family, I did not have the impression that reproductive and symbolic relationships in China were governed by what we would call the "phallic." First, the difference between the two sexes is not so great. Second, the two sexes are not at war with one another, for "man" is in "woman" and "woman" is in "man." The relationships we would call "sexual" do not focus on transgression, so they are not rooted in a quest for part objects, in perversion, or in other such phenomena. What governs this scene is the onset of genitality, which is contingent on getting through the oedipal stage (although I hesitate to use this psychoanalytic jargon), and it lends the street, the workplace, and such holidays as the First of May a calm, relaxed, "maternal" allure that is secure without being romantic, and strong without being violent. Chinese writing provides the closest approximation of this rhythm.

At any rate, it is impossible to speak about Chinese socialism without acknowledging that it emulates a different model of sexual difference and thus of the roles that women should play. There is no guarantee, of course, that the efforts being made today will not be engulfed in the tide of an ever-present revisionism or in a return to the bourgeois system. In this respect, as well as in an economical and political context, the "struggle between the two defense lines" is not a slogan but a phenomenon of daily life.

Just as the feminine is the antithesis of the masculine, feminism may be the antithesis of humanism. We want to resist ideologies that create only inversions, yet we know that each woman must recognize her own minimal degree of feminism and her own temporary arena. In that perspective, women's struggle cannot be detached from revolutionary struggles, class struggles, and anti-imperialist struggles. Our primary focus is on the notion of the subject and its explosion and on the inscription of heterogeneity and difference. Such questions are evaded by feminism, which posits that women are "self-sufficient entities" having "their own identities" and which demands such things as "giving women names." How might we conceive of a revolutionary struggle that was not also a discursive revolution (not an upheaval of language itself but an upheaval of the theories seeking to explain such upheavals)? Does feminism perhaps contain elements of a dominating ideology? And what will occur if its "demands" pertain only to the "social realm"?

Feminism may constitute merely a demand for the most vigorous rationalization of capitalism. Valéry Giscard d'Estaing, who wants to do away with Gaullist archaisms, has created a post called the Secretary for the Status of Women. It is better than nothing, but it's not really it. In the wake of fascism and revisionism, we should have learned by now that any sociopolitical transformation is also a transformation of subjects because it alters subjects' social constraints, experience of pleasure, and, more fundamentally, language. Today's new political phenomena are communicated by new types of music, comic strips, and groups of young people (so long as they do not seek refuge in their marginal status but participate in the contradictions of political life). In my opinion, if the women's movement has a purpose, it is to participate in such trends. In fact, the movement itself is one of the most radical components of these recent phenomena. The negativity of the women's movement makes both "right" movements and "left" movements aware of what they themselves repress: that "class consciousness," among other things, cannot occur without the unconscious of the gendered speaker. When the feminine acts as a demystifying force, it runs the risk of identifying with the principle of power it believes it has surmounted, as when the hysterical saint offers her jouissance to the social order, albeit in the name of God.

This brings up a question: who plays God in contemporary feminism? Is it Man? Or is it Woman—his replacement? So long as a libertarian movement (including feminism) fails to analyze the relationship between power and overtly religious or secular spirituality on the one hand and an exertion of power on the other, and so long as it fails to stop believing in its own identity, it will be exploited by this power and spirituality. Therein lies the last hope of spirituality. The solutions to this predicament are infinite, for what is at stake is the shift from patriarchal society, class, and religion (that is, from prehistory) to . . . to what? Does anyone know? Whatever "it" is, it will have to confront what remains repressed in discourse along with relationships of production and reproduction. "It" could be either "woman" or "oppressed social classes," for they share the same struggle and always appear in tandem. In my view, the first goal of the movement should be to express this connivance with ideological and political endeavors. Yet this would mean that we would have to change our style and to distance ourselves a bit from the notion of working "among women." It would also mean that each woman would have to fight against the sociocultural archaisms that continue to pervade her environment.[5]

9

"unes femmes": The Woman Effect

This interview was conducted by Elaine Boucquey. The transcription was edited by Kristeva and published in a 1975 issue of the Belgian feminist journal *Les Cahiers du GRIF*. The translation is by Ross Guberman. In "Julia Kristeva in Person," another interview in this book, Kristeva explains that she chose the title "unes femmes" because she wanted "to celebrate women's singularity and uniqueness without reducing them to a generic category of 'women' comparable to 'the proletariat' or to 'men.' " She begins by defining "feminine identity" as an element in economic regulation, but also as the "woman effect" and the "maternal function." According to Kristeva, the woman effect is "neither power nor language but the silent support that allows them to function and surpasses them." Turning to women's subordinate position, Kristeva warns against attempting to identify with power, urging women instead to "become a source of negativity and harassment, pushing power to its limits and then struggling with it." She points out two dangers that subordinated women can face: phallic identification and a regression manifested as hostility toward psychoanalysis or a rejection of intellectual work and unique creations. Regarding artistic production in women, Kristeva states that women can rely on the repressed but violent love-hatred they feel toward their mothers, yet she expresses doubts that cultural production can be assigned to one gender or the other. In conclusion, she argues that any generalization about women should serve merely as a way to help women express their uniqueness.

The specificity of feminine creation cannot be discerned until we define the *feminine identity* that we seek to find in such creation. I believe that one could define what might be called the "feminine identity" in two ways. First, it could be seen as a major element in the regulation of economic rationality. I say this because the emancipation of women creates a female workforce essential to the economy, but it also helps curb population growth and forces traditional familial structures and antiquated morals to respond to the demands of the day. So the emancipation of women keeps archaic ideologies from making social hypocrisies even worse and from causing explosions that could affect more than just those on the left. One example of how the "feminine condition" is intrinsic to economic rationality as well as to its self-regulation can be found in the recent vote that the French National Assembly took on abortion laws. The vote disregarded the de Gaullesque and perhaps religious objections to abortion, participating in the modernization undertaken by a new technocratic and liberal bourgeoisie and supporting the progressive needs of the lower social classes. Thus the problems facing women and their identity bear on another axis of cohesion and social development: not one of *class-consciousness* but one of relationships involving reproduction as well as something that could be termed the *unconscious*.

Yet "feminine identity" has another important feature. By emphasizing the biological and physiological characteristics of feminine identity, one could see it as a symbolic effect of the way the subject experiences social cohesiveness, power, and language. In this context, which will frame my remarks here, the feminine question could be compared to "the woman effect," but also to the "maternal function."

In our monotheistic-capitalist societies, "the woman effect" entails a specific relationship to both *power* and *language*, or, if you will, to the power of language. This particular relationship is based not on appropriating power and language but on being a source of silent support, a useful backdrop, and an invisible intermediary. I have called this modality of the linguistic (and social) functioning of language the "*semiotic*."[1] The semiotic is heard in rhythms, intonation, and children's echolalia as well as in artistic practice and in discourse that signifies less an "object" than a jouissance. I shall return in a moment to the way the "semiotic" manifests itself linguistically, focusing now on the social element that enables this "woman effect" to be neither power nor the language system, but the silent support that allows them to function and surpasses them.

We find this social element, for example, in primitive societies in which women are the objects of exchange that constitute power and are indispensable to the exercise of power even though they do not participate in it directly. Another example might be the way a woman is subordinated to the paternal name and to paternal authority (as defined by the patriarchal family) even though she is a substantial and indispensable source of support for this family (although perhaps not in the most obvious way). In that situation, we find ourselves in a dialectic between master and slave that assigns the "woman effect" the role of the slave. Put in such a position, a woman possesses an implicit awareness and knowledge of this structure and thus of social power as a whole, since the slave knows more than the master. So the "woman effect" is sometimes the hidden and even more fundamental side of both secular power and religious power, for all gods are sustained by a loving obedience that is beneficial for both parties. One could also say that the "woman effect" may be adopted by a man, as with the male homosexuality that Freud believed to be at the base of such social institutions as the army and the school.

When a woman is placed in this subordinate position, she has two options. Even though she is excluded from power and language, she possesses the hidden, invisible element that allows them to function. On the one hand, she can become a source of negativity[2] and harassment, pushing power to its limits and then struggling with it. This is the classic role of the hysteric, who runs the risk of exploding into a symptom that is revolutionary in the positive and constructive sense of the word. Yet she can also lay claim to power until she identifies with it and supplants it. One might wonder if some aspects of the feminist agenda do not fail because they attempt to identify with power. Such attempts make women into a counterpower filling gaps in official power—or into a promised land consisting of an ultimately harmonious society believed to consist only of women who know the truth about the mysteries of an imaginary society lacking any internal contradiction. This phantasmatic cohesion is governed, moreover, by an archaic mother with paternal features. According to some socialist tenets, utopian societies are conceived on such a model, such that a sexually ambiguous (though ultimately paternal) being guarantees social cohesion. A leftist utopian tradition could thus transform accommodation into an acknowledgment of women's rights, so long as it did not mean that the other sex is an *other*, a source of contradictions, an impossibility, or a destroyer of social contradictions. In the end, recognizing feminine "specificity" and "creativity" associates them with structures and identities borrowed from paternalistic or monotheistic societies. Because such societies do not recognize feminine specificity, they try to put it aside, subdue it, and make sure no one talks about it. Yet the women's movement would have another reason to exist if it could become what Hegel calls "the eternal irony of the community," a permanent disagreement with what is held in place, or a source of humor, laughter, and self-criticism—as well as a criticism of feminism itself.

In other words, women face two dangers, as do men who find themselves in a submissive position. First they risk regressing to the pre-oedipal stage and the archaic mother and to the illusion that one can attain an idyllic society that lacks internal contradiction. Then they risk identifying with the phallic power that they want to possess or share, an identification that requires that they stop harboring contradictions and playing the role of the other sex. Could you give some examples of these two pitfalls?

An example of phallic identification would be the role that women played in the putsch in Chile against Allende.[3] They identified with the reactionaries because the Right spoke a language that addressed femininity, children, and the household, while the discourse of the left focused only on the class struggle and neglected libidinal factors. Some female Chileans attacked the partisans of Allende, accusing them of being libertines and homosexuals. Leftist discourse should have been more attentive to these libidinal factors. When the right speaks a language that responds to such concerns, it can attract female support that is regressive and totalitarian even though it disempowers classical rationality by presenting itself as an anarchistic gesture against the Law.

A fascination with women's movements can sometimes arise, particularly in developing countries. Western Europe faces another danger:

although the technocratic and liberal bourgeoisie guarantees the sustained growth of women's rights (moving toward a dialectical and enlightened integration of women into the Law) in the name of a post–May 1968 radicalism, other women perpetuate unconsciously the very oppositions they are trying to undo. As a result, these women offer other women a model of "fluid" discourse or "pre-oedipal jouissance," produce female creations of mediocre quality ("since a woman created it, it must be good"), and yield to persecutory fantasies (right-wing, objectively speaking) about intellectuals who are too quickly branded as "paternalistic," if not "homosexual."

It seems to me that the leftist analysis of the situation has not paid enough attention to libidinal factors, nor has it paid enough attention to strictly economic ones. The Left restricts itself to relationships of production and disregards human reproduction. Yet reproduction is one of the most important elements of production, for it ensures that the producer and the consumer will be properly cared for.

Women are often reduced to being a force of production that need only be granted class-consciousness. Although this goal is extremely important, it cannot be accomplished as it might have been in the nineteenth century. We should use psychoanalytic interventions to respond to libidinal needs rooted in relationships of reproduction and production, needs that have become a glaring social reality. If not, leftist discourse will be unable to account for new phenomena—women, young people, drugs, the media. That is the problem with fascism today. Since the 1930s, fascism has attracted avant-garde forces that have unwittingly confronted strict rational discourse. These modern currents have thus become engulfed in totalitarianism or in a mystical irrationality.

You have offered an example of phallic identification. Could you give an example of regression, the other danger that looms over "subordinated" people?

The women's movement has become a rallying cry for various forms of resistance or hostility toward psychoanalysis. Things seem to be changing in America, although not without some difficulty; but in Europe we still have a long way to go. Female opposition requires that women stand together (while remaining flexible) against the Law, the Name of the Father, and so forth. On that note, I would like to mention some essays Lacan wrote in 1938 that describe the transformation of the Western family. Lacan claimed that the decline of the father's image and the increased role of the mother create a crisis because they encourage the return of the repressed to take on some dangerous and totalitarian forms. The psychoanalytic response to this crisis in the monotheistic regulation of the Western family has been to specify and to reinterpret the authority of the law—not "dad's" authority, but the Name of the Father: since the returned repressed was obviously repressed, it is obliged to disobey the paternal law. At that point, we are faced with anarchy, a return to an absolute archaic mother (without an other, without a father), and a complacent attitude toward regression and even madness.[4]

Yet feminism cannot condone the repression of the mother for the sake of preserving the Law.

Of course not, which is why we look for ways to use "aesthetic" or "intellectual" sublimation to enable the repressed to speak. This goal is shared by the avant-garde literature created since the turn of the century (Mallarmé, Joyce, etc.).

Freud's discovery of the unconscious and of the father's role in constituting the social group should not be in dispute, for this discovery implicates men as much as women, as does his notorious notion of "castration." The most we can do is give increased attention (which Freud was unable to do in his pioneering studies) to the pre-oedipal stage, to the relationship between the speaking subject and the mother, and from there, to a position that is no longer transcendental but immanent and thus more flexible and less encumbered with repression and social restraints. What is needed in the West today is a reevaluation of the "maternal function," seeing it not as explosive and repressed but as a source of practices considered to be marginal (such as "aesthetic" practices) and a source of innovation. Men as well as women are seeking this, and they are turning in particular to the women's movement.

Could you give a concrete example of the second danger faced by a repressed person who feels free because she believes she is protected from social restraints and so finds herself in a state of social and psychological regression?

Such regression occurs when intellectual work is rejected and the "concept" is declared to be masculine and something that women should avoid. It also occurs when people are suspicious of unique creations: no exceptions or no proper names are allowed, and the individual is absorbed into a group whose constraining character is forgotten. (This raises a question: what does a community of women repress?) Finally, it occurs when psychosis is encouraged implicitly. When we contemplate a creation made by a woman writer, we fail to see how dramatically exceptional she is. Instead, we appropriate her name after she commits suicide and after neglecting her when she was still alive ("die, and the group shall recognize you") in the name of a femininity understood to be a return to the pre-oedipal mother.

How can we avoid these pitfalls and focus our attention on creating?

It is hard to know for sure. Having listened to others as well as to myself, I would say that we must not repress this archaic relationship to the mother, this phase (or mode of symbolization) that I have termed the "semiotic." Instead, we must endow it with its own expression and artic-ulation while not holding it back from the sort of "symbolic" and more intellectual manifestation that can bring it into our awareness. In fact, all *creative* activity, if you want to use the word "creative," presupposes the *immanence* of libido and the symbolic process along with their dialectal-ization and harmonization, if you will. Innovation is never the repetition of the paternal discourse or a regression to an archaic mother. It presumes that the subject, let's say a woman, is able to take charge of her entire archaic libidinal apparatus (which is unconscious and egoistic) and to invest it in a symbolic articulation. If a theory is truly new, whether it has to do with linguistics, literature, chemistry, or physics, it always involves a deeper localization of libido in the symbolic. Since our society consid-ers mastery as well as logic and syntax to be masculine and rhythms, glos-solia, and the pre-oedipal stage to be related to the mother and by exten-sion to the woman, one could say that a creative act is a function not of difference but of sexual *differentiation* between these two axes.

Do you mean all creative acts—those by men as well as by women, and in all domains?

What we call "art" is characterized by a more patent immanence of the semiotic to the symbolic. Art transforms language into rhythms and transforms "aberrations" into stylistic figures. Art is the "incestuous" side of language, as reflected in its dependence on the mother's body and its relationship to the pre-oedipal stage. As Mallarmé put it, art introduces "music into literature." This phenomenon is particularly noticeable in works of modern art created since the turn of the century, which participate in a process that closely resembles schizophrenization. Nevertheless, such works succeed where the schizophrenic fails, because they attempt to free themselves from logical constraints and the law, returning instead to the maternal body and remaining in the realm of rhythms and glossolia by *proposing*, inventing, and reformulating a new discourse and a new universe. Examples of this can be found in Artaud, in Joyce's umbrella words, in the surrealists, and in the modernist texts written by the Tel Quel group.

So what happens when the person who formulates this reunion with the mother is a woman?

I said in the beginning that "feminine identity" is the "woman effect" and the "maternal function." The maternal function has to do with the pre-oedipal process and thus aesthetic practice. The pre-oedipal stage is defined by primary, oral, and anal satisfactions, by a lack of differentiation among need, demand, and desire, and by a piecemeal body that is not yet identified as one's own body because the identity of the ego and the superego already depend on language and the father. The individual's socialization thus requires that this primitive relationship with the mother be repressed or sublimated. The incest taboo, which is constitutive of the social order as well as the order of language, is in the end a mother taboo for the boy and for the girl. Yet the man finds a maternal substitute in his sexual partner, while the woman is forever exiled from this archaic territory because her sexual partner is usually a man. For a heterosexual woman, the mother is the rival, which explains why the love and hatred directed at the mother are so violent. In most cases, the woman experiences a very repressed combination of love-hate, one that can be a powerful stimulus for symbolization, that can lead to the psychotic deviations of hysteria, and that can be manifested in the more mediated and productive form of sublimation and of aesthetic products.

If fathers were to take care of infants and give them their bottles from the earliest days of their infancy, would that change the basis of the question?

Yes, I think that would change things around. For example, I had the impression in China, where the gap between the sexes is smaller, that this split is not as painful for the child.

In our societies, female homosexuality or identification with virility can come to a woman's rescue, for she is exiled forever from a maternal territory that she must lose in order to become heterosexual. These are two ways for female libido to satisfy this frustration, but they are weak and do not make up for the basic deprivation. This is perhaps what one could call *castration* for the woman. What happens when a woman, who struggles (as do all speaking beings) with "castration," makes these discoveries with the mother, which, when formulated, incite her to change the symbolic codes of a society, that is, to invent a language? It seems to me that artistic "products," fetishes, the "work," media attention, and praise are less gratifying and carry less weight for women than for men. Virginia Woolf may have been very intrigued (if not anguished) by the positive response her work received, but this response did not give her enough narcissistic gratification to eradicate the permanent anguish that led her to decompose language and to destroy her identity to the point of madness and suicide. Proust has his mother and Madame Strauss to support a gratifying image, and Kafka's lovers and Joyce's Miss Weave served as the maternal relief that enables a man to keep going. But when a woman's paternal image collapses, her image of her mother or of maternal substitutes may appear derisive and short-lived. The risk of psychosis seems greater for such a woman, as does the desire for death manifested as a desire for self-effacement.

It is important to note, however, that women who write are characterized not only by a certain return of the mother but by the way this submersion is *organized* in painting, music, or the written word. Once we began to write, we are no longer engaged in a connivance with madness, regression, or a simple nostalgia for the archaic mother. The essential ingredient in all forms of practice is the struggle for a work of art that is produced and then immediately started anew. Creating a work of art obviously requires a certain lifting of repression that is already an unveiling of risk and dangers: the struggle between symbolic authority and the drive-based call from an archaic mother is always present and is at the very heart of the creative process.

Is this experience more difficult for women?

On the one hand, once the repression that constitutes us as our fathers' daughters and as wives and mothers has been analyzed, we are led to borderline experiences that stem from this specific relationship with the mother, a relationship based on an intense love-hate. Yet we are more fragile than men because identifying with such fetish-objects as books and fame offers a derisive support against the violence of this relationship and this fundamental frustration.

Does this lead to a different sort of writing? Perhaps one that is more violent?
Women still have a great deal to teach us about the hatred underlying the love that Christianity considers to be at the root of all production.

That aside, I am increasingly convinced that we must avoid assigning genders to cultural productions, saying that such-and-such is female and such-and-such is male. I believe the problem lies elsewhere: how can we offer women the economic and libidinal conditions they need to analyze social oppression and sexual repression so that each women might realize her specificity and difference in the context of what is *unique* about the way she has been produced by the vagaries and necessities of nature, families, and societies? What is the point of asking a woman to write like every other woman? Any generalization made about the feminine condition should merely be a way of enabling each woman to speak about her own uniqueness. This act of speaking is no more "male" than it is "female;" it cannot be generalized, for it is specific and incomparable. Only then can it be an innovation or a potential contribution to a civilization that is lucid and aware of the constraints it imposes without creating new forms of totalitarianism.

10

Feminism and Psychoanalysis

This interview was conducted in 1980 by Elaine Hoffman Baruch and was published, along with the interview with Perry Meisel also included in this book, in a 1984 issue of *Partisan Review*.[1] The translation is by Brom Anderson. After some brief remarks on narcissism and the borderline personality, the interview turns to Kristeva's relationship to feminism. She describes "women's protest" not only as a "movement of sociological protest" but as a "protest that consists in demanding that attention be paid to the subjective particularity that the individual represents, in the social order, of course, but also and above all in relation to what essentially differentiates that individual, which is the individual's sexual difference." And for Kristeva, sexual difference is rooted not only in "biology" but in the linguistic and symbolic "representations that we ourselves make of this difference." She goes on to criticize attempts to link logic and theory with men and the realm of drives and the "unsayable" with women, adopting instead a position that acknowledges the importance of scientific and theoretical discourse for women without disregarding "the particularity belonging to the individual as a woman." She also questions the practice of "speaking for all woman" and warns against "practicing feminism in a herd." Kristeva then discusses *Powers of Horror* and her famous notion of the abject. Abjection is "something that disgusts you, for example, you see something rotting and you want to vomit [. . .] an extremely strong feeling that is at once somatic and symbolic [. . .] rooted in the contact that every human being carries on with the mother." Finally, Kristeva discusses the abject mother and the paternal function. The interview concludes with remarks on the family, culminating in the assertion that love "is the only thing that can save us" and in a condemnation of any attempt to "wipe out" the symbolic moment of love.

Do you feel that France is as narcissistic a society as critics such as Christopher Lasch have said that the United States is?
Narcissistic? What does it mean?

Well, concerned only with the self, to the exclusion of institutions, such as the family, such as even political institutions.
What I can say is that French culture is an extremely chauvinistic culture. That is to say, it is preoccupied with national values. It is interested in its own past. It treats its tradition as a model, and it suffers from being closed toward the outer world. Yes, it's a form of narcissism. But the idea of the "self" is not a French idea. It is an idea belonging originally to Anglo-Saxon psychoanalysis, and it doesn't fare very well in French psychoanalytic literature. It's not a key idea, if one is talking about psychoanalysis. Are individuals in France narcissistic? I wouldn't say that. One would have to make use of other categories. The French are more hysterical, more paranoid, not so much narcissistic—if one can generalize to this area. Personally, I would avoid national diagnoses. I don't think there is a national psychology; there are individual differences.

You do have what is called the borderline personality in France also?
Yes.

What direction will psychoanalysis have to take in order to treat the borderline personality?
That is a very interesting question. The French authors who are beginning to get interested in these problems have been influenced by people such as Winnicott and Fairbairn. To come to terms with this problem,

ELAINE HOFFMAN BARUCH 114

one would have first of all to reread Freud, and to see, every time he speaks of his neurotic cases, how he treats the problems of narcissism. It is at these moments that the question of the borderline might be understood, for this has to do with serious deficiencies at the level of narcissism.

And then another direction that we might take to understand these patients is to pay attention to discourse—and it's here that the contribution of Lacan is important. He taught us to listen to what he calls, following linguistics, the signifier. So one would have to try to follow these patients at the level of their speech, with all the unconscious implications that their speaking may have—implications inscribed in their speech at the level of the signifier. That is rather difficult, because the discourse of the borderline is fragmentary, difficult to follow, full of gaps, without logical order. It would be necessary for the analyst to implicate himself much more profoundly than in the case of neurotics, in order to be able to associate on behalf of the patient.

When did you decide to become an analyst?

I was working on language, particularly situations where it does not yet exist—that is to say, in children, and where it no longer exists, that is, in psychotics. And as I worked in these linguistic situations, I realized that I found myself or put myself in a relation of transference to the people I was observing, and I wanted to experience these transferences more personally. I came to realize that there is no such thing as a neutral meaning, and that a signification is a signification one gives to someone else. It was therefore necessary to contest the whole of positivist linguistics, and I wanted to put positivist linguistics on trial by starting from a precise experience of the transference.

In an interview that you did once for Psych et Po, which was translated in a new anthology edited by Elaine Marks called New French Feminisms, *you said, "There can be no sociopolitical transformation without a transformation of subjects, in other words, in our relation to social constraints, to pleasure, and, more deeply, to language."*[2] *Elsewhere you have spoken about the importance of language for structuring experience, and so have other French theorists. American feminists speak about the importance of language also, but I think they are talking about something quite different. How can we change women's relation to social constraints, to pleasure, and, especially, to language?*

I don't know what American feminists have in mind when they speak of the important role of language; I must admit I don't know much about American work in this area. When I said the sentence you have quoted, it had to do with the following: very often in France a certain sort of feminism has posed itself solely as a movement of sociological protest, which consists in making of women a sort of social force or motor that would ultimately take on the role played in Marxist theory by the proletariat. Here is a class or social group that is oppressed, that is not paid well enough, that does not have its proper place in production and in political representation; and this oppressed class, this oppressed social stratum, should fight, essentially, to obtain recognition—economic, political, and ideological.

I, on the other hand—and I am not alone in this—think that women's protest is situated at an altogether different level. It is not first of all a social protest, although it is also that. It is a protest that consists in demanding that attention be paid to the subjective particularly that an individual represents in the social order, of course, but also and above all in relation to what essentially differentiates that individual, which is the individual's sexual difference. How can one define this sexual difference? It is not solely biological; it is, above all, given in the representations that we ourselves make of this difference. We have no other means of constructing this representation than through language, through tools for symbolizing. Now these tools are common to the two sexes. You speak English if you're English, and you speak French if you're French, whether you are a man or a woman. So how do we situate ourselves in relation to these universal tools in order to try to make our difference?

Here the position of some feminists has seemed to me rather strange and regressive. Certain feminists, in France particularly, say that whatever is in language is of the order of strict designation, of understanding, of logic, and it is male. Ultimately, theory or science is phallic, is male. On the other hand that which is feminine in language is whatever has to do with the imprecise, with the whisper, with impulses,[3] perhaps with primary processes, with rhetoric—in other words, speaking roughly, the domain of literary expression, the region of the tacit, the vague, to which one would escape from the too-tight tailoring of the linguistic sign and of logic. This is, so to speak, a Manichean position that consists in designating as feminine a phase or a modality in the functioning of language. And if one assigns to women that phase alone, this in fact amounts to maintaining women in a position of inferiority, and, in any case, of marginality, to reserving for them the lace of the childish, of the unsayable, or of the hysteric. That the valorization of this modality of expression can have a critical, if not a subversive function, is obvious; but I think that it is not sufficient either. On the other hand, other women say that we must appropriate the logical, mastering, scientific, theoretical apparatus, and these women consider it extremely gratifying that there are women physicists, theorists, and philosophers. In saying this they preserve for women an extremely important place in the domain of culture, but this attitude can be accompanied by the denial of two things: on the one hand, of the question of power, and on the other, of the particularity of women.

In other words, one can fit oneself to the dominant discourse—theoretical discourse, scientific discourse—and on the basis of that find an extremely gratifying slot in society, but to the detriment of the expression of the particularity belonging to the individual as a woman. On the basis of this fact, it seems to me that one must try not to deny these two aspects of linguistic communication, the mastering aspect and the aspect that is more of the body and of the impulses, but to try, in every situation and for every woman, to find a proper articulation of these two elements. What does "proper" mean? That which best fits the specific history of each woman, which best expresses her. So you see that I would be just as much against the slogan, "All women should master the dominant discourse," as I am against the position that asserts that all this is part of the game of power and that women must express themselves in literature. I think that the time has come when we must no longer speak of all women. We have to talk in terms of individual women and of each one's place inside these two poles. One of the gravest dangers that now presents itself in feminism is the impulse to practice feminism in a herd. At first this was perhaps important, because people cried out, "We demand abortion," "We demand the social advantages we have been denied," but now this "we" is becoming troublesome. There have to be "I's," and women have to become authors, actors, not to hypostatize or overvalue those particular kinds of work, but so that this perspective will push each one of us to find her own individual language.

I would like to ask you about your new book, Pouvoirs de l'horreur [Powers of Horror].

It is mainly a psychoanalytic book, but like all psychoanalytic books, it is somewhat self-analytical, like—I am going to make a pretentious comparison—Freud's *Interpretation of Dreams.*

Your subtitle is Essai sur l'abjection. *How would you translate the term* l'abjection *into English?*

It may be impossible. *L'abjection* is something that disgusts you, for example, you see something rotting and you want to vomit—it is an extremely strong feeling that is at once somatic and symbolic, which is above all a revolt against an external menace from which one wants to distance oneself, but of which one has the impression that it may menace us from the inside. The relation to abjection is finally rooted in the combat that every human being carries on with the mother. For in order to become autonomous, it is necessary that one cut the instinctual dyad of the mother and the child and that one become something other.[4]

There are two rather well known books in the United States right now; one by Dorothy Dinnerstein, called The Mermaid and the Minotaur, *and the other by Nancy Chodorow, called* The Reproduction of Mothering. *Their thesis is that the exaltation and the degradation of women stem from the fact that mothers rear children, and that if fathers or men were to have equal responsibility for the rearing of infants all our sexual malaise would be eliminated, all the problems having to do with women's inaccessibility to culture would be ended. How do you feel about this idea?*

If there is a sort of rage against mothers, it is not only because they take care of the child but because they carry it in their bodies. And that is something that men, even if they handle the diapers, can't do. I think it is here that a certain desire is rooted, a certain negative desire, a certain rejection of the maternal function—a fascinated rejection. Moreover, the fact that men do the same work as women with regard to the education of children or their early upbringing will certainly change things in the psychic functioning of children, but I don't know if it will do so in the way foreseen by these feminists. In fact, it will decimate the paternal function. I mean that it will render ambiguous the paternal role. Up to the present, in the division of sexual roles, the mother takes care of the child, the father is farther away. The father represents the symbolic moment of separation.

And you feel that that should be retained?

If we do what they call for, that is, if the fathers are always present, if fathers become mothers, one may well ask oneself who will play the role of separators.

Couldn't they both be? Couldn't both sexes be both nurturers and differentiators somehow?

I would like to think so, but it would be very difficult. What seems more likely is that many borderline children will be produced, and it will become necessary to find a third party, that is to say, the school, all those medical sectors of the different "psy's": psychoanalysts, psychiatrists, psychotherapists, who will play the paternal role. The number of helping institutions for early childhood, for schoolchildren, that are forming now in our society is extraordinary, and one may well ask oneself what their function is. These people, of course, replace the failed mother, as is remarked only too often, but it is above all to replace the nonexistent father: to play the role of the separator, of someone who comforts the mother in order to permit her to take her role in hand. The question is not so much what must be done in order to allow children to develop so they will accede to the various elements of human culture. And I think that what interferes with that access is the underestimation of the paternal function.

Nancy Chodorow, whom I mentioned before, would say that the function of the father has nothing to do with his sex, and that someone female could play the same role of separator. '

Yes, certainly; that's why I say "a third party," who could be the woman psychotherapist to whom one can bring the child.

Let me get back to that problem of not being able to overcome the biological fact of the mother carrying the child, never mind rearing it. How would you feel if the biological revolution were to go so far that the reproduction of the infant took place outside the womb? Would you welcome that possibility, which I no longer think is quite so much of a fantasy as we had considered it even five years ago?

I think that we are all caught up in moral scruples, and we tell ourselves that in the near future such a prospect is to be avoided, for ontological and ethical reasons, for the various experiments that could be done in this area should have guarantees. We aren't very clear in what domain, but we have the impression that we are exposing ourselves to an arbitrariness that is not very far from the experiments of the Nazis that hover on the horizon. This is a defensive attitude, which I cannot help. But I think that nothing will stop "progress" and that, as you say, this will be the case someday. Assuming that, the question to ask ourselves is, "How will sexual roles be distributed? What will fathers do and what will mothers do when the child is no longer carried in the uterus?"

Here we are in the face of humanity whose character is completely unforeseeable. In the present state of things, one attitude one might have, a defensive one, would consist of saying, "There must be preserved, along a straight Freudian line, the distribution of the paternal function, on the one side, and the maternal function, on the other, so that the speaking subjects who are constructed, psychically and not just biologically, can have the "normality" that we think of as theirs. And what is this normality? It is that which succeeds in getting along, surviving, in the oedipal triangle. This position seems to me more and more untenable. I think that we will not be able to hold on for very long to this position—the fathers on one side, the mothers on the other. There will be mixtures of these two functions, which will give rise to a very different psychic map of humanity. One will no longer have the good neurotic caught between Daddy and Mommy. One will have a psychic structure much closer to what is seen now as borderline, I suppose, which does not necessarily mean that it will be outside the social order.

Without going so far as reproduction ex utero, what do you think the future of the family will be like? What changes do you see occurring?

This is difficult to say. I think that you are asking me what is, in the end, a social question. Now, I take very seriously the threat of a crisis—an economic crisis affecting the whole world. There are two solutions to this. I think that this threat of a crisis, which is real, stems from the entrance of the third world on the scene, from the lack of resources, and, of course, from the way these problems are handled. Either, then, this crisis will be resolved through a war of extermination, or—and I am inclined personally to believe the second alternative—it will find a solution in, to put it brutally, sovietization. If we are lucky, our ruling groups will find reformist solutions to the internal conflicts of the Western countries, which will move the Western world in a social-democratic direction. This sort of society, at first, will have to maintain itself by relying on certain conservative forces in the domain of morality, of sex, of the relations of individuals to one another. It will have to avoid having too many explosions, too much violence, too much free acting out of desires. So there will be a consolidation of the family. There will be a politics of birth rate to favor women staying at home, while at the same time giving women part-time work, to satisfy women who work away from home while at the same time taking care of their children. In fact this is just what has been happening in Eastern Europe, with lesser means and via a totalitarian regime. Those regimes, too, are feeling the crisis and will be driven to a relative liberalization—if there is no war.

What do you see as the place of love in this new conservatism of the family?

It's the only thing that can save us. One would have to try, in this situation, to save some territories of freedom. This would be in the realm of affect: a place where people could explore the limits of their discourse, of their thought, of their manipulation of colors and sounds, of words, of whatever you like, so that they express themselves as they wish. But the space of freedom for the individual is love—it is the only place, the only moment in life, where the various precautions, defenses, conservatisms break down, and one tries to go to the limit of one's being; so it is fundamental.

People such as Kate Millet in Sexual Politics *and Shulamith Firestone in* The Dialectic of Sex *claim that love is a myth propagated by men for the control of women.*

Love is not something fixed; there is a history of love. In certain instances, it is possible that it has been a means of blackmail by one sex of the other—and essentially, of the female by the male. But that is a vision, perhaps through the wrong end of the telescope, which doesn't interest me very much because if you look at things that way the whole of culture oppresses women. A madrigal, or Shakespeare, is antiwoman. What does one suggest as an alternative? I for my part say that the love relation is the only chance to go through narcissism toward the recognition of the symbolic moment. And I would look with horror on a humanity that tried to wipe out this symbolic moment.

II

Women and Literary Institutions

This interview was originally published in Alice Jardine's and Anne Menke's *Shifting Scenes: Interviews on Women, Writing, and Politics in Post-68 France*, a collection of interviews with such well-known French women writers as Hélène Cixous, Marguerite Duras, Luce Irigaray, and Julia Kristeva. The translation of the interview with Kristeva is by Katherine Ann Jensen. The first five questions were submitted to all the writers, and one additional question was tailored to each woman's specific work. In the interview with Kristeva, a brief conversation with Jardine and Menke follows each of her answers. The interview focuses on the relationship that women writers have with literary institutions—including the public, the university, independent research groups, academic disciplines, the "canon," and "standards" of greatness. Kristeva argues that "writing 'as a woman' [. . .] should be subordinated to the necessity of writing in one's own name" and suggests that when women enter the traditional institution of the university, they must exercise caution to avoid adopting the "combative and virile qualities" that can be a detriment to their personal happiness and their creative output. Responding to the hypothesis that the growth of interdisciplinary work in the academy stems from the increased importance of women's writings, Kristeva claims that we are "moving toward a future that effaces sexual difference" and toward a "life of difference [. . .] in other forms." She celebrates interdisciplinary work, particularly in neurobiology and psychoanalysis, but does not believe that it is "necessarily female or male." Like many of the writers in *Shifting Scenes*, Kristeva resists the notion of a "canon" and claims that "there are already no more master thinkers." She believes that questions pertaining to the crises of everyday life are more germane than those concerning the canon. Finally, she urges women not to reject organized knowledge but to use their "sensitivity to the mother-child bond" and their interest in language that "recall[s] archaic situations" to find "objects of thought of knowledge" that men have not discovered. She also warns that replacing one set of literary standards with another does not mean that one has moved outside epistemology or outside an "existing rationality."

Question 1: What does it mean to you to write at the end of the twentieth century?

It means trying to be the most personal I can be by eluding all forms of pressure, whether that's from groups, the media, public opinion, or ideology.

And what's the implication of this personal writing?

I'm not sure, but it's a way to preserve a margin of surprise and of the unknown.

And is the effect of the unknown important for you?

Yes, because contrary to how it seems, I think we're seeing a kind of standardization of mentalities, of information, and of education. It's difficult to preserve individual voices, personal voices inside this standardization.

Which helps to explain the boredom that seems to be around?

Absolutely. The personal is really a guarantee of freedom.

Does what you're calling "speaking in a personal voice" have anything to do with the concept of the individual as it was constructed at a given historical moment, or is it something else?

It's probably something else. That is, the notion of the individual is historically dated and supposes different ideological "sedimentations," but this notion of the individual also changes according to the places in which it's used. Obviously, to say "individual" in Moscow means something different from what it means to say it in the United States; it doesn't have the same value. But nonetheless I keep the word's connotations of liberty and rebelliousness. Perhaps we could keep this function for it when speaking of the twentieth century.

Question 2: Is it valid or of value to write as a woman, and is it part of your writing today?

Yes, for me it's really a necessity, but I have the feeling that it depends on what I was saying in the last question, on the need to write in my personal name. This seems to me to protect against the risks involved in writing "as a woman," for that can end up being a kind of uniform: writing as all women write. So I think that the necessity of writing as woman can be maintained under the condition that this be subordinated to the necessity of writing in one's own name. Otherwise there is a risk of making writing uniform.

In what you've written about poetry, you talk about the semiotic versus the symbolic.[1] *The semiotic is closer to the body and can be communicated in language through rhythms, for example. Does the personal effect you were speaking about come from the body, and if so, is it important in this sense to write as a woman? That is, does the female body have different rhythms and sensations than the male? Should sexuality enter into this personal effect on account of the rhythms of writing?*

Sexuality is different; it can be expressed on different levels, on the level of style or in the recognition of some sexual thematic. It can also be on the cognitive level. I'm not at all one of those women who believes that when one is a woman, one must express oneself in a subterranean, elliptical, or rhythmic language. That can be one solution, but it's not the only one. We can simply change the objects of thought. The terrain of thought is not necessarily male, in my opinion, and women can do something right now by presenting new objects of thought.

Question 3: Many women writing today find themselves, for the first time in history, at the center of institutions, such as the university or psychoanalysis. In your opinion, will this new placement of women help them to enter the twentieth-century canon, and if so will they be at the heart of this corpus or (still) in the footnotes?

I think there are two sides to the problem. Obviously, it's an important gain for women to be in the institution, whether that's the university or psychoanalysis, and we must rejoice at this. This must be consolidated, this placement must be made more significant, and women need to be in more decision-making positions. But that doesn't mean that once this has been achieved, the battle is won. I believe one has to remain constantly vigilant. At least that's been my approach. One can't fall asleep, can't close even one eye. One has to be in a constant state of wakefulness and struggle. Otherwise, whether one is in the university or in psychoanalysis, even in apparently important positions, one's personal work won't be noticed or appreciated. I wonder, though, if this is the case only for women. I think that men too, if they fall asleep at their chairman's job, will be finished. I think that for all individuals, though perhaps especially for a woman because of all the resistance, gains cannot be considered definitive. Important gains have to be consolidated, and that's where all the work begins. One must remain in a permanent state of vigilance and combat.

Let's say that a woman does manage to incorporate this personal effect into the work she does inside the academic institution. We know that ideology and the institution are masculine. Given that, do you think this personal effect will be recognized, or is it going to disappear again? That is, I'm trying to see whether the fact of being inside the institution . . .

Should I say, guarantees recognition?

Yes, guarantees recognition. Because I don't find that to be the case.

I think that we're in a completely uncertain situation, because you can say neither that you must be absolutely on the outside in order to be an individual and personal and to continue research, nor that you have to be inside in order to continue research and to transmit it. I think it's a question of an individual fighting spirit—almost animal-like—for someone to remain vigilant while being on the inside. That might also be the case for those on the outside who manage to make their marginality known yet not get buried in a kind of permanent demand for marginality. For me, there's no guarantee in either direction, and I think you have to emphasize that nothing's won in advance and no situation is comfortable. Women have to understand that the battle will go on forever. But this is something that the tradition of woman—the woman-mother, the homemaker, and the woman-object—could never accept. For there are benefits to marginality, to being outside history: you can rest, you can do nothing, you have some small pleasures—which aren't simply secondary but can be extremely important. Now that women have entered the institution, there's also a heavy emphasis on combative and virile qualities that quickly can get blocked and result in women acting like bosses. And at that point, one loses the open structure that is as necessary for personal life, for personal happiness—I was even going to say for personal pleasure—as it is for creation. So the necessary ideal is a kind of balance between the inside and the outside. But that depends on a permanent vigilance and a constant working on oneself.

Question 4: Today we are seeing women produce literary, philosophical, and psychoanalytical theory of recognized importance; and parallel to this, we are seeing a new fluidity in the borderlines among disciplines and genres of writing. Will this parallelism lead only to women being welcomed alongside men, or to a definitive blurring of these categories?

What struck me in your question and what's currently in debate is the issue of the blurring of sexual difference. We would seem to be moving toward a future that effaces sexual difference, in parallel perhaps with other differences. It would seem that humanity must prepare itself for the fact that men could be women and women men. That's a fairly troubling problem to which there are two solutions. First, let's say that this really is going to happen, and that in the twenty-first century there will be no difference between the sexes. There will be a kind of perpetual androgyny even to the extent that—as certain fictions say—men will give birth, and from that point on, the difference of reproduction, which up to that point had been women's realm, will disappear.

I think that if this happens, if we are witnessing a blurring of sexual difference—and why not consider that hypothesis—then two phenomena will accompany this fact. The first is that we're going to witness the end of certain kind of desire and sexual pleasure. For, after all, if you level out difference, given that it's difference that's desirable and provokes sexual pleasure, you could see a kind of sexual anesthesia, and this in an incubator society where the question of reproduction will be posed by way of machines and bioscientific methods in order for the species to continue. That's extremely troubling, first, for the individual's psychic life whose leveling off rules out desire and pleasure, and second, for the individual's creative possibilities. What can that individual invent that's new, surprising, or evolving? By moving toward this sexual homeostasis, won't we see some sort of symbolic homeostasis and therefore very little creation? Or then, again—since the kind of societies and psychic life we've known up until now haven't tolerated this homeostasis—won't new differences be invented? But in that case, won't they also be very problematic? For example, in certain marginal societies, we already see victimizing attitudes created within androgynous couples, as well as extremely violent sadomasochistic practices that can go so far as to libidinalize death. On the other hand, other differences might be emphasized, making them extremely heterogeneous and therefore capable of attracting desire as well as a desire for death. These could be racial difference, for example. An extreme version would be that while there'd be no difference between men and women, we'd hear instead, "Arabs are filth; I hate them and I'll kill them."

I think this possibility exists; it's already quite visible in certain age and social groups. For example, at adolescence, or menopause or andropause, when the individual is in a state of agitation, this kind of ideology or attempt to regulate difference and psychic life can seem very appealing. Apart from that, there are periods when perversion seems self-evident and can be legalized. Perversion becomes the social law. Having said that, I actually think society is going to defend itself against this, because, on the one hand, repression works against these zones of paroxystic pleasures, and, on the other, there are a number of rationalizations being elaborated now that will slow down this kind of behavior. But I think we will see a reformulation of difference.

I imagine the end of this century—since we are really talking about science fiction—and what will come afterward as a life of difference but in other forms. That is, ones that recognize in a more marked way than at present the bisexuality of each sex, not that the feminine won't be dominant in the female and the masculine in the male, but there will be more recognition of women's right to power and affirmation, and so on, and of men's possibilities for passivity and all sorts of behaviors that are coded as feminine, like tenderness, interest in children, all that. So there will be redistribution of this kind, but while maintaining differences.

So much for the question of the sexes. As for fluidity among disciplines [. . .] I'm particularly interested right now by the possible or impossible encounter between neuroscience and psychoanalysis, two realms that have been irreconcilable up until now. With research in its current state, it's hard, really, to see, for example, the bridge between testament with different antidepressants and psychoanalytic treatment. Yet all the work of certain researchers is moving toward creating models in neuroscience on the one hand and in psychoanalysis on the other that can, if not communicate, at least ask questions of the other science. Well, that's where we are for the moment, while recognizing, nonetheless, the enormous gap between biochemical treatment and psychic representation. And the abyss between cells on the one hand and representation on the other remains, for the moment, unbridgeable.

Do you find that women's presence in this . . .
This kind of dialogue?

Yes, does their presence help blur the categories in question? Is there a historical or ideological reason why women entering this debate would encourage this dialogue?

Well, the work I'm familiar with in this area isn't necessarily female or male. For the moment, I don't see a particular contribution [by women]. But it's possible that insofar as women are especially interested in the psychic aspect of things or, in other realms, in bodily functions—for example, the relationship between menstruation and psychic life—they might be inclined to ask overlapping questions. But that's just a hypothesis. In practice, in the group in which I work on these matters, there are two women, and the rest are men. I don't think that men, because they're men, are cut off from this kind of issue.

This difficulty of crossing boundaries may be more evident in American universities—for example, in women's studies, where there is a demand for interdisciplinary work. There are always men around saying, "No, you can't ask those kinds of questions because they're about literature, or psychology, and we cannot blur, we cannot mix these things up."

Perhaps it's like this overall on the university level, but is the same true in research groups? Right now, I'm reading a book by Morton Reiser called *Mind, Brain, Body: Toward a Convergence of Psychoanalysis and Neurobiology.* He's someone who asks these kinds of questions about psychoanalytic-neurobiological relationships. I find he's too reductive and so I don't agree with him, but at least he's asking questions that bridge disciplines. He cites work by some biologists, one of whom is a woman. On the basis of biology, this woman is asking questions about the relationship between social conditioning and learning and cell modification.[2] These factors aren't necessarily psychological—because we're talking about animals—but are external factors of behavior, society, and conditioning that influence the cell. So there is an example of a woman whose interests overlap. Perhaps what we need to question here is precisely the institution. The university institution is actually quite conservative, but research groups are something different.

I think, rather, that it's because historically we see these two things at the same time—women in institutions and the blurring of boundaries between disciplines—that we relate them. Is there really a link between them? Or do we find one now when, for the first time, many women are in the institution and in research groups? Maybe they don't have anything to do with one another? Perhaps it's a coincidence?

The framework is important, though. For example, as you say, society is masculine. But it has created frameworks where contamination is possible. At the university, we tend to say, "Don't touch, everyone remain normal, we're conservative, but even so, we'll let ourselves have a small research group where anything is possible and where there will be mixtures and blending; afterward, we'll see." But on the overall university level, that won't really come about for another fifty years.

If it's that soon.

And the human sciences[3] are even more conservative; the emphasis now is on neuroscience and possibly on psychology. That raises a lot of problems in any event. Many neurobiologists say, "All that psychoanalysis stuff is crap. Soon we will discover pills that will get rid of all mental illnesses; so we don't need to bother with the psychic aspect." Then there are psychoanalysts who are completely closed to any relation with neurobiology, and sometimes they're right, because there can be all sorts of abuses leading people to believe that a pill can get rid of your problems, which isn't true. But I think we can find interesting bridges.

Question 5: Given the problematic and the politics of the categories of the canon, and given the questions we've been dealing with here, do you think your oeuvre will be included in the twentieth-century canon, and if so, how will it be presented? In your opinion, what will be the content of the canon?

Well I was just thinking of a play on words here. One has the canon and the gunpowder in the canon. One day there will be no more canon, only powder, nothing in fact but a screen of gunsmoke [*de la poudre aux yeux*]. What I'm trying to say is that it seems to me that the question you're asking is really about education and the transmission of information. I see this transmission as if by a TV with fifty to a hundred stations, each different, transmitting very different information—although they cancel one another out—since one often has the impression they all participate in the same ideology or, in any case, in something held in common and not easily discernible but that is perhaps a form of resistance to anything surprising or to anything that could undermine the norm. In any event, it's my impression that soon there won't be a canon, at least not in the current sense of the word, given this plurality of information that the media have already started to transmit and that the schools and universities work against. When you see what's being taught in the universities and then, on the other hand, what people read and what movies they see, what music they listen to, there's often no correlation. So sometimes you say to yourself, thank goodness for the university, because a certain classical culture is maintained. But conversely, it's not clear that this classical culture is maintained such that it's integrated within modernity. At times, classical culture is maintained in such a way that it's completely rejected and unassimilable in the modern world, and so one emphasizes even more its expulsion through this kind of [university] transmission. So we're going to see a sort of sabotaging of formal education and university information by the plurality of communication; and in that framework, the canon will be exploded, reduced to powder—it will be pulverized and pluralized. For example, there are already no longer any master thinkers.

The example of France, a centralized, Jacobin country, is instructive from this standpoint because up until five or six years ago, the canon was heavily imposing; there were ranking members that everyone repeated or imitated, or tried to align themselves with. But now, we see all this work being neutralized, like on a TV where nothing makes any sense. At this point, then, the issue for me is not about knowing whether I'm going to be maintained in an institutional canon, which in some universities will be transmitted as but a vestige of the past, a kind of relic, whereas people aren't at all interested in all that, [for they live] in a culture where everything possible is done to blur the canon or make it impossible to transmit. The question is to know whether one can ask interesting questions, or pose problems that interest people in the twentieth century. It's a question of the whole problematic of adaptation to evolution, and at the same time, of nonconformity to fashion, which is a giant and tricky slalom. This supposes both the possibility of being able to listen and a self-accountability where one tries to impose what one believes to be a personal truth. From then on, what may arise as an interesting practice is not a canon but [a way of posing] problems that can respond to the crises people live from day to day.

So even if people continue to teach this canon within the university, even if French high schools continue to teach Lagarde et Michard, *and so on, in your view, all this has died, it's not anything to fight against?*

I think that in the form it's taught, it really is dead. There's also the other side of the problem: how do we react to the leveling out and anesthetizing of thought that this "multichannel communication"[4] produces? In such a case, there might, in fact, be a way to show that Racine and Homer are readable today and that even a kid who watches Zorro can think so, too. But then, you have to find ways to make this reading correspond to current tastes.

And the dinosaurs will disappear themselves?

Or else just stay the way they are, like a sort of . . .

Vestige . . .

. . . of a dead culture. I've recently read a thesis on cultural survival that puts these things quite clearly. The man who wrote it took street names and translations as signs of the canon. Well, who names streets? The municipality, the establishment. If you name a street Bernanos, you think Bernanos is in the canon. But when a guy passes Bernanos Street, he doesn't have any idea who that is. It's an empty name, it contains no information. Or Jussieu. Who knows who he was? He was some scientist, but even the majority of our students in humanities here at Jussieu don't know that. It's the name of a metro stop. A canon, if you like. But does that really make sense as a means for a culture to transmit itself?

On the other hand, if you look at what's going on in translations, there's a certain kind of translation that's done by pressure groups—publishing houses obviously have lobbyists with their own tastes and ideologies, and so on. But given the mass-media status of publishing as well, there's an enormous number of things that get translated and that aren't coded. Detective stories or other things that aren't considered valuable are more readily translated than Balzac. Antonin Artaud or other important writers who are considered to have marked culture are rarely translated. So there's a dilution that shows that outside transmissions canonized by pressure groups, outside classical culture and the establishment, there's a culture of desire, almost a cathartic culture, one of expenditure, of pleasures, which becomes not a new canon but a new corporation [capable of] exploitation.

Question 6: In the diversity of your work, one always finds the epistemological problems that have been posed throughout time examined from a contemporary perspective. This perspective is a knowingly critical one, and since it is also that of a psychoanalyst, it must necessarily take sexual difference into account. How is it possible to work in that way without at least appearing to repeat on a theoretical level the historical gesture of organizing knowledge by relegating women-subjects and their texts to the background?

I don't happen to agree with the position that because the gesture that organizes knowledge is based on effacing sexual differences in the name of an absolute or neutral subject, women should refuse that gesture. I think that there are different manifestations of culture, and knowledge is one of them. Women must take their place inside the cultural field by trying to discover objects of thought or knowledge that men haven't. In doing this, then, do women respond as women? No doubt they do, if one considers that we are always constituted bisexually and that a woman who makes the historical gesture of organizing knowledge her own gesture is exhibiting her phallic component. I don't see why women shouldn't exhibit that component. However, once they do exhibit it, from the moment they create new objects of knowledge, they also reveal their specificity, which is not phallic but which has to do, for example, with their sensitivity to the mother-child bond, which is something that men can't necessarily delimit. Or another example is women's interest in the modulations of language that don't come from the language of everyday communication but that recall archaic situations.

So I would keep this way of operating and consider it valuable and interesting. I also think men can find analogous objects of knowledge through their bisexuality; women don't have a monopoly on this. But I believe that to insist on sexual differences doesn't prevent thinking or even demanding both permutations, and that work done by a man can also be done by a woman. Otherwise, we regionalize culture and consider one aspect as female, another as male, and in that way, we castrate the essential polyvalence of subjects. Nonetheless, I would like to insist again that within this organizing gesture, the tonality a woman would bring—in the way she presents a new object, or in the way she treats it—is totally particular. We're not going to keep a woman from playing Bach because Bach was a man.

I completely agree with you within the context of working on our own historical moment. But women working on other historical periods have had to confront the fact that most of what's called phallocentric thought—the thought we have inherited from the fathers, this entirely historical philosophy—must be completely questioned because it was created only by men. This is a real problem for feminist critics who work on past texts: how not to repeat the historical gesture that has effaced the texts that somehow didn't fit in?

What do they have to do if they want to rehabilitate these texts? Possibly they will change the standards, but these women will remain within the framework of conceptual thought. So they'll remain within the gestures of Western knowledge, but they will say, "There used to be criteria X and Y, but I'm going to invent a criterion Z that hasn't been considered by men or by those who evaluate texts in men's name, and I'm going to consider that such a woman, who was thought of as obscure in her time, has qualities." But by adopting this perspective, they're still operating with Aristotle's categories, with criteria of thought based on good and less good, within existing rationality. They're not placing themselves outside epistemology.

CULTURE

I don't like photographs. I fail to recognize myself in those fixed moments and poses, those fragments of lost and forgotten time that leave no impression on me besides an occasional feeling of discomfort that bears little relation to the remnant that I see before my eyes. Still, that remnant is the only one that exists; it alters the moment I actually experienced when it doesn't erase it forever. In our image-filled world, we believe only in what we see. There, I remain a foreigner. If my body and mind still hold interest, I believe you will find them not in what appears to the eyes, but in an invisible intensity of which I seek the meaning, and not the mere appearance.

That said, I accept with a bit of emotion the editor's invitation to include here some photographs, some signs that may bring me closer to the reader. In the end, a child's expression of fear or defiance, an adolescent's pose of joy or attraction, and a few points along my path as a woman and an intellectual have helped me realize with a touch of nostalgia and joy that these flashes of memory continue to flourish inside me.

Through the museum of circumstance, then, I would like to share with you this memory of an ever-present underground life—not a past, but a malleable immanence that never stops developing, however secretly. These photos point to this immanence, like forgotten odors that revive, for lovers only, the very passions that created them.

—*Julia Kristeva*

1942
Taking my first steps in Bulgaria
with my mother, Christine

1944
At home on the sofa dressed in
the Bulgarian national costume

1948   In Sofia, right after the war, with my father, Stoyan Kristeva

1951   May 24, the Festival of the Slavic Alphabet; I am wearing the scarf awarded to the "top student"

1966   Studying in Paris

1970   With Philippe Sollers and several members of the Tel Quel group

1970   At a conference in Kuwait on the "Palestinian and Arab Socialist Movement"

1973   In China: The Tel Quel delegation in Luoyang

1973   In China: With a school principal in Shanghai

1973   In China: With Roland Barthes in front of the Pagoda of the Great Goose in Xian

1973   In China: In front of the baths of the Imperial Concubine in Xian

1974   Arrival in New York, at the invitation of Columbia University

1976   In New York with my son, David

1977   With Philippe Sollers vacationing on the Ile-de-Ré

1985   With David on the Ile-de-Ré

1991   At the Collège français of Moscow University, then in St. Petersburg

1994   In Jerusalem

12

Memories of Sofia

This interview was conducted in 1992 by *Le Nouvel observateur* for a special issue on European cultural capitals. The magazine asked thirty well-known figures to write an essay on a designated city, and Kristeva was a natural choice for the piece on Sofia. The translation is by Ross Guberman. Kristeva offers a free-form reflection on her native city, combining poignant memories of her childhood, a brief history of Sofia, and musings on Bulgaria's relationship to Europe. She also alludes to her second novel, *The Old Man and the Wolves*.

What does Sofia mean to you?

I am attached to Sofia in the same way one is shamefully yet loyally attached to women who are disgraceful because they have lived too much. With no Renaissance or baroque treasures and no panache to speak of, Sofia is one of the most commonplace capitals you could ever imagine. Middle-class residents and old-fashioned intellectuals rub shoulders with peasants in a 1.2 million–resident city that would be drab were it not for the sparkle of its honey-colored paving stones and the ringing bells of its churches. To be blunt, Sofia is depressing, marred by a dirty mist and a heat that pins it down to the foot of the Vitoche mountain, not to mention the endless lines in which my father, mother, or sister and I would wait for four hours just to buy a pound of cherries.

My childhood unraveled right in the heart of Sofia. For me, Sofia can be boiled down to the Saint Nedelia cathedral, with its little gardens, its snowy slopes on which I would throw my toboggan, its secret rooms, and its nervous believers. My father, a faithful man whose beautiful voice added to the Saint Nedelia church choir, would bring me to the cathedral before dawn so that I could take communion without being spotted. I eventually rebelled, not because I was bothered by the dissidence of the act but because of universal reason, which is, I still find, harder to understand and to embody than faith is. My rebellion did not stop me from hiding in Saint Nedelia's dark corners, from smelling its incense, from hiding under its tables that were filled with boughs and painted eggs at Eastertime, and even occasionally from ringing its bells, which would make an unwanted disturbance that amused small pockets of children while frustrating priests and parents.

I learned later that I was not the only person to have been drawn to this magical site. The center of Sofia has not changed in seven thousand years. Neolithic excavations say as much: Sofia is the only European city that has stubbornly preserved its heart for so many millennia. The Thracians were the first people to leave signs that still can be seen today, for Thracian coins, which can be found near Saint Nedelia, date back to the first millennium. Close by is the stunningly symmetrical Saint George church, which was constructed during the fourth century, covered with frescoes beginning in the tenth century, and made into a mosque during the sixteenth century.

With his bright eyes and high cheekbones, my father claimed that we were Thracians. Even so, I refused to see him as Spartacus, because he didn't have red hair. He did speak in Latin, however, and we lived in the memory of Sofia more than in its cement buildings. Serdica, which was the name the Romans gave to the Thracian city that Philip II conquered in the fourth century B.C., was a central city in the Roman Empire. It grew under Marcus Ulpius, who named it Ulpia Serdica after himself, and it prospered further under Marcus Aurelius. Constantine the Great, who founded Constantinople, even dreamed of making it into his capital: "Serdica is my Rome," he said.

The Thracians and the Byzantines resisted Slavic invasions for a long time, and the city did not become Bulgarian until the year 809, under the reign of Kroum Khan. Known as "Sredets" for the following two centuries, the city was captured by the Byzantines, who renamed it Triaditsa. This did not protect it from other conquerors' invasions, however. Finally, in the twelfth century, Tsar Ivan Asen II recaptured it and made it into a central part of the Second Bulgarian Empire. At the end of the fourteenth century, the capital acquired the name Sofia. Sofia's refined lords, however, could not withstand the Turkish invasion. Prosperous at first, the capital declined during its five hundred years of Ottoman rule. At the time of its independence in 1878, Sofia was an unimpressive city. People sought to beautify it in the narrow, decadent style of the Balkan countries that had already begun to confuse themselves with "Balkanization," that disaster of fratricidal misery.

This didn't bother us at all. We held on to a glorious memory in which Sofia was a worthy part of culture. It mattered little if it was European culture or world culture, for it was Culture. I shall say nothing about Cyril and Methodius, who invented the Cyric alphabet, the source of our national pride, for Sofia was not really at the heart of their adventure even if the medieval civilization we owe to them flourished inside its walls. Since Sofia is nothing more to me than a springboard to time regained, what I would most like to remember is the Boyana church. This little church, which was built in the early part of the eleventh century, had a section added in 1259 that housed eighty frescoes depicting 250 characters. The portraits of Dessislava and Kaloyan are the missing link between Constantinople and Saint Mark's of Venice. The same year—1259—also marked the founding of the Sorbonne. Europe is a story of religions and paintings in which Boyana sparked Renaissance art. Do you think I am exaggerating? Go see for yourself, now that Europe appears simply to be an entity onto itself.

Of course, Sofia contains not only monuments but men and women. It must have been difficult not to succumb to the waves of invaders that surged onto this crossroads between Europe and Asia. Like everywhere else, people allowed conquerors to go about their business: Attila the Hun, the Wisigoths, the crusaders, the Turks, the Russians, and I will leave it at that. Some people resisted, of course, but Europe ignores them because it sees no value in a parcel of Orthodox territory that it believes to be innately Russian.

Personally, I knew Levsky. This nineteenth-century deacon had a habit of hiding in the Dragalevtsy monastery, near Sofia, where we sometimes spent our holiday alongside groups of vacationers. Levsky fought against the Turks. After he was arrested, he smashed his skull against the prison wall to avoid torture. You can visit the Levsky monument right in the middle of Sofia. I myself would go to the stadium to yell, "Go, Levsky!" against the soccer players of the "Popular" Army, for Levksy enjoyed the sympathy of the disaffected. Levsky is not only a monument but also a soccer team, just as Danton is a subway stop in Paris and Charles de Gaulle is an airport. That is how memory works.

Yet memory can also become mummified. Along with Moscow, Sofia is the only European capital to have a mausoleum, one whose mildew ripplings are barely dissipated by the scent of roses. Georgi Dimitrov—some people probably still remember both this anti-Nazi and the Reichstag trial—was laid to rest under a cream-colored marble temple in the mausoleum's red-tinted sarcophagus. To cover up the massacres, dead people cloaked in makeup were put on display. Aghast, we paraded in front of this cadaverlike memory.

The mausoleum is now empty, but I am not certain that the heart of Sofia has caught its breath. A few months before the fall of the Berlin wall, I saw a city invaded by wolves, that is, by hatred, brutality, and corruption. An old man who dared to say this out loud, a Latinist, a European, was assassinated by these wolves. I made this story into a novel.

The wolves appear to be changing. They go from one place to another; they learn new ways to meet their goals. More elaborate "affairs" develop—shadowed by incompetence and misery. Some of the wolves will become men. Or at least it seems they will—slowly though it may be. This makes me think of the end of the Roman empire and of Byzantium. Sofia was an important city in Byzantium, a city of memories. If memory lasts, nothing is impossible. For the moment, indifference and forgetting are bearing down on this part of the world. Europe hopes to construct itself without taking the Balkans into account. One can understand why. In Sofia, however, the old man's new allies dream in Latin, in Byzantine, and in European. Because this extremely discreet city has lived too much, it is still too early to tell. Fifteen years from now, I will meet you in Sofia.

13

America: A Society on the Move

This brief but incisive interview with Catherine Francblin appeared in 1976 in the inaugural issue of *Art Press International*. The translation is by Ross Guberman. It is similar in content to the lengthy conversation among Julia Kristeva, Philippe Sollers, and Marcelin Pleynet published in a fall 1977 issue of *Tel Quel* and translated as "Why the United States?" in *The Kristeva Reader*. This interview introduces many themes that will reappear in Kristeva's later remarks on the United States, including the "archaic" tendencies of the American left; the sophistication of American theater, painting, and dance; the way the "Protestant," "old-fashioned," and "repressed" side of America relates to its penchant for spiritualism and orientalism; and the differences between the women's movement in France and in the United States.

To begin with, could you say a few words about the role of intellectuals in American life? How would you describe the ideological and political position of their work?

The notion of intellectuals, defined as "the members of a society who put the impossible into words," is no doubt a bourgeois construct associated with the predominantly French ideologues of the Enlightenment. I find it even harder to know how this notion functions in the United States than in France. The little bit I've seen in the States suggests that at least two distinct groups of American intellectuals specialize in the humanities: the first works for academic institutions, primarily universities, and the second is made up of avant-garde writers and artists and is part of the counterculture. These two camps remain autonomous entities, so much so that the violent subversions of the counterculture hardly ever affect the ideological workings of the more mainstream groups. This division is mirrored by individuals themselves: although young people have been struck by the uprising of the beat generation, they continue to be "good" students and remain staunch believers in the values of the academy.

Since American universities have sustained a tradition of humanist rationalism that reached its peak in Europe during the seventeenth and eighteenth centuries through Descartes and the Enlightenment philosophers, they are quite liberal yet rather archaic. An academic such as Chomsky would thus be less inclined to explore French research on language and psychoanalysis than would a counterculture writer such as William Burroughs. In contrast to France, where Tel Quel might be seen as the "underground" of the Collège de France and Lacan the "underground" of the Académie Française, the movements of cultural protest in the United States stand entirely apart from any such intellectual "superstructure." This division has allowed for subversive acts that appear to be quite radical and sometimes are. Yet when Europeans appear to be working inside an institution, their activities may display a stronger undercurrent of deep protest because they are disturbing the very foundation of rationality.

Are these rationalist-humanist universities explicitly political?

They are often "committed" in the existentialist sense of the word. Even so, the American university brand of Marxism leaves cultural archaisms intact because it fails to bring politics to bear on such problems as signifying practices or the subject's relationship to language and the unconscious. So American Marxists seem archaic when compared with the capitalist economy or the underground movements. In my view, these leftist currents have not absorbed the essence of May 1968, which was a movement of political and ideological protest verging on a cultural revolution. As a result, the academic left in America finds itself in an objective complicity with the Soviet Union. Even if its members lambaste the concentration camps, the only thing they are able to contrast to the United States is Eastern Europe. From Kissinger to Chomsky, they have all distanced themselves from Solzhenitsyn. The archaism of "leftist rationalism" is never so obvious as it is in the United States—and it is rebounding here in France.

Do you believe there is something that could be called American thought, given that Americans have no philosophical tradition and display no interest in Marx and Freud, and yet are extraordinarily sophisticated in such domains as painting? Does this set up an opposition between the United States and a community of European thinkers?

I believe that one could draw such a distinction. Americans express their pain through painting, theater, dance, and even pornography—practices that are certainly not ideational. Their system of thought falls directly under the spell of a repression that stems from the ever-presence of Protestantism and the immanence of transcendence (itself a vestige of British royalty). Americans invest in "old-fashioned values," and as soon as they try to contemplate a possible "connection" to the process of meaning and the subject, they find themselves turning to "wild" or "oriental" ideas. This lends a spiritualist flavor to their social protests when it doesn't function as a foreign body. I believe this reflects the very nature of American society, particularly the influence of Protestantism, which has intensified the repression and enabled it to function optimally in a consumer society. Perhaps that is what it was meant to do. The Catholic tradition seeks to reinforce the current downfall of the French psychoanalytic or "aesthetic" revival. So American intellectuals who want to think of these disturbances as signifying practices and to consider this "link" in a materialist way are drawn to French work on Freud and his followers (such as Marcelin Pleynet's study of American painting). Americans consider such work to be an external phenomenon, since the only discourse through which intellectual Americans (like those from the Eastern bloc) can analyze—or dissolve—their culture is spiritualism, defined as the orthodox religions of the Orient or the various esoteric movements of the West.

One hears that certain parts of the country have some latent fascist tendencies . . .

Mainstream middle-class Americans are clearly preoccupied with the nation, with the family, and with many other conservative mainstays. Since this tendency has no violent undertones, it is apparently not fas-

cism, yet it is rooted unconsciously in the phenomenon of totalitarianism, that is, in total repression. Is American society prone to fascism?
I would be more inclined to say that since America is broadly diverse
and has access to many outlets (cinema, pornography, pop music, and
so forth) that are able to free up fantasies and drives, it protects itself
from the threat of any ideology, including that of the state or the
employer. Pornographic shows appear on television every evening,
which may make the American Midwest less prone to fascism than are
the debates of the Communist party in the USSR. I have been particularly impressed by the incredible resiliency of the American system,
whose inner workings create a space for subversion because one can
always arrange for small liberal pathways that will enable society to
guarantee its own survival. That is why I doubt we can expect much
from the States in the way of revolution, which does not mean there is
nothing left for them to accomplish because everything is controlled
by the government. On the contrary, America is in the midst of a long
process of disintegration driven by a growing number of danger zones.
Modern art is a more recent example of these zones, and so are drugs,
blacks, women, and the like.

*Speaking of women, how has the women's liberation movement taken shape
in the United States?*

American women still face many economic problems such as unequal
salaries and limited professional advancement. Because of this enormous resistance to women's social recognition, feminist movements
have found an eager audience. A magazine such as *Ms.* tries to reach all
women and thus loses its radicalness; it contains many articles that a
French woman could find in *Elle*. On the other hand, if certain feminist groups have displayed fascist strains, the Americans are more aware
and critical of this risk than are the French (see Susan Sontag's articles
in the *New York Review of Books*). Although the current movement is
quite diffuse, it has already managed to remove the aura of guilt surrounding the sexual ambivalence of both genders. Homosexuality is
dealt with more liberally over there than it is in the Catholic countries
of Western Europe. American tolerance releases a sublimation that has
returned, explicitly or implicitly, as a core element of American art (it
may also be at the base of "aesthetic" experimentation and classical
"thought").

By giving "men" the opportunity to experience themselves as "women" and vice versa, this effort to taint dependence (as well as the archaic Mother) with a bit of guilt eases "sexual relations." Since such relations do not exist,[1] a man and a woman could meet each other only if they both experienced themselves as ambivalent beings. That is why Americans believe quite strongly in the couple even as they enfeeble sexuality. American campuses have witnessed an increase in blatant flirtation and in everything associated with the neurotic tribulations of romantic love. This disaffection with sexual relations may also stem from a repression manifested as a deferred effect of pornography, but I am more inclined to believe it is rooted in the emergence of a subjectivity that permits sexual bipolarity. And what will be the result of all this? The sort of ennui that looms over Scandinavian countries? Or will it lead to new forms of expression? The answer remains to be seen.

14

Psychoanalysis and Politics

Edith Kurzweil conducted and translated this interview for a 1985 issue of *Partisan Review*. The tone of the interview is warm, open, and conversational. In the first part of the interview, Kristeva criticizes the American literary academy, accusing it of falling prey to an exaggerated form of deconstructionism that disregards questions of ethics and history. She also addresses the notion of psychoanalysis as a political and interpretive praxis, arguing that psychoanalysis, which provides an antidote to pure intellectual speculation, can free up some of the impasses presented by excessively formal literary study and can function as a form of political commitment in its own right. She then describes some of the internal political struggles of the French psychoanalytic movements. Finally, Kristeva claims that psychoanalysis provides a way of understanding foreignness and exile. For the remainder of the interview, Kristeva gives us a rare glimpse of her political opinions, discussing candidly her views on François Mitterand, socialism and the French Socialist party, the American left, the dangers of political naïveté and idealization, and the way the United States influences French national identity. She concludes with some hopeful words about the future of cultural exchanges between Europe and the United States.

When I first knew you, you had written about women in China,[1] and you were very involved with the publication Tel Quel. You were primarily a writer. Soon you were very much interested in questions of semiotics and deconstruction. What made you become a psychoanalyst?

Well, as soon as I began working in France, I got interested in literary criticism and in the feminist and political issues you just mentioned. This led me to try to analyze some of the "avant-garde writing," which, I believe, begins with Mallarmé at the end of the nineteenth century and goes through surrealism. (Tel Quel is an extension of this movement.) So in order to apprehend the formal construction and logic of a work, and of the human experience it expresses, I wanted to understand the psychological functions of language in critical situations. Such situations for the most part occur before language exists—in infants or in the disturbed language of psychosis. I then tried to analyze the acquisition of language and psychotic language as critical discourses. For neutral description or observation is not enough: I had to involve myself to understand how the people I hear are contributing to the transformation of a relationship. Therefore I went into psychoanalytic treatment and wanted to become a psychoanalyst. This was my intellectual motivation, but there was a whole range of personal motivations, such as living in exile, not belonging to a culture or to my native language. This is a common situation in the modern world, where we often are strangers in exile and live in hostile surroundings. For me this situation was painful, and thus it pushed me to know more about myself, about exile as more than a sociological fact, as part of my psychic structure: some people choose to be foreigners not only in response to political pressures but because they have never felt at home anywhere. Psychoanalysis helps in understanding this situation.

Are you saying that your own personal history pushed you both toward understanding and studying French literature and, then, toward understanding yourself via psychoanalysis?

Yes.

Why, I wonder, don't more people do that? After all, so many people have been in similar situations and don't go into psychoanalysis or use literature to resolve their problems. Obviously talent has something to do with it.

I don't really know. But my family, early on, pushed me into a cultural milieu. Literature was important to us, so we couldn't imagine—particularly in Eastern countries where religion was banned and political issues became dogmatic—that children could grow up without art and literature. They always were a part of me. But you are asking why more literary people don't go into psychoanalysis. I think that literary criticism, after formalism, and particularly after structuralism, got too abstract. This is interesting, because when you try to describe more precisely how literary form functions, when you get to the eternal logic of texts and get into abstractions, you often tend to lose its human aspects—its importance to the reader and writer. In other words, we cannot see the inner dynamics, the inner motivations, or the results of reading *on* somebody who reads. That is why I think psychoanalysis may be a viable extension of formalistic studies, so that these studies don't reach a sort of impasse.

Does that mean that you do not support the popularity of French deconstruction among American literary academics, for whom it has become somewhat rigid, and that their pursuits are too formalistic for you?

Yes. I have the impression that Americans have picked up French theoretical development only partially and that it has become a sort of monopoly. It goes beyond the essentials of symbolic forms, sometimes quite dogmatically; even its most enthusiastic French proponents are less dogmatic than the Americans.

That's exactly my impression.

For instance, when we say that we try to analyze metaphysical presuppositions, and when we question the notions of "meaning," or "form," as well as the dichotomy between meaning and form—we know that we cannot *entirely* get away from these metaphysical statements. We assume that there always is a sort of dialectic between the metaphysical postulates and something else, and this dialectic enables us to consider such fields as ethics and history. In America, the so-called deconstructionists think that, because ethics and history belong to metaphysics and because metaphysics is criticized by Heidegger or his French followers, ethics and history no longer exist. I have been amazed when lecturing at American universities, for instance, when trying to understand Mallarmé's formal involvement at the end of the nineteenth century in relation to French history, to religion, the state, the arts, and the bourgeois parties—someone in the audience always asks why I speak about ethics and history when those notions already have been deconstructed. Not even the most dogmatic French deconstructionists ask such questions.

Yes, many of us feel the same way. But do you think that the people who invite you are more familiar with your positions of five or ten years ago?

Maybe. But I don't think that they were quite so formalistic even then. Still, there is some sort of misinterpretation, since formalism is newer than are historical and ethical interpretations: some people focus on it and forget its context. I wrote my first paper in France for Roland Barthes's 1966 seminar about Mikhail Bakhtin.[2] He soon became an important figure. But I spoke about a book by Bakhtin on Dostoevsky, and about another one on Rabelais, which already were considered poststructuralist or postformalist.[3] Bakhtin accounted for what happens in the literary forms of Rabelais and Dostoevsky, but did not disconnect these formal aspects from the surrounding history and ethics. He looked at the aesthetics of the carnival in relation to the church, and so on. I was interested in how he already considered form as part of historical and moral issues.

Unfortunately, in America we divide intellectual life into disciplines.

Yes, it is a universal academic tradition.

From what you said, I gather you believe the French are more playful than the Americans?

Yes. On the one hand Americans are more extremist and on the other more tolerant. Those tendencies in structuralism, for instance, or what you call the deconstructivism of Derrida, have been developed in a very sharp and absolute way. In France, they are not the only important, or unique, orientations. They exist in a cultural tradition and at a cultural intersection that allows for other positions—both classical and ideological. At one time we suffered from a strong tradition, but such a tradition also prevents new inventions from taking over, from considering themselves as unique and absolute.

In Paris, of course, you always have many more interdisciplinary discussions in the real sense, rather than conferences that call on people from various disciplines.

Yes, this is true. And this was particularly important in French universities after 1968. Yet it also gave rise to something useless, because people representing different epistemological models often cannot talk to one another; they stay on parallel discourses that don't cross or meet. That is why we now change the very objects of our analyses. When we want to be interdisciplinary, we choose an interdisciplinary topic and address it from the different kinds of discourse. For instance, in my university we now have a research group on the theme of crisis: what is a crisis—in literature, philosophy, ideology, religion, and so on. We go back to the sixteenth century, and look at it in the seventeenth, nineteenth, and twentieth centuries. In order to analyze such an ambiguous topic, we do so in terms of linguistics, sociology, philosophy, psychology, and so on. Thus every scholar is obliged to be on top of all these discourses, rather than wait for the various specialists to supply their own expertise.

In other words, as one used to say, you have to make it all your own.

Yes, it supposes that you don't belong to your own discipline alone but that you broaden and enrich it.

Personally, I've always found this very appealing.

Well, it may seem *un peu dilettante,* but it's not.

I wanted to ask you something else, about your work as a psychoanalyst. It seems to me that it's one thing to be in therapy and another actually to treat patients. You must have had a great deal more training and, I assume, a didactic analysis, so that you really are engaged in two enterprises. Do you find that the two mingle?

Literary criticism and the practice?

Yes. Do you find that seeing patients and sitting behind the couch or across from it, whichever way you do it, and listening to people's problems over and over again helps you with your literary activities?

Yes, it helps. And it does something else. I'll try to explain what it does, and how this illuminates literary work. Theoretical development, I believe, achieved a very high level of speculation, of abstraction, and thus brought something new into European culture. But also this abstraction presupposes a split from practice that is a sort of "malaise" in our culture. Hannah Arendt talked about it in the controversy over distinctions between work and labor, and between practice and speculation.[4] Literary and philosophical work is speculation. At the same time, you get more involved by helping people and by changing real situations. After all, one of the post-Hegelian—that is, of the Marxist— issues was to unite separate fields of human activity. So far, the various solutions have been more or less dreadful, because they either betrayed the purity and sharpness of intellectual work or proposed practical solutions that were dogmatic and somewhat dangerous. Psychoanalysis, it seems to me, can bring them together. We have to reach a very subtle liberation; nevertheless it is liberation, speculation, and so on, that cannot exist without practical involvement: it arises in the cure, helps it, and is realized in it. Hence we achieve a very particular connection, which does not even exist in the sciences. This is why psychoanalysis is a very special field, and why I went into it—at least, it is one of my reasons. I did not want to remain in only abstractions and theoretical observations about writers or artists. In psychoanalysis, I *think* and I *do*; it's very interesting. This helps my literary criticism because I now am in a better position to understand the writer's motivations in changing religious, ideological, or sexual languages, forms, and themes. I can also surmise what happens to the personality of the writer, and his impact on the reader. Psychoanalysis helps me to understand both reception and creation. Because writers on the couch are telling stories, they are permanent writers, maybe not always very gifted ones. But from time to time I have the impression that we sometimes hear more interesting stories on the couch than are being published. (When I said that on television, I had many demands for analysis.) From time to time, these stories are told in a very imaginative way, in terms not only of content but of style. This does not always hold true, but when it does, my patients' stories are more dramatic than the superficial stories of best-sellers.

I have been puzzled by something else. When you did decide to become a psychoanalyst, why did you become a member of the classical psychoanalytic group rather than join the Lacanians, whose ideas, one would have assumed, are closer to your own?

I can tell *you* why, but I have not told the newspapers. First there were personal reasons. I knew Lacan very well; he was a friend, and he was intellectually important to me. But I wanted to keep my psychoanalysis apart, in a private domain of exploration, away from intellectual pre-occupations. Thus Lacan was not the right person to analyze me. Aside from these personal reasons, I considered the Lacanians somewhat too politicized and thus less interested in clinical problems than in intellectual power. By politicized, I mean that they were too concerned with questions of succession and power in psychoanalysis, in the group itself, and in competing with other groups. In the 1970s, and especially after Lacan's death, my impression was confirmed. This may not have been their fault alone, since they were rejected by the International Psychoanalytic Association and reacted against this rejection by denouncing the IPA. I thought this was archaic, and that psychoanalysis ought not relive conflicts that exhaust people in political struggles that have little clinical importance.

But don't all analysts belong to a school, be it Lacanian or any other, and need to justify their positions? And don't they all need mentors to get patients? Or do French psychoanalysts recommend patients to members of other psychoanalytic groups?

Well, I suppose it is important to belong to a society, not only in order to get patients but mainly for exchanges, clinical and theoretical discussions with colleagues. But things have changed. My patients are not sent to me by members of my institute alone, they also are referred by others. This means that tolerance of different approaches has increased, and that you are appreciated for what you are. When I have a patient I cannot take care of, I often send him to a friend from my institute, but if I believe he would be better off with someone from another, I send him there.

Is that partly the result of such groups as Confrontations?

Maybe. That group helped this trend to take hold, but it no longer is very active. Yet many people shared this way of thinking, and its ideas continue to work.

I had that impression the last time I was in Paris, although I also noted that there was tremendous chaos. One couldn't even find out what was going on.

That is true. But much depends on what generation you belong to. People older than I have been fighting so hard against other people that they now hate them, or if they don't hate them, they are unable to have relationships with them. My generation, I believe, is more eclectic. For theoretical reasons, we feel that we have to know what all the others have done, even the Kleinians, the Freudians, and the followers of Bion and Winnicott. So we have a sort of psychoanalytic Babylon, but it's useful: you no longer want to be pure, to belong to one and only one group. You want to know what *all* psychoanalysts have done, in the hope of someday hitting upon *the* pertinent synthesis. So I am not disturbed by the heterogeneity of approaches; in fact, I think of it as an essential part of clinical work itself at this very moment.

Yes. You know, of course, that things are different in this country.

Yes. But in a sense the French institutes as institutions also need their divisions. Otherwise the institutions could not maintain themselves. Each group has to defend and define its own identity. The people who are in their forties, however, don't conform. They meet with "outsiders" and borrow their techniques.

Now that you are so involved with psychoanalysis, do you think less of politics? Where do you stand politically? Do you support Mitterand and the Socialist party? Tell me a little about that.

You may be right. I am less involved in practical politics, because I think that I now can be more useful as a psychoanalyst. I no longer need to add an *engagement* to my intellectual work, because psychoanalysis itself is an *engagement*. But this doesn't prevent me from having political opinions. I don't involve myself so much in politics, because to some extent this would be against psychoanalytic ethics. I do not want to be too visible on the political scene, to be too much of a public person. I want to preserve a sort of neutral and more enigmatic personality, because this is the only way to work with patients' unconscious. For if they think of you as rightist or leftist or as something else, their own freedom, I think, may be blocked.

Yes. But even if you don't appear in public or on television, I assume that you do have your own politics. Do you discuss politics with friends?

Yes, of course. I have personal opinions and positions. I also discuss political problems with my students in the university. But this runs parallel to psychoanalytic practice, and this presupposes more reservation than political work. Thus political discussions remain for me separate from psychoanalysis.

I would assume—maybe I'm wrong—that you must have been pleased when Mitterand got in. But by now, almost none of the intellectuals any longer support him.

No, they don't.

How do you explain that, and what is your sense of this situation? How have you been making this transition?

My experience, I believe, was particular. As you know, I lived with socialism in Bulgaria, and cannot in this sense be considered a French intellectual. Some of the latter were quite enthusiastic when Mitterand took over the government. I thought that in the Western countries we already have a utopian socialism. I hoped he would not destroy this utopia, because when you try to realize a utopia it usually dies. I was persuaded from the beginning that it would be a failure . . .

When you say socialism, do you mean socialism or democracy?

I know there is a difference between the Eastern countries and Western socialism, but when the French were attracted by the socialist government, they did not properly perceive this difference. I think they thought that in France they could not have an Eastern regime, but they also thought that some of its practices could be implemented. It appeared impossible, for instance, to retain a liberal economy, in a liberal state whose administration increasingly would take care of everybody. Also, one of the early aims of Mitterand's government was to do away with unemployment. But this meant more centralization of the state, and it supposed that France would withdraw from the European market. Such policies could not be realized along with the idea of tolerant Western socialism. Hence the socialists were in an unresolvable contradiction.

You mean they mixed up the Marxist ideal of socialism with the actual type practiced in the Soviet Union?

There was a sort of mixture between components of Marxist socialism, and their possible implementation in a Western liberal country. Because this contradiction couldn't be overcome, they first went somewhat too far in the Marxist direction and then had to go back to a liberal capitalist economy. Now some polls show that even people who, for instance, were for Pétain during the war also voted for the Socialist party. Its platform is very imprecise intellectually, ideologically, and politically.

In other words, French socialism isn't working the way it was meant to?

No. That's why intellectuals have the impression that politics no longer is essential. For a while they thought that socialism was coherent ideologically. But socialist policy turned out to be a permanent compromise. Intellectuals did not know what to do with it, so they turned to the right, which already has been severely criticized and which doesn't propose any consistent program.

But in a way this situation could have been predicted.

For me it was predictable. But intellectuals in bourgeois countries don't have as much political experience and therefore suffer from a sort of naive enthusiasm. They are idealistic and think that some ideals, because ideally good, can be applied without compromising. This type of politics, in fact, is the end of what some call political religion. But we are familiar with the failure of religious ideas, although there may be a return to an interest in sacred experiences. Essentially, religion in politics replaced religion. Everything was to be resolved by some sort of political arrangement. After the socialist failure, however, political religion seems to be finished. This may turn out to be a new liberation: our spirits are freer, and we no longer feel the weight of the global solution.

I would agree with you, but then, one still finds these ideas and a political naïveté on American campuses.

Yes, maybe because you have not experienced the power of leftist groups.

But do we always have to be hurt and dominated in order to learn something?

Unfortunately. Freud was very pessimistic, and events have confirmed his beliefs. But maybe what I'm stating is a generalization: human beings have to experience personal failure before renouncing their ideals. Maybe the French and other socialist experiences have proven that ideologies don't correspond to the demands of the modern world. Maybe now people will begin to look more seriously at the reasons for this failure and then sober up these American leftists.

Well, we have tried this a number of times.

I often have been shocked by these attitudes on American campuses. Less so this time.

For some, it seems to me, the experiences of previous generations are forgotten.

Yes. This is true about the Holocaust phenomena as well as about the experiences of leftist politics. It is very disappointing.

What do you think we can do about it?

Write, and try to explain.

But then people have to read us.

Yes, they don't read very much. I've been told about this, and that the younger generation is very Reaganite.

Yes, some are. But I have a lot of students who come from working-class families, and it is interesting that many of them are more on the right. They want to work and to succeed. They often are against welfare programs: because they work, they feel that all others can work too. So it's mixed. But then, you have their opponents as well.

Yes. You think that leftists and enthusiasts are not as numerous as they were some years ago.

You know very well it's not always a question of numbers. A small critical mass, a small group of vociferous people who get signatures can get things moving.

The left is often very active; it has its rhetoric.

Yes, it also has its listeners. So it can get much farther than its numbers would warrant.

But don't people change when they get to be twenty-five, get involved in other business?

It depends. Many do. But you now have also the third or fourth generation of the very wealthy, who, for reasons of social conscience, do not think politically but feel that it is politically correct to oppose whatever the government says and not to think about it. Many of the affluent middle-class "kids," the so-called 1968 generation, have the same reactions.

Yes, this is very strange. Just yesterday, I talked with a friend of mine about a person, and I said that I was told that this man was too radical. But my friend wondered how anybody could be too radical. For him, I realized, it is natural to be radical, that is, to criticize every time whatever is proposed. I tried to explain that when I say that "somebody is too radical," I mean that this man approaches problems not by thinking autonomously but with prepared reactions—which means that for him everything must be opposed. This really is an avoidance of thinking.

Absolutely.

But he said, "Oh, I've never thought about that." He assumed that to be honest means to be radical. He did not realize that to be radical may not always be the only honest attitude, that it may simply be more facile.

Of course, it's so much easier to go along with your friends than to examine every issue, to decide to go with one thing but not with another, and take responsibility for the consequences.

It is very difficult not to go to extremes, to opt either for the new conservatism or for the new leftism. These may be two poles, and you cannot talk about them globally. To have a more moderate position, one must try to weigh every case in a specific way. And this is less acceptable. That is what is expected from the intellectuals.

Yes, that's right.

It's supposed to be adult.

But it's difficult to be an adult. Actually I was going to ask you about the American Strategic Defense Initiative, the so-called Star Wars, and about the French attitude of going it alone, or not going it alone.

Well, the French attitude has to be understood in relation to the French tradition. At present, the French are afraid of losing their identity— because of the influx of immigrants and of the weakened economy, among other reasons. This generates feelings of inferiority in the majority of the population, and not only in the government—whether it will be rightist, or leftist. People imagine that in order to preserve their national identity, they have to possess strategic as well as economic— but essentially military—strength. The exaggerated pride in military power, I believe, is equated with preserving national autonomy. So we have to question whether this need is an archaic attitude belonging to a bourgeois or feudal state, or whether it helps preserve national and personal individuality. The French want to counteract the uniformization of the world, which they feel is developing as a result of both the conflicts and the compromises between the two superpowers. They perceive the conflicts between the Americans and the Russians but think that the superpowers agree somehow on eliminating the other cultures. That is a big cultural danger, even if economically it seems inevitable. Thus they aim to preserve a plurality that, in terms of economics, may seem utopian. Nevertheless, it is a good utopia to preserve.

Sure. Are you saying also that the French feel it's okay to be patriotic?

Yes, they are returning to a sort of patriotism. But not when it means going into the army. French students are antimilitaristic. They will not want to fight for France, I believe, because that would be old-fashioned. But the image of France is important to them. This is new and doesn't belong to the 1968 mentality. It has developed in connection with the immigration problem, which parallels the antiracist developments of different groups such as the *Ne Touche Pas Mon Pot* [Don't touch my buddy]. There is a tolerance toward others *and* pride in being French. This is difficult to appreciate, and either of these two tendencies may prevail. At present, they both exist. National pride is very obvious, very noticeable, and all the parties—left, socialist, and traditional right—are aware of it. So they try to win votes through national and patriotic propaganda.

Is this truer for internal politics than for foreign policy?

For both.

I get the feeling that in terms of foreign policy, the French feel they must defend themselves and must preserve democracy at any cost.

This is true; you have to preserve democracy. If the Americans were to preserve our democracy, then they would be our invaders. Since we would be dependent on them, it no longer would be *our* democracy but the American one.

Yes, of course. On the other hand, there is a certain convergence of interests, just the same, between France and America, insofar as we are both democratic countries, more or less, and the Soviet Union is not.

Yes, exactly. This was de Gaulle's position way back—to remain in the Western bloc. There still is no problem with that, I think, even if the socialist government questioned it in the beginning. Within this bloc, however, the French want to preserve a sort of independence. Other European countries do not have the same attitude, but they have the same preoccupations. They express them in different ways, according to their own traditions. In England, it is less necessary to affirm autonomy toward the United States, maybe because people share the same language and culture. The Italians, for example, cannot allow themselves to be very independent. But the French remain proud for having invented human rights, the independent bourgeois state, and the real ideal of left solutions—as a result of the French revolutions. It depends, of course, upon who formulates the position for French independence. But even if a classical rightist government were to govern France—and this probably soon will be the case—it will maintain its independence, maybe in a less dramatic way. It will be a question of rhetoric, but basically there is an agreement about the national independence.

Yes, but still, when you talk of independence, you speak of an independence that will not allow the Soviet Union to invade, if it had the chance. And this is true for the right as well as the left, which is in a way different from American leftists . . .

Exactly. It was very important for Mitterand, for instance, that the pacifist movement did not develop in France. The French think that in the pacifist position there is a naïveté about Soviet power. For when pacifists say that they also want to prevent Soviet nuclear arms experiments, it's just wishful thinking. They have no way to pressure the Soviet government. This sort of naïveté has not been very developed in France, although there is a small pacifist movement that is dominated by the Communist Party. Almost everybody knows that those people are, as we said in our Marxist days, objectively allied with the Soviets. Yet such movements exist in Britain, Germany, and Holland. Clearly, French independence is related to the United States as well as to the Russians. But the balance is not often easily maintained. In third world situations the French position at times seems quite ambiguous, and it is difficult to preserve national independence about the third world against Americans and against Russians. I'm not sure that they remain neutral all the time: and their position occasionally can be used by dogmatic Marxists in Latin America.

It is being used, of course.

This goes along with my original statement, when I said that the French try to be independent from America as well as from Russia, and that their position is not always so ideal, or so moral or neutral. Some practical policies, as for instance the support of the third world, objectively happen to be helpful to the Russians.

Yes. Are you saying that French politicians are aware of this and cannot do anything about it?

Some of them are aware. The Mitterand government is quite heterogeneous. I suppose that some of its members are aware and think it's okay; others are aware and try to prevent it. But neither their external policy nor their internal policy is very coherent.

Isn't that always the problem with democracy, where whatever you do is open and discussed publicly, and certain consequences follow from that alone? Since we've covered a lot of ground, I want to ask you one last question. You've been coming to America quite regularly in recent years. Do you have any new impressions, other than those we already have talked about?

It is difficult to have general impressions because I see only some people from universities and a few intellectuals around publishing houses. I have the impression that the problems about leftist orientations, the sort of naive enthusiasm, is less widespread than some years ago, and that the Reagan policies generate very critical attitudes. Nevertheless, the people I meet in the universities now may be more doubtful about their ideological choices than before, even if they don't always revise these choices, although they seem less convinced of their ultimate truth. Also, I think that more and more Americans are interested in a sort of European way of thinking, of living. I read, for instance, some articles on feminism and then discussed them with friends, and they thought that American feminism had gone into a decline. So they proposed to fight this decline by borrowing elements that have always been a part of the French feminist discourse—such simple things as not systematically rejecting men but living with men, and not considering maternity or seduction to be in opposition to the glorious image of woman. And I noted much more interest in European culture and, in particular, French culture. I also have been struck by the decline of some well-established university reputations and by the fact that a number of state universities are trying to take over, to be more active, less traditional, and more inventive. They try to have more links with students, they encourage young researchers in the humanities, organize exchanges of students and researchers with European universities. This augurs well for a better cultural understanding between Europe and America in the future. The present period, however, seems to be one of mutual withdrawal and suspicion.

15

Interview: The Old Man and the Wolves

This interview was conducted by Bernard Sichère and was first published in a 1992 issue of *L'Infini*. It appeared in an English translation by Léon Roudiez in *Partisan Review*. Although the interview is based on Kristeva's second novel, *The Old Man and the Wolves*, much of the conversation addresses politics and contemporary culture. This interview shows Kristeva at her most pessimistic, describing a world tainted with pain, disorder, mourning, violence, apathy, depression, barbarity, and banality. She defends her idea of a contemporary "civilizational crisis," supporting it with her account of a recent trip to Moscow. Commenting on contemporary intellectual life, Kristeva claims that we must free ourselves from "consensual ideology" and "moralizing, euphoric discourses," adopting instead an "analytic, relentless position" that takes negativity into account. Although she acknowledges that psychoanalysis needs to confront some serious issues (excessive literalism, internal power struggles, the media's appropriation of psychoanalytic jargon, the rapid growth of psychopharmacology), she contends that it continues to furnish us with a "living discourse." At the end of the interview, she claims that the age-old dichotomy between the "right wing" and the "left wing" may no longer be relevant, and she lambastes a political culture in which no one admits guilt. She challenges "writers," as opposed to "intellectuals," to reinvent the political realm, "even to circumvent it." Speaking specifically about her novel, Kristeva notes that the

Santa Barbara she describes combines the collapse of the East and the malaise and banality of the West. Suggesting that her novel serves as an antidote to "a deep crisis in language," she describes it as a "grafting of what comes from another culture, another mentality, onto the language I adopt and that I assume welcomes me." Also addressed are the characters of Stephany, whose "truth-seeking" is said to counterbalance the overarching negativity of the novel, the couple Alba and Vespasian, and the Old Man, whom Kristeva affectionately likens to her father.

Two features of your second novel distinguish it from the first, it seems to me. Thematically, there was in The Samurai *a sort of emphasis on the positive aspects of the main character as well as on her intellectual, erotic, and domestic journey, whereas* The Old Man and the Wolves *brings to the fore a dark, negative dimension, an outlook on the world that is more pessimistic. The second feature involves form: why is there, in this new narrative, a scrambling of codes and genres (clipped dialogue, allegory, first-person narrative), and such an increase in the variety of voices, so many metaphors?*

In connection with what you call negativity, I would refer to Hölderlin's well-known query, "Wozu Dichter in dürftiger Zeit?" and rephrase it by asking, "Of what use are novels in times of distress?" The thrust of my new book stems from the conjunction of the personal shock of mourning (the death of my father, who was killed in a Sofia hospital through the incompetence and brutality of the medical and political system) and a public unease—the acknowledgment, which was indeed barely present in my first novel, of a general disarray in a society—to begin with, our own. As a psychoanalyst (that is one of my frames of reference), I am sensitive to the collapse of minimal values and the rejection of elementary moral principles. I found it imperative to choose the form of the novel instead of a theoretical form (as was the case in my earlier essays), because I realized that the novel form was a better way to portray that distress. On the other hand, within the novel form *métaphore* operates, giving form to infantile psychic inscriptions that are located on the border of the unnamable. On the other hand, by elaborating *intrigue* one enacts the dramatic essence of passion, the intolerable aspect of love as it is necessarily coupled with hatred. In comparison, the ability of theoretical discourse to take on *métaphore* and *intrigue* seemed to be far behind the form of the novel. Recent French novels most often reject metaphor and avoid drama: "good taste" demands a certain amount of restraint. For my part, I have not ceased reading Proust: "Truth shall arise only at the moment when the writer, taking two different objects, will posit their relation [. . .] in a metaphor. The relation might be uninteresting, the object mediocre, the style awful, but so long as that has not taken place, there is nothing there."[1]

The allegorical dimension, for instance, which is indeed central in *The Old Man and the Wolves*, needs to be understood in that context. In contrast to *The Samurai*, my second novel is anchored in a pain to which allegory aims to give significance without fixing it, instead irradiating it, having it vibrate, in an oneiric way, according to each reader's personal framework of ordeals and choices. Thus the fictional city in the novel, Santa Barbara, might be located in the heart of Central or Eastern Europe, but it also suggests an American megalopolis, or some continental city: it harbors a fountain that strangely resembles the one at the Pompidou Center, and the Oasis Bar in the novel brings to mind a rather fashionable spot in San Francisco. Santa Barbara's very name suggests to me first the surrounding barbarity but also, by alluding to an American television series, the surfeited elements of American society and that vulgarization which constitutes one of the aspects of contemporary savagery. In short, the novel's negative diagnosis first applies to the collapse in the former Communist countries of Europe, but at the same time I did not want to exclude the West, the malaise of our society.

And the wolves? To what extent does this key metaphor illustrate (beyond its explicit reference to book 1 of Ovid's Metamorphoses) *what you have just said?*

Those threatening wolves, setting wildly upon their victims, recall the invasion of the Red Armies, the establishment of totalitarianism—my readers in Eastern Europe have had no problem identifying them. More deviously, the wolves are contagious; they infect people to the extent that one can no longer make out their human faces. They symbolize everyone's barbarity, everyone's criminality. They finally signify the invasion of banality, which erases the entire criterion of value amid the racketeering, corruption, wheeling and dealing.

Nevertheless, making this all-pervasive violence or barbarity contemporary doesn't play off only on the level of the wolves. It also is reflected in the narrative fragmentation in the novel that you mentioned, in the multiplicity of codes and voices. In the novel's Santa Barbara, which is comparable to the declining Roman Empire, history cannot unfold in a naive, indubitable manner, nor can the characters themselves embody stable identities. Hence the presence of *Doppelgänger* in the book: the Professor and the narrator's father, but also Alba and the other Alba who is discovered drowned. The shiftings in the narrative, the duplication and dissemination of identities, refer to the obvious fact that we are experiencing contemporary culture in a process of metamorphosis. Does it have to do with the return of the gods, as set out by Heidegger? Does it involve another fictional experience, and if so, which one? For the time being we are in the gothic *roman noir*.

But doesn't the book's shift to the first-person narrative, spoken by Stephany, the investigator, change the perspective from the dark, negative dimensions we have just conjured up?

Absolutely. Stephany doesn't play her part on the same level as the others. As soon as she speaks, the oneiric, confused universe of the novel's first section assumes the shape of a detective novel; it means that a crime has been committed and that it is possible to unravel the truth about this crime. A truth-seeking effort takes place, thanks to Stephany Delacour, who will show up again in other episodes, for in the book there are a series of mystery novels. So the "twilight of the gods" that makes up the first part of the novel acquires a meaning in the second part, which is simply the setting of a course, the shaping of a plot: *it is possible to know.* Henceforth, an ethics of knowledge, let us say, is involved.

Consequently, I feel that to call my novel pessimistic is inaccurate. As long as the investigation is being carried out, the crime is challenged, and death does not prevail. Stephany introduces the vigilance that is the resistant force of life, if not of hope. In the third section of the book, Stephany imposes her diary upon the mystery novel, as a counterpoint.

Her subjective experience, her sensibility as a woman, a child, a lover is a veritable counterweight to death and hatred. If Stephany is able to undertake this investigative work and confront crime, it is because she doesn't ignore her personal experience, because she is plunged to a point of rapture, and not without cruelty, into the pain that mourning imposes on us: mourning for her own father, until then repressed, awakens on the occasion of the Old Man's mourning. As a consequence, the character of the journalist-detective introduces a certain psychoanalytic tonality in the book. Without this interior space sculpted out by mourning but given shape by other erotic upheavals— for mourning is an eroticism full of undulations, without the smooth visage of joy—no working-out of truth is possible. No investigation, no knowledge. Some based their aesthetics, for example, on Goethe, others on Rousseau, or Rimbaud; I consider myself a contemporary Freud. A possible wager: what about a novel that would be cognizant of Freud? Is such a novel possible? Would it attract readers? For my part, it is enough that the novel is disturbing.

The barbarity you alluded to earlier seems to me to be essential. Part of the opposition your book has encountered, I'm sure, has to do with its illumination of what is unbearable in our society, with people recognizing themselves. As I was reading the book—and what you have just said confirms it—I found two images of barbarity; criminality, violence, on the one hand, and on the other what you have termed "banality." Could you tell us a little more? To what extent does this duality reflect the distinction suggested by Guy Debord in Commentaire sur la société du spectacle *between the "integrated spectacular" germane to the Western democratic societies and the archaic survival of tyrannic forms that, a short time ago, characterized communist societies?*

The Old Man and the Wolves is set in Santa Barbara—a city that also evokes the violence of our own societies, their racketeering and delinquency. At the same time violence has become banalized, a trivialization that is no less frightening. The psychoanalyst detects it in the speech of certain patients. We are basically dealing with the image of a *depression* that integrates aggression but under the ruinous guise of an erasure of meaning. That is what I depict in the character of Alba. Alba is one of those depressed persons who considers herself to be "void of meaning." She views her actions as neutralized, impossible to describe, even in the extreme, murderous facets that they might exhibit. A true depression of meaning itself takes place, and the insignificance into which the melancholy person sinks is not merely an individual, "pathological" occurrence. Because of its amplitude, it assumes the seriousness of a societal event, a civilization crisis.

I should like to add something about the nature and the extent of that crisis. I have just come back from Moscow, where I have a series of lectures at the French Studies Institute in Moscow's Lomonosov University. I was struck by the pervasive crisis over there, the way in which it seemed to be the very realization of the crisis I portrayed in *The Old Man and the Wolves*. I recognized Santa Barbara. No one any longer respects authority; no one any longer occupies the seat of power, particularly in the university, where there are students but no semblance of rules and regulations; and no one is in charge. I am puzzled by contemporary studies of Soviet or Russian society that, knowingly or not, minimize the extent of the catastrophe, which is not only economic but also ethical. In the face of such general decay, there is at the moment a massive regressive return to religion, which effectively serves as a solace but also a way to flee reality. The French Institute, which, on the other hand, enrolls a large number of very qualified and critical-minded students who are eager to learn, constitutes a fortunate exception in that landscape.

Basically, the most disquieting symptom, here as well as over there, the major consequence of which I have called banality, is the tendency that could result in a loss of interest in the psyche. In Western societies today, the most common temptation is to prescribe medicine to appease people's anguish rather than guide them to confront the pain of living.

In this respect, I refer, in *The Old Man and the Wolves*, to Hölderlin's *Der Tod des Empedokles* [The death of Empedocles] and *Mnemosyne*, from which the Old Man explicitly quotes, to the waning of the gods, which arouses in the Old Man a strange mixture of nostalgia, doubt, and fear. On the other hand, Alba in her own evil fashion takes up a theme dear to Heidegger: the "protective heed" provided by being. Alba perverts the heed. She believes that paroxysmal conflict carried to the point of hatred is the only truth. That is her very own punctilious nihilism. She hates without feeling guilty, she ends up untouchable, "at home," proud within the supposed truth of her hatred. That is the dreadful part of it—the unscathed conscience, with neither unease nor hardship, present at the very core of hatred, which might go as far as murder. Within the reverberations of Hölderlin and Heidegger, to which the Old Man and Alba harken again, the insistence of the question remains. In opposition, what strikes me in today's world, and this is why I speak of the loss of interest in the psyche, is the feeling that the very possibility of questioning has been closed. We have become unscathed in evil just as one might have been immaculate in love.

You have just talked about your bleak impressions of Moscow, which suggest the state of the whole former communist bloc. What strikes me at the same time in this picture of Russian society is the absence of any reference to what has been for years the work of dissidents. Have they disappeared through a trap door? Don't they have anything more to say? Must one conclude that their historical role has come to an end and that their ethical values could not possibly constitute a frame of reference today?

I have no global hypothesis, and there exist without doubt several partial answers. On the other hand, these dissidents fought essentially for Western values, such as democracy and the rights of man. The current regime presents itself as defending and embodying these values and would seem to be rendering yesterday's struggle out of date. At the same time, it is clear that we are not witnessing over there the triumph of economic and moral principles being loudly proclaimed, but instead widespread wheeling and dealing, passivity and incompetence. Democracy has not yet been born, and what claims to pave the way for it isn't acceptable. So people wonder what is to follow the destruction of totalitarianism. And more basically, whether this is truly a renewal or only a masquerade of the old, a ruse. The former dissidents seem puzzled. Listen, for instance, to their doubts concerning the factitious coups: is the old regime really dead, or is it masquerading under a new *nomenklatura* more smoothly attuned to the image-making process than the previous one, greedy for money but yet incapable of creating it and managing it?

Having said that, we also have our own responsibilities. We must depict and try to think through the unraveling of the social fabric of the East, which the Spring 1991 issue of *L'Infini* reported on. Did the media follow up? Of course not. They told us not to interfere in "the process." But who can grasp the meaning of this process? Finally, we must remind ourselves that we are not immune from peril, not penned up in a small protected space. What goes on over there concerns us very closely, if for no other reason than that we shall be called upon to pay for it—financially and morally—for the sake of European solidarity.

In your novel, the Professor is a strong and moving character. He is simultaneously called the Old Man and Septicius Clarus, and acts as a Doppelgänger to Stephany's father. He is as complex as a Latin scholar (why Latin, by the way?), at the same time skeptical, ironical, and troubled; a figure of the ethical resistance worried about his impending death; a referential third party to the disciples Alba and Vespasian; a wise old man; a paternal, loving image for Alba.

Why a Latin scholar? Aside from the fact that my father was one of those cultivated people who could express themselves in Latin (ridiculously pretentious, wasn't it!), it seemed to me that, more than Greek culture, the culture of the Roman empire just before the advent of Christianity was already in harmony with our own. With Ovid, Suetonius, and Tibullus there was a modern, Christ-like sensitivity that echoes our own anguish. I might also add that I summon up Latin culture and language as a way of calling attention to French as an endangered language. For there is a withering away of language just as there is a general withering away of culture, perfectly clear to you and me, as members of the teaching profession.

What I am suggesting here may appear quite ambitious, coming from someone who is a foreigner, a migrant. But it seems to me that in the face of a deep crisis in language, there are two possibilities. The first consists in turning back toward tradition in a loving, proud, reactive, nostalgic fashion. The other, which I uphold in this novel, is the grafting of what comes from another culture, another mentality, onto the language I adopt and that I assume welcomes me. In this case, it means grafting onto the body of the French language and syntax an experience of sorrow and hurt that originates elsewhere and is perhaps liable to awaken other effects.

Could we return to the Professor as father figure? Such a figure, of course, cannot be disassociated from the work of mourning that the daughter (Alba or Stephany) must carry out after the father's death. But what kind of mourning is it? And what ethics emerge out of it?

The theme of mourning is central, and the Professor is foremost a father in the novel. A father's love and love for the father does not constitute a fashionable theme, since every contemporary artist who wants to be worthy of the name begins by defiling the father. Can you imagine? A likable father? Nevertheless, love for the father is not only an antidote to the barbarity of the novel's Santa Barbara but also an experience that Stephany lays bare with a certain lack of modesty, as if it were the secret, not always an idyllic one, of her passion for life, her combativeness. For what makes Stephany Delacour run? Sensuous and indecent as they are, her dreams tie her to an Old Man—the Professor, the Ambassador, who knows?—who is far from being a master, even less so a hero, but who remains an enigma at the very bottom of a sea of insignificance or brutality. This orphaned, suffering, uprooted father is certainly an image of the law. But it is neither a stern law nor an abstract law. The Professor is not a superego; he is a man endowed "with a body" who is present with the full weight of his psychology, his affects, his fears. A rebel, if you wish, and at the same time a man of sorrows, in a certain way a Christ-like figure. What needs to be done under these circumstances is to prepare a place for possible law, and I might also say that it involves new images of atheism that fit the situation we are experiencing, at the end of a world.

You have written about a similar father image in Tales of Love *and notably about his humanism. It was already that of a traveling, skeptical scholar who embodies what you sketched out in* Strangers to Ourselves. *It accords with a humanism that doesn't belong in the realm of principle or idea but is embodied in a singularity. The most profound message the dead father appears to transmit to his daughter lies in this realm: "Don't give in where your singularity is at stake."*

Absolutely, but this message is precisely the ethical message of psychoanalysis. In a manner even more singular, Stephany writes that she is "a detective in search of emptiness." "The emaciated hand still holds the stiletto and I make out the word 'Nada.' Nothing. Nothingness crept into me with the smile of a father whose pain made him sing. I am nothingness." And again, "Atheism, which is said to be inaccessible to women, who are always in quest of illusions, that is, of a father-mother lover, opens up for the one who is inhabited by the desert bequeathed her by the dead father. The choice is henceforth restricted and dangerous. Seeking childhood—a kind of madness. Or wandering—independence played over and over again."

What strikes me about the couple Alba and Vespasian is both the extreme violence that is brought into play within them, a potentially criminal violence, and at the same time the violent image of the man as presented by the woman, without her removing herself from the picture, so that as a result we have a reduction, through fiction, of two singular symmetrical manifestations of violence.

With respect to "the couple," as to all the other configurations in the novel, the bottom line is to know whether fiction can aim for truth effects (this obviously implies that it take charge of the death drive and its expressions), or whether it should, on the contrary, reassure us by reinforcing some communal illusion. "Always protest against the domestication pact," says the Old Man. I have obviously chosen the first alternative. Vespasian not only stands for a caricature of masculine violence; he is also an individual without inner life, almost psychotic, "either an active monster or monstrously insignificant"—one can't tell which. You have surely met people who are like that.

In opposition to a certain kind of feminism that idealizes the victimized spouse, Alba doesn't give in to Vespasian and his destructive, murderous tendencies. Moreover, the story of this imaginary couple comes close to assuming in its entirety what I happen to have heard from the couch—for instance, about murder wishes and attempted poisonings. Quite simply, the novel tells what one most often conceals. We thus encounter once more the question, Can a novel tell the truth? If so—and this has nothing to do with "being seduced"—who can accept that truth without feeling unmasked, betrayed, exposed? Must we then consider a metamorphosis of the novel? Not really. Police investigations, mystery thrillers make the unveiling of cruelty plausible, almost bearable. That is why I intend to pursue the mystery genre—a game. A way of continuing analysis. Following Freud, Lacan reminded us that the truth of love lies in hatred. An ethics of the written word implies that one should become aware of hatred, and psychoanalysis is also and perhaps foremost the analysis of hatred.

In what way do you think one should bear witness to those ethical components that are at the core of your novel and at the core of your own discourse?

Is this the raison d'être of today's intellectual? How do you envision the intellectual's intervention in the face of violence and the banality of evil?

It seems impossible to me to hold a discourse that ignores negativity. We must free ourselves from the consensual ideology that surrounds us, from the deceitful putting forward of a rallying discourse that is being called for everyone in order to get rid of "problems." Up against such a general condition, which I recently described as a "national depressive syndrome,"[2] I don't believe it is appropriate to seek a reassuring discourse that would take over from the "positive" discourse we have known, which was Marxism. I should like to pursue this further in order to answer your question. I believe it is more than ever necessary to examine seriously, in opposition to moralizing, euphoric discourses, the theoretical work that we earlier engaged in at Tel Quel. You spoke of this work in your book, *Eloge du sujet*. Others have attempted to stigmatize that work with such terms as "structuralism," "theoreticalism," or even "antihumanism." Actually, it was a critical, not a nihilistic discourse, as some tried to argue. It seems that people claimed to have been terrorized by what we stated then, and I am ready to believe that. They were terrorized less by technical language than by a critical, cleansing, undermining will that in truth they recognized. How does one dispose of such demystifying technique? By embracing the world created by the media or the empty discourse of hope. I feel that it is harmful, even criminal, to keep illusions going, for this amounts to encouraging new pitfalls. One mustn't be afraid to disappoint, if that is the road to knowledge and truth, in the face of the "national depressive syndrome" I spoke of. The analytic, relentless position that I uphold is preferable to the manic rehabilitation of depression under the guise, for instance, of nationalistic fundamentalism or the soporific television rating games.

Doesn't that imply that an intellectual should be less cut off from reality, less ensconced in a superb solitude?

Something like that. My "commitment," a very microscopic one, is to analytic listening. It seems to me that we are surrounded by a sea of distressed persons, but they are given no representation. They are not represented where true power resides—beyond politicians, who have less and less, and of course beyond intellectuals, who have none. Psychoanalysis is indeed a privileged listening post, but one should invent and diversify listening posts in order to compensate for the general deficiency of the symbolic markers we are talking about. Consequently, the analyses we are able to produce, that I produce for my part on the basis of my clinical experience, could be put to practical use, doubtless not by media intellectuals, the stars of the system, but by those I might call "basic intellectual," those who play their parts in educational centers, schools, mayors' offices, and new microspaces that need to be opened, to be invented. It is in that direction that one should give a concrete extension to the ethics of listening, an ethics that would be different from the militant ethics resting on a deceitful discourse.

What precise place do you allot to psychoanalysis in that sphere, and, as you see it, what is the status of the psychoanalytic movement?

One hears people say that psychoanalysis is dead, and in some ways they are not completely wrong. Many psychoanalysts and analytical societies are in the process of self-destructing, both in the guise of an excessively dogmatic obedience to the letter of Freud's text and of sectarian splinterings around the remains of Lacan. In spite of that, however, there exists a living, fruitful psychoanalytic discourse, and such a discourse is aware of unavoidably competing and conflicting with two contemporary trends. The first of these is inflated media growth; one now witnesses a takeover of the analytic language by the media, with all this implies in psychic laziness, fleeting narcissistic mirages; at the same time there is a careful shunting aside of the reality of suffering and the necessity to confront such suffering with a full knowledge of the facts.

The other trend is the inflated growth of the neurosciences. One should not, of course, reject the knowledge gained from those sciences; one must learn to work with them. But it is absolutely appropriate to resist some of the things that have been propagated, such as the pharmaceutical bombardment of individuals to the extent that their individual responsibility is taken away. Everything concerning the "soul" is being ignored, and by "soul" I mean that psychic space whose protection and creativity lie at the heart of Freudian thought. This is where psychoanalysis appears to me to still play a part today, involving both resistance and awakening, and in protecting culture or what is left of it.

We have spoken of the intellectual and his role without directly mentioning the political dimension. The intellectual you speak of—should one call him "left-wing"? Does that phrase have a meaning for you? Are you, are we, on the left?

One can't brush that question aside, but the answer is far from simple. Such a bipartition, such alternating between two political and ideological poles, the "left" and the "right," has long been a safeguard of our democracies, but I believe that it no longer plays that part. What strikes all of us is indeed the massive *uninterest* in the political game on the part of citizens, particularly the fact that they no longer care to vote. Even more so, politics to a large extent has been reduced to a technocratic setup that allows a political personality to call himself or herself "responsible but not guilty"—and this means that all subjective and moral dimensions have been reabsorbed, eliminated, by the inexorable march of a bureaucracy that is more and more anonymous and responsible to itself alone. There are no more culprits, just as there is no crime in Santa Barbara: since good and evil don't exist, total bureaucracy, another version of totalitarianism, has trivialized and animalized the human.

Read *The Old Man and the Wolves*; Santa Barbara is where we are. Nevertheless, I would tend at this moment to maintain the distinction you have made between left and right by giving it a particular content. In the history of the West, left-wing thought seems to me linked to an ethical requirement that includes at the same time the dead ends of revolutionary movements and the Terror and the lessons to be learned from such dead ends. Basically, I am not concerned with giving the idea of the left an objective meaning in itself, starting from such-and-such a content or principle. I would rather define "the left" at the locus where the question of politics, and above all of the limits of the political (from the viewpoint of symbolic formations, that is, the acquisition of culture and knowledge), can be formulated and dealt with.

One would obviously need to say much more and ask the following question: what should be, today, the appropriate political approach to social welfare policies or to the practice of democracy? It seems to me that the traditional practice of democracy through a delegation of power to political parties, which goes back to the traditional model of voting in the Greek city-state, is no longer the most appropriate or efficient representation, when faced with the speed and efficiency of media coverage, on the one hand, and on the other the polymorphism of the individuals that make up our societies.

I had a specific point in mind: To say in what manner we are in spite of everything "left-wing"—isn't this particularly a way of resisting such a vague free-for-all, which uses the collapse of the communist world as an excuse for exp ressing hatred of all people's liberations and engaging in a rather disturbing witch-hunt?

One hunts all kinds of witches. If not Heidegger or Céline, it is Marx and the deluded auto workers of Billancourt. Santa Barbara, the city of *The Old Man and the Wolves,* is the city of resentment, at the antipodes of thought. Certainly, new forms of political life need to be invented on the basis of genealogy of the present form of political life (particularly the two-party system). But isn't the part of the *writer,* as distinguished from that of the "intellectual," as it has always been in the past and today is more than ever, one of defining this political realm in order to reinvent it continuously, even to circumvent it? In order to conceive, utter, and describe unusual, free, and strange bonds between irreconcilable individuals? Writing is an anarchic act, obviously redeemable but desperately obstinate. Writing is aimed not at the *political* man and woman but at their *being.* Nevertheless, it is precisely from the realm of being that the unconscious disrupts the civilized spectacle and reveals us as barbarians, prey to death. The Old Man had that vision, and he died of it—unless he was murdered.

I am a part of his story.

THEORIES

16

General Principles in Semiotics

Pierre Oullet and Charles Bauer conducted this interview in 1976, and it was published in a 1977 issue of the Canadian journal *Etudes littéraires*. The translation is by Ross Guberman. As Oullet states in his introduction, the interview addresses the possibility of "semiotics as a general science, as a science of the general, as a generic science, and as a science of the generalizable." Kristeva's answers go to the heart of the debate surrounding semiotic theory: the general versus the particular, the text versus the reader or theoretician, and neutrality versus subjectivity. Throughout the interview, she challenges the idea of general principles in semiotics, suggesting that such notions are grounded in a "classical rationality that is historically and socially determined," a rationality that "is merely one approach among many." Kristeva claims that "there is no general Text" and that semiotic research is never "neutral," but "committed and thus unconscious." She advocates a hermeneutic, interpretive approach to semiology in which both the reader and the writer are considered to be decentered speaking subjects—and so suggests that psychoanalysis should play a greater role in semiotic theory. In Kristeva's view, semiotics should focus on specific processes of signification and on language practices in particular situations, searching for "new and diverse spaces that can be interpreted in the context of the subject's complex and critical experiences with meaning."

Contemporary semiotics is both a hermeneutic science targeting the speci-
ficity of particular principles and a heuristic science striving to create (to
simulate or to generate) models for a relatively vast array of semiotic
assumptions grounded in universal principles or generic features. In your
opinion, what is the relationship between a semiotics of interpretation and
a semiotics of modeling? Does one of them (here, a semiotics of modeling)
precede the other, or should they be seen as two autonomous entities?

Your question alludes to the history of semiology. The origin of semiology can be traced to the Stoics, who replaced *being* and *logos* with the
system of signs. It expanded under the influence of the medieval theories
of the *modi significandi* developed in the context of Christian theology.
Semiology was then subjected to a logicopositivism focusing on the
question of *general semiotic principles.* Yet it seems to me that contemporary semiology, as defined by Saussure and Peirce and by its concern
for the decentered speaking subject of the Freudian unconscious, challenges explicitly the notion of general principles. Semiology defines
itself today as a diverse and polyvalent approach to different discursive
practices, each of which implies a particular situation for the speaking
subject and a particular set of signifying articulations. Although the
"semiological" dimension of these different approaches comprises questions about the sign, the signifier, and formal systems, the articulation
of these questions is always particular and differentiated, which prevents us from making generalizations about them.

You also mention the way semiology has relied on logicomathematical models. Although contemporary semiology operates inside the
ever-decaying corpse of ancient philosophy, where *being* and *logos* are
replaced with the *system of signs,* it is also formed in a space in which the
pure sciences, mathematics in particular, touch on notions of the sign,
meaning, signification, and the entire realm of language. Working from
this point of convergence, semiology has "appropriated" the development of formal studies, that is, of logical and mathematical theories
offering new modes of inquiry. So I would say that such notions as
Thom's theory of morphogenesis[1] or Zadeh's theory of "fuzzy sets"[2] play
a role in semiology because they present specific objects for formal
study. When these structures are used as models of an object, however,
the situation changes and becomes more complex. Such applications
are rooted in the structuralist conception of semiology, which used
phonological models to analyze myths and used logicomathematical

models to analyze narrative structures. This earlier conception of semiology fell to the wayside because it proved to be little more than the grafting of external forms onto a signifying operation that may—or may not—be appropriate to them. The problem lies in the status of the theory being applied, a problem faced by any subject (here, a semiotician) who uses a specific model to read a text. So we are faced no longer with the classic problem of logicomathematical modeling but with the earlier problem of *interpretation* (in the context of which it would be useful to perform a Freudian reading of Peirce). We are no longer interested in proving that a model is valid or that there is a one-to-one correspondence between a model and a particular signifying system. Instead, we must turn our attention to particular signifying spaces.

Does that not make semiotics a system of endless interpretations unable to establish any general principles or modes of regulation that may not be universal but may be generalized for a specific context?

Recent generalizable theories in language science have proved to be generalizable only for a specific area of language or a specific linguistic experience—syntax, phonology, or certain structural rules. No general rules have been found that apply to the totality of the signifying processes. When we use mathematical systems or operations to engulf the signifying process in certain formulae (which is entirely possible), we are merely grafting a given mathematical finding onto an interpretation. I find such applications to be much less interesting than interpretation itself, which presents in my view the most fruitful line of inquiry.

Will semioticians return eventually to comparative linguistics and to a new form of philological study, as Benveniste has suggested in an interview with Pierre Daix?[3] Since you believe that the grafting of formal systems makes no sense, and your Erkenntnisinterresse *is completely different from that of scholars working in the tradition outlined by Peirce or even Frege, Carnap, and Lieb (a tradition that attempts to construct a system that could serve as a model for all other signifying systems), could we speak about the status of historical and philological studies that seek to determine what can be understood through semiotics, through something formal or at least formalizable? An example of this renewed interest might be your seminar on* La Traversée des signes, *which includes work by philologists, among others.*

Although the field of philology is believed to be defunct, it continues to hold great promise because it goes beyond a presumptuous logical abstraction and focuses on the specific processes of signification. One of the goals of my seminar on *La Traversée des signes* was to place the internal processes of signifying systems in the context of different cultural and historical determinants. We discovered that the very substance of the Western "human sciences"—*metalanguage* as a system able to describe the way signs work—is clearly not the only way for human beings to appropriate the "signs" of which they are made. Other means, such as the different forms of Chinese writing (see François Cheng's article in *La Traversée*)[4] or the Buddhist or Brahmanist practice in India of implicating the body in "signs" as a complement to knowledge, broaden the horizons of our metalinguistic paradigm. Yet this does not mean that we should disregard the metalinguistic approach or challenge the scientificity of sign system research. In fact, I believe that we should maintain this scientificity. We should also note the difference between the realm of a text or a work of art, and thus of a directly subjective implication on the one hand, and the realm of knowledge on the other. When I draw attention to these different "sign" and "knowledge" practices in Asian systems, it is to stress that our approach and our semiology depend on history. This history is not linear, as nineteenth-century thought would suggest, but a mosaic of attitudes displayed by the speaking subject toward signs and meaning. It is a series of signifying practices.

Recent work in literary semiology suggests that semioticians have an increasingly mimetic and identificatory approach to the object of their study. Less emphasis is being placed on the heterogeneity of a text treated as an object of knowledge, and more is being placed on the undifferentiated and homogeneous space in which the text and its reader form a unit. How do you view these efforts to identify with the text?

The tendencies in studies on sign and meaning that you mention result from the realization that the act of applying a model to a text is a much less innocent act than that of applying a model to a sentence. A text always calls for a reading that emphasizes the instinctual and unconscious elements of the semiotician's interpretation.

Some of these recent studies strive for a complete identification with the text by interpreting it for the sake of the reader's knowledge, just as a writer might do. Such an approach could indeed be termed "mimetic" or "identificatory." Once we cease to acknowledge an external object, which is what occurs in the metalinguistic approach, we create literature "about" literature. Yet when we strive for writing rather than for an object of knowledge, we often wind up inventing a repetitive style subjected to the remnants of classical or symbolist writings or, at any rate, of writings that have already been produced. This is the case with certain French philosophers who try to write as if they were writers.[5]

According to another approach, which I myself advocate, the inevitable stage of identification (which is the stage of reading and interpretation) must be followed by a search for knowledge. The second stage consists of a return to the apparently neutral realm of metalanguage—first to Husserl's "thetic phase," which posits the existence of a real object guaranteed by predication, and then to the syllogistic and metalinguistic knowledge that the thetic phase is accessible.[6] Thus the second stage uses all available materials to describe the identification preceding the text. Relying on the models you have mentioned may help describe the prior or primordial relationship one has with the text, yet the models would then be used not in the logicopositivist sense of the term as in logic or physics, but in the sense of ideas subjected to a certain number of transformations.

Do the exteriority of the object and the neutrality of the subject not also depend on the type of text or object being studied? When the ethnologist (or ethnolinguist) is working at a site, is he not much less "implicated" in the social network that provides the information about the language or text studied? In other words, is his approach to his informants not much more neutral?

Anthropology has transposed the models of our thinking onto the external site of "wild" thought. It has outlined some of the particularities of our thinking, but it has also preserved the metaphysical assumption that the speaking subject (here, an ethnologist) is neutral because his object is external. Yet this neutrality is guaranteed only through a theoretical presumption that ignores the question of the ethnographer's own assumptions about his workplace and his enunciative situation.

The ethnographer's work consists of two stages. The first entails decoding texts and using his familiarity with a language to derive the literal meaning of a message. Here, of course, the semiotician is not subjectively implicated. Yet as soon as the semiotician advances to the more complex level where he analyzes the structures of a myth and its social or intertribal implications, he faces the same problems he would face if he were analyzing a text written by a modern writer such as Céline. I am obviously referring not to any personal or psychological problems he may have but to the specific economy stemming from the subject's decentering through nature and culture. In summary, I am speaking of the problems of psychotization, of multiple individualities and attempts to restructure society through social structures of kinship or other symbolic and cultural codes.

To put my previous question a bit differently, I would say that the literary objects of Western modernity resemble idiolects because they reflect a personal use of language and meaning. Ethnosemiotic objects such as myths and rituals, on the other hand, are much more decentered from the person and the individual, so they offer a way out of the self-reflexivity that seems to encumber contemporary semiotics.

Discourse on the sign and on meaning is aware that it is a self-contained entity. In fact, its attempt to pursue objects that cause it to close in on itself is the very source of strength that allows it to prevail. It brings us closer to the neuralgic moments of the speaking subject's identity and unity that I use modern art to describe. Modern art offers us a way to address the problem of *universality*, not through a conception of sign, meaning, and structure that is limited historically by classical rationality but through the principles of other signifying systems, cultures, and attitudes of the speaking subject and through principles that acknowledge that the sign, meaning, and identity have been decentered. So when I look to Céline's writings, I focus on the relationship between his experience of language and meaning and the tradition of apocalyptic literature, which is something that may be generalized, a specific break in the array of possibilities that the speaking being is able to signify. What is needed, then, is a typology of signifying practices that shows that the type of modeling we have learned from the pure sciences, one that encourages the search for "generalizables," is rooted in a certain rationality that is historically and socially determined, a rationality that is merely one approach among many.

Linguistics seeks not to study specific languages but to study these languages to find out how the linguistic mechanism itself works. Since liter-

ary semiotics is interested in specific texts, why is it not also interested in "textual mechanisms"?

There is no general Text. Mechanisms may be generalized, but only for certain types of texts corresponding to certain types of attitudes the speaking subject may display toward meaning and signification. I myself have described one of these attitudes, one that intrigues me because it has to do with psychosis and the crisis of individuality and institutions. Other attitudes certainly exist.

If we must abandon hope of finding generalizable aspects of formal systems, can we at least hope to find, through what you have termed "the connection between biology and meaning,"[7] certain empirical universal principles that would be linked, for example, to notions of heredity? Such universality would apply to certain prelogical processes of spatiotemporal referencing that arise during language acquisition because children master situational and enunciative limits before they have a fully developed system of enunciation. This hypothesis (which is related to the localized hypothesis of inflected grammatical systems) could be understood in the context of what you term "semiotic" and oppose to the "symbolic." Might we consider that an opposition set up in ontogenetic terms could also be stated as a hierarchy of restrictions in a model of semiogenesis?

Certain theories of language acquisition posit a set of spatiotemporal and operational reference points preceding the formation of the child's syntactic and grammatical structure. These reference points could be considered part of what I call the "*semiotic*," but the semiotic is always contingent on the symbolic. In other words, what is "prior" to language is accessible only through the very process of language. Some have posited a heterogeneity between the semiotic and symbolic that could enable us to create fluid structures, but this heterogeneity is always already conceived through language. When children perceive structures of time and space, moreover, they do so in the context of parental language. The symbolic functioning of parental language provides a vantage point for their perceptions. I am clearly not referring here to the hypothesis that certain mental structures are innate. I am simply noting that if we set aside the hypothesis that the symbolic is hereditary, it becomes clear that the sociohistorical context makes it so the semiotic is already created through the symbolic. If children are placed outside their social context, they may be able to develop an instinctual mapping, but they cannot necessarily develop the structures that are the preconditions of language—the structures that precede language acquisition but are already much more complex than those governing the animal's adaptation to its environment.

What relationship does semiotics have with current research in psychoanalysis and neurology? Would it be possible to posit an intermediary element coordinated with the bio-communication system? Might we assume that neurological processes interact with symbolic processes (in the sense of the Lacanian "Symbolic") and that semiotics is the catalyst between them?

In other words, you are asking if any neurophysiological reality corresponds to the semiotic code other than the articulation of neurological functioning defined as the neurons' transmission of a certain excitability of tissue prompted by internal stimuli and the articulation of language. Given the current state of linguistics and neurology, we have a long way to go before we can answer your question. For now, we must continue refining our analysis of language practices in particular conditions, especially in borderline states of psychosis or parapsychosis. Only then can we return to neurology and its findings. The problems of neurological maturation clearly reflect verbal and symbolic expression, but we are not yet able to describe the reciprocal effects of these two domains. We are still developing the sciences of neurology and semiotics. We semiolinguists must refine our analyses of signifying phenomena by giving attention to the speaking subject, for the speaking subject is what links the structure of meaning to the neuron.

While describing your attitude toward a literary text, you have alluded to a sort of psychoanalysis without transference. Mustn't we distinguish between transference in the literal sense and the identificatory network that occurs outside the analyst's office, such as the one that occurs at Mannoni's institute where children and young people find themselves in a permanent identificatory network even though they establish no transferential relationships—which in any case are forbidden because children and young people should not see the "other" as a madman or as a mother, uncle, brother, or sister? But to return to the matter at hand, do you really believe it is possible to speak of a psychoanalytic approach to a text that would break free from the clinical experience of transference?

Psychoanalysis is primarily a clinical experience made possible through transference, but it is also a way of reading texts. When it is used to read texts, the text itself becomes the locus of transference. Research by a theoretician of signification is never neutral, but committed and thus unconscious. If every analysis begins by describing the semiolinguistic specificity of a text, the analyst will be forced to adopt an attitude toward the text that I term "transferential-toward-the-text"[8] as soon as interpretation enters the picture. This occurs in every reading, regardless of how neutral it may claim to be. The presumed "neutrality" of the structural analysis of narrative, for example, guarantees absolutely no objectivity. Instead, it guarantees merely a restriction. Lying somewhere between this attitude and the attempt to create (low-quality) literature, the modest domain of analytic semiology is capable of prompting a search for new and diverse spaces that can be *interpreted* in the context of the subject's complex and critical experiences with meaning.[9]

17

Intertextuality and Literary Interpretation

Margaret Waller conducted this interview in New York City in 1985. It was published in *Intertextuality and Contemporary American Fiction*. The translation is by Richard Macksey. Kristeva speaks lucidly about her well-known notion of intertextuality, expressing her intellectual debt to Bakhtin's notion of dialogism while emphasizing that the intersection of voices surrounding an utterance concerns not only the semantic field but the syntactic and phonic fields. She introduces a psychoanalytic element into the notion of intertextuality by suggesting that the intertextuality of the creator and the reader make them "subjects-in-process" whose psychic identity is put into question. Commenting on Nerval, Kristeva then contrasts modern poetry, described as "more openly regressive" and direct, with the modern novel, which is said to result from a "working-out" of the self. She claims that the modern novel could thus be seen as a "kind of continuous lay analysis." Other questions have to do with melancholia (Kristeva was working on *Black Sun* at the time of this interview), psychoanalysis (which is said to link theory and practice more fortuitously than does Marxism or political commitment), and the political structure of the United States. Kristeva concludes by discussing her plans for writing fiction, including the project that would eventually become *The Samurai.*

How do you conceive of intertextuality? What are its formal and intrapsychic aspects? How do you distinguish it from Bakhtin's dialogism?

One should perhaps emphasize the history of this concept, which has come to have rather wide currency, I think. Many scholars are using it to deal with important rhetorical and ideological phenomena in modern literature and in classical literature as well. I have a certain idea of the concept. At the beginning of my research, when I was writing a commentary on Bakhtin, I had the feeling that with his notions of dialogism and carnival we had reached an important point in moving beyond structuralism. French literary criticism at that time was especially fascinated by Russian formalism, but a formalism that limited itself to transposing notions proper to linguistics and applying them to the analysis of narrative.

Personally, I had found Bakhtin's work very exciting, particularly his studies of Rabelais and Dostoevsky. He was moving toward a dynamic understanding of the literary text that considered every utterance as the result of the intersection within it of a number of voices, as he called them. I discussed my reading with Roland Barthes, who was quite fascinated and invited me to his seminar—it was 1966, I think, and the seminar was held at 44 rue de Rennes—to make a presentation on Bakhtin.[1] I think that my interpretation remains, on the one hand, faithful to his ideas, and demonstrates, on the other, my attempts to elaborate and enlarge upon them. Whence the concept of intertextuality, which does not figure as such in the work of Bakhtin but which, it seemed to me, one could deduce from his work.[2]

All this is by way of showing you, with as much intellectual honesty as possible, the source of the concept of intertextuality, while at the same time underscoring the difference between this concept and that, for example, of dialogism. I see the following differences. In the first place, there is the recognition that a textual segment, sentence, utterance, or paragraph is not simply the intersection of two voices in direct or indirect discourse; rather, the segment is the result of the intersection of a number of voices, of a number of textual interventions, which are combined in the semantic field, but also in the syntactic and phonic fields of the explicit utterance. So there is the idea of this plurality of phonic, syntactic, and semantic participation. I think that what is new with regard to Bakhtin is seeing this intervention of external plurality at different levels—not only at the level of meaning but at the level of syntax and phonics, too. What interested me even more—and this seems to me unique—was the notion that the participation of different texts at different levels reveals a particular mental activity. And analysis should not limit itself simply to identifying texts that participate in the final texts, or to identifying their sources, but should understand that what is being dealt with is a specific dynamics of the subject of the utterance, who consequently, precisely because of this intertextuality, is not an individual in the etymological sense of the term, not an identity.

In other words, the discovery of intertextuality at a formal level leads us to an intrapsychic or psychoanalytic finding, if you will, concerning the status of the "creator," the one who produces a text by placing himself or herself at the intersection of this plurality of texts on their very different levels—I repeat, semantic, syntactic, or phonic. This leads me to understand creative subjectivity as a kaleidoscope, a "polyphony" as Bakhtin calls it. I myself speak of a "subject in process," which makes possible my attempt to articulate as precise a logic as possible between identity or unity, the challenge to this identity and even its reduction to zero, the moment of crisis, of emptiness, and then the reconstitution of a new, plural identity. This new identity may be the plurality capable of manifesting itself as the plurality of characters the author uses; but in more recent writing, in the twentieth-century novel, it may appear as fragments of character, or fragments of ideology, or fragments of representation.

Moreover, such an understanding of intertextuality—one that points to a dynamics involving a destruction of the creative identity and reconstitution of a new plurality—assumes at the same time that the one who reads, the reader, participates in the same dynamics. If we are readers of intertextuality, we must be capable of the same putting-into-process of our identities, capable of identifying with the different types of texts, voices, and semantic, syntactic, and phonic systems at play in a given text. We also must be able to be reduced to zero, to the state of crisis that is perhaps the necessary precondition of aesthetic pleasure, to the point of speechlessness as Freud says, of the loss of meaning, before we can enter into a process of free association, reconstitution of diverse meanings, or kinds of connotations that are almost undefinable—a process that is a *re*-creation of the poetic text. I think, then, that this kind of writing, whose formal aspects I try to stress along with its intrapsychic aspect—and I think we must never discuss the one without the other—can be accounted for only by a reader who enjoys the complexity of the text and who places himself or herself on both levels at once.

This logic and dynamics, which may also be applied to classical texts, seem to me to be absolutely necessary for modern texts. This is true for poetic texts, which are characterized by great condensation and great polysemia: as examples I can cite the writings of Nerval or Mallarmé in particular. It is also true for the modern novel. The texts of Joyce are a very special example of this type. It is impossible to read *Finnegan's Wake* without entering into the intrapsychic logic and dynamics of intertextuality. Yet this is also true for postmodernism, where the problem is to reconcile representation, the imposition of content, with the play of form—which is, I emphasize again, a play of psychic pluralization. And here, in postmodernism, the question of intertextuality is perhaps even more important in certain ways, because it assumes an interplay of contents and not of forms alone. If one reads Faulkner without going back to the Bible, to the Old Testament, to the Gospels, to American society of the period and to his own hallucinatory experience, I believe one cannot reconstitute the complexity of the text itself. This is valid for more recent literature as well. Once again, this question of content is to be understood not as being about a single content—"What does this mean in the sentence?"—but as a content that may be dispersed, traceable to different points of origin; the final meaning of this content will be neither the original source nor any one of the possible meanings taken on in the text, but will be, rather, a continuous movement back and forth in the space between the origin and all the possible connotative meanings.

Given the applicability of the concept of intertextuality to modern texts that call into question the very concept of genre, would you agree with Bakhtin that the novel is the type par excellence of this polyphony?

Yes, I do agree, but provided we understand that ever since the rise of the novel in the West we have had an interminable novel, and the word becomes the generic term for a drastically expanded experience of writing. The term *roman* can now be applied to poetic writing incorporating a narrative element. It can also be applied to *récits* of a journalistic type that integrate the possibility of narrative, provided the category can be expanded. It can be applied as well to the intermingling of auto-biographical elements with essays and theoretical texts. These are all *romans*—as long as we understand "novel" as an intersection of genre and as a generalized form of intertextuality. If one identifies the novel with intertextuality, then every contemporary type of writing partici-pates in it.[3]

Even if it is poetry? Even if it incorporates. . .

Poetic elements, yes. Obviously, if you are dealing with writing that is very fragmentary, very elliptical, as certain modern poetry is, then it is difficult to talk about novelistic elements. I will use the term *novel* when the narrative moment is really present, which is not the case with cer-tain poetic texts that are quite chopped up. To these texts, then, we will apply the word *roman*, but the question of intertextuality persists.

So the concept of intertextuality encompasses both novel and poetry, even if the novelistic element can be taken today in a very broad sense. Intertextuality is perhaps the most global concept possible for signify-ing the modern experience of writing, including the classic genres, poetic and novelistic. And to the extent that these genres, in the classic sense of the term, are unrecognizable in the modern novel, perhaps we will be, as it were, freed from our obsessive appeal to genre if we accept the terms of intertextuality in characterizing the experience of writing.

Yes, but if I understand your global definition of intertextuality and of the novel's importance to it, then what is important is the narrative element, the récit element, even if it is fragmented, dispersed . . .

That defines the novel.

Yes, that's it.

Precisely. And I think it's an interesting distinction to maintain, at least in what concerns me, from the point of view of psychic activity. It is true that I see intertextuality as being just as applicable to modern poetic writing as to modern novelistic writing. But perhaps within this broadened concept of intertextuality, which concerns all contemporary writing, one can maintain a distinction between poetic and novelistic experience. For me, this distinction is interesting because it indicates different levels of psychic unity and, in a certain way, some of the writer's possible defenses with regard to the crises that writing assumes.

In the narrative experience the subject has access to more options for working things out with respect to moments of crisis, hallucination, loss, and risk of psychosis. The poetic experience is more openly regressive, if you will; it confronts more directly the moments of loss of meaning, and perhaps also the maternal, the feminine, which obviously represents the solicitations of sexual pleasure and gratification and, at the same time, risk and loss of the self.

We can see this clearly in Nerval, to take a writer from whom we have some distance. When he writes a poem, which is very often a struggle against schizophrenic collapse or the threat of melancholia—"El Desdichado," for example, the Dark Prince, "the black Sun of Melancholy"—the symbols mean a number of things one can inventory by using dictionaries of esoterica; but that's not the point. The essential point is precisely the polyvalence of the symbols, and the fact that we can add other connotations that perhaps even Nerval didn't recognize. If one also takes into account musicality, rhythmicity, alliteration, and so on, this type of writing is obviously a temptation to go down as far as possible toward the semiotic, toward the confrontation of the subject with the object of loss, nostalgia, melancholia—in other words, that maternal form which may be conjured up as a dead mother, an absent mother. And it is an attempt to go down—note that the poet compares himself to Orpheus descending into hell—an attempt that is totally vulnerable because it assumes the possibility of self-loss, and at the same time accurate, because the poet pursues the vulnerability of the psychic experience to the very edge of nonmeaning.

But what one can see is that when the poet feels he has won out in this regressive quest, he expresses his triumphant emergence with a narrative, or at least with the opening of a narrative. We see this in the first line of the last tercet of the sonnet: "Et j'ai deux fois vainqueur traversé l'Achéron" [And I have twice as conqueror crossed the Acheron]. So Nerval uses an "I," with a verb in the perfect tense that moves us away from the poetic sense of fusion dominated by semiotic processes. He distances himself; he places himself in time. He begins again to tell a story in which, instead of mythical, esoteric, ambivalent, and indiscernible characters, there will appear two aspects of the feminine figure: the yearnings of the saint and the cries of the witch—the mental and the carnal, if you will, the sublime and the sexual. It is as though from that point onward one is dealing with protagonists in conflict, and beginning to tell a story. But it stops. It's a poem, and a narrative is not continued. Nonetheless, what I want to say is that the moment of triumph and mastery over the experience of conflict is the point at which narrative begins.

And this narrative overture Nerval will use more than once in his work. He will have real problems in writing works like *Sylvie* and *Aurélia*. These incorporate not just the apparent or staged problems of the picaresque novel, which plays with a narrative that is broken up and rearranged in a radial pattern because this structure is conditioned and motivated by adventure itself, by the idea of adventure. Nor is Nerval's a case of a dismantling of the narrative mode, as in the *nouveau roman* with its attempt to overpower narrative logic. It is simply his inability to keep himself on a temporal line because the massive, archaic past will not go away. This remote past bursts out, breaking and destroying the narrative line. At that point we are seeing a polyphonic, intertextual narrative ruptured and broken by poetry. The phenomenon demonstrates that the subject of utterance is having difficulty keeping himself in the narrative mode. The poem does not turn out like a novel, properly speaking.

I chose this example to show to what extent narrative construction is the result of a "working-out" of the self, but also a defense and consolidation of the self in relation to its experience of crisis. I want to remark, too, upon the fact that in the contemporary world narrative writing, novelistic writing, doubtless takes on significance against a background of religious crisis, where we have no sacred discourses for reckoning with our experiences of crisis and rejoicing. Or else such discourses, when they do exist, are called into question as parts of a past difficult for modern society to accept without extremely problematic regressions. In this context, novelistic writing is an immense and very powerful means of guiding us most deeply into our crises and farthest away from them at the same time—a kind of repeat descent and reemergence such as Orpheus could not achieve, a sort of Orphic experience, but that of a conquering Orpheus, a possible Orpheus, an Orpheus triumphant.

This is why the modern novel, which incorporates the poetic experience in an intertextual manner, is a tremendous opportunity for the sublimation of our crises and malaises. It is a kind of continuous lay analysis, and often perhaps weaker than psychoanalysis because it may lack the ideational means, the knowledge, the why and how of the psychoanalytic enterprise. But it may often be a more powerful tool than psychoanalysis because at times it presents us with situations that rarely appear in psychoanalytic treatment. Certain writers manage to lead us as deeply as possible into our malaises, where we seldom go except in dreams, and without always bringing back adequate accounts of those dreams.

I am struck by your definition of literature as a continuous lay analysis. You are currently working on melancholia and the imagination, and Nerval is one of the authors you will treat in this new book.[4] Who will the other authors be? Why those and not others? And why nineteenth-century authors in particular?

It's a book that comes largely out of something observed in psychoanalysis: the high frequency of depression in the contemporary world. This is a very current phenomenon, even if it is unfashionable because we have no ideological or theoretical discourse valorizing depression. It eluded civilizations that enjoyed suffering or depression, and that indulgence was perhaps, sometimes, a way of aggravating the disorder, but also a way of helping people get through such periods. Our society is much more action-oriented, and those who are sad, or terribly boring, who move at a slow pace or do not speak, cannot be objects of fascination. We move them to one side and try to forget them.

There are civilizations, as I've said—the fifteenth century in particular, but also the nineteenth—that have tried to take depression into account after periods of religious crisis as at the end of the Middle Ages, or the end of the rapid rise of the rationalistic bourgeoisie with its belief in the goddess Reason and its crisis of religious values. The goddess Reason was an eighteenth-century idea that the nineteenth century called into question, and there was a subsequent return to the spiritual, the irrational, which signified not only a crisis in formal religion—"God is dead," Nietzsche said—but also a crisis in the belief of reason. So against this background the explosion of depression and melancholia attracted attention, and there was an attempt to find aesthetic forms and discourses to account for it. One can find such things, such rhetorical events, occurring again in modern and contemporary literature. One might see many of Faulkner's texts, for example, as tending in this direction. The American South, specifically Flannery O'Connor, is shot through with depression, but it knows it can find a way out. And then there are certain texts of Sartre, *Being and Nothingness* and *Nausea* in particular, that bear traces of attempts to redeem periods of depression. One can find these, too, in the nineteenth century—more direct than the modern examples, perhaps also more naive and therefore more striking.

I have tried not to write an encyclopedia of texts concerning and discussing depression. In the first place, I couldn't do it, and I also wanted to reserve part of my book for clinical experience and what I hear coming from the couch. In particular, I have tried to report on certain configurations of female depression, which seems to be a question of current interest. So among those texts or, rather, artifacts that have dealt with melancholia or presented themselves almost as courses of treatment, I have so far chosen three great works. I think now that I will stop there, but I'm not sure: I may add a fourth. There will be Holbein, the great painter, so sober and restrained, who, between Catholicism and Protestantism, tried to maintain a humanistic line, but precariously so, simultaneously serious and . . . at the limits of the possibility of representation, as though at the limits of artisticity. One wonders how it is possible to write and paint with so much restraint and sadness. I treat his work mainly through his painting, *The Dead Christ.* Then there will be Nerval, "the black Sun of Melancholy," his sonnet "El Desdichado," but also *Aurélia.* And Dostoevsky, insofar as he examines in a very explicit way the relationship of melancholia to religious crisis within the context of a political situation, which is, in fact, a current concern. One may wonder whether the choices of certain modern terrorists are not parallel to the terrorist choices of Dostoevsky's characters—Kirilov, Raskolnikov—whose actions range from suicide to the murder of a stranger and seem to be phenomena recurring in the modern political world. But Dostoevsky makes it possible for me to see them with more distance and, perhaps, with more objectivity. The reader, moreover, is bound to be struck by the similarities to the present day and can no doubt make the connection between terrorism and melancholy himself or herself.

And this same book will also be about your practice of psychoanalysis, especially female depression?

Actually, I will try to make depression comprehensible by presenting different types of patients, not all of them women. But I have also written a chapter where I concentrate more on various aspects of female depression.

I was wondering, because your "authors," so to speak, are men, and I was wondering about this gap . . .

I'm trying to find a woman author, too, but I'm having a lot of trouble because either I have to choose a very well known woman author, and in that case the temptation of cliché or repetition is too great, or else . . .

But couldn't one say the same of Dostoevsky?

Not so much, perhaps, from the point of view of depression. What has been written about him has dealt more with his religion, his relationship to epilepsy, his polyphony. The presence of and apologia for suffering have been emphasized less; whereas with women authors, this element, I think, was seen right away. The suffering of Virginia Woolf, or Sylvia Plath, or Charlotte Brontë has often been discussed. I have wondered, by the way, whether it wouldn't be interesting to suggest, as an example of women writing melancholia or on melancholia, the work of a woman psychoanalyst. But I've not finished yet, so I'm not sure . . .

We'll wait and see. Can you see something beyond psychoanalysis, or are you so comfortable with it that the question of political commitment, or anything else, doesn't even come up? Is there anything missing, theoretical perhaps, or practical, that bothers you, in the sense that it indicates to you that there is still another stage to get to, not now, but later on?

You mean, do I feel comfortable or do I . . . You seem to have the impression that I feel comfortable for the present with doing psychoanalysis. If one feels comfortable, one doesn't do psychoanalysis! Psychoanalysis is a response to an enduring uneasiness that is not necessarily a simple existential uneasiness but rather an intellectual discomfort. And I believe that psychoanalysis is the discourse of the intellectual life, if the intellectual life is also characterized by this uneasiness and a constant questioning of meanings, heritages, doctrines, and appearances. Now psychoanalysis as I understand it—I know this does not correspond to the various and often controversial portrayals of psychoanalysis we may receive in America as well as in France—has the advantage of being a fusion, if you will, an intertextuality of practice and theory. It is the great obsession of our culture.

At the end of the nineteenth century, we constructed quite advanced and very abstract theoretical systems that found themselves at a certain point in a state of culpability—that is, cut off from practical experience. At that moment, the available solutions were two. Either one could follow this development to its logical conclusion by pushing the isolation even further and shutting oneself off in a universe of metalanguage meeting metalanguage—analytical philosophy, among other things, or at least one possible version of it—or one could, dialectically, try to make theory and practice meet. The consequences of this second strategy are Marxism, various forms of socialism, of political commitment, and so on, that are not innocent and that can often lead to catastrophic results, as much because they may involve an abdication of the intellect as because they represent a social and political dogmatism that betrays any moral aspirations.

I believe psychoanalysis has the advantage, with Freud's innovations, of linking theoretical work with action, of being a bridge between contemplation and efficacy, between theoretical construct and treatment. And you never have one without the other. You cannot be a good theoretician, a good analyst, without being a good practitioner. If you are one or the other, either something is wrong in your practice or something is wrong in your theory. One often hears, "But there may be people with a lot of insight who don't produce theories." I can't say that theory must necessarily be written down, but in their insights these people already have concepts of how they function, and of how the psyche functions—so a certain modalization is present to guide them in their practice. This point seems to me very crucial for the analytic adventure.

The second point is that psychoanalysis is a discourse that is not closed, contrary to certain images presented by certain kinds of analytic practice that portray it as the mere repetition of Freud. We are in a continuous confrontation with the living discourses of society—the new malaises and symptoms, but also new ways of relating to image, public life, sexuality, biology, and procreation. With regard to all these, psychoanalytic discourse is called upon to break new ground, to be a sort of continuous creation, if it wants to keep up with people and to make it possible for them to find their own ways of responding to these existential questions. Expanded in this way, analysis does not at all appear to me to be a closed system that we will someday have to discard. It incorporates and displaces discourses. The practices of the teaching of literature and literary criticism can be nourished and enlightened, finding both resources and greater lucidity, only through contact with psychoanalysis.

You have often spoken of the United States in your writings. I am thinking in particular of the article in Polylogue . . .

"From Ithaca to New York."

Yes, in that, and also in "My Memory's Hyperbole," which you wrote for The Female Autograph. *You were talking there primarily about France, and about the sixties and seventies . . .*

And it ends that way?

It ends—

—with America.

With America and the United States. Right. So why America? Of course it has to do with your personal life, with the fact that you are here every three years. But would there be other reasons?

Yes, there are many reasons, and it's true that we must perhaps begin with personal reasons—especially in the case of a psychoanalyst—we all know that! I must say that I am very fortunate to have been invited by Columbia University to come every three years and teach in the Department of French. It's a very good university, and the students always welcome me with a great deal of kindness and curiosity. They ask questions that stimulate me a great deal because they have a way of listening to theoretical discourse "psychologically," existentially. Their questions always stem from an experience that may or may not be connected with the concepts, but it is always stimulating for the one to whom the questions are addressed. So there has been a sort of adoption of me at Columbia that is very flattering.

But I think we must go a little beyond that, since there are a number of reasons that have always made me feel very favorably disposed toward American life and the American experience. First of all, I say this in the context of a certain centralization of political, administrative, and ideological life in France that is our legacy from royalty, from Bonaparte. American feudalism—the polyvalence of centers of decision-making in the publishing and academic worlds, but also, I believe, in the government (and I admit I've had little opportunity for observing the latter, but it strikes me that it works in this way)—seems to be a more favorable and adequate response to the problems people face today than the centralization of Europe in general and of France in particular.

Second, there is a big problem facing European communities today, that of racism or polyracism. We are turning into a polyracial or polynational society. From across the Mediterranean, masses of Arabs, Africans, and so on are spreading through France. The political structure of France, on the one hand, and the French mentality, on the other, are not capable of taking in this phenomenon because they are extremely strong and coherent and find themselves absolutely incapable of absorbing these "invasions." We find ourselves in a sort of face-off, with conflicts that threaten to result in catastrophe in the coming years. I am not necessarily speaking of right-wing political groups, who play up such things and take advantage of the malaises. Those groups, in my opinion, ultimately are used by parties on the right *as well as* parties on the left in a rather subtle and dangerous political game. But that's all part of the current scene.

I simply think that, even if it is a long-term prospect, there must be a resolve to recast our ways of thinking, which is very difficult, given our cultural heritage. From this point of view, American society, which is a society of immigrants, already a conglomerate and a mosaic, can provide an example of how, *practically*, to resolve these questions. That said, I do not think the American model can be exported to Europe or that we can have the same attitude as Americans, since the conditions are not the same. You do not have the cultural heritage France has, which is a kind of identity that feels itself invaded and reacts to that invasion. So we will have to find our own solutions, but the example of American tolerance, of American pragmatism, of dealing with the other on various levels of daily existence while allowing him his autonomy on the levels of his deep cultural and religious choices—these kinds of solutions are interesting for Europeans to envision and contemplate. Thus the American model continues to interest me very much.

However, perhaps I have failed to stress something that exists in the articles you mentioned and that is extremely important in terms of the intertextuality of the world. Europe, to my mind, remains a locus of civilization, of the art of living, and of that capacity to assume the law without forgetting pleasure. Americans, perhaps, are in the process of discovering and trying to assimilate this lesson from Europe, after having an offended attitude with regard to what they consider to be European arrogance. I have often heard American friends speak of feeling rejected by the prestige that Europeans believe they have, which leads Europeans to be a little condescending toward representatives of American civilization. Well, I think things have changed somewhat in that regard, and I think the American world—perhaps because Europe, too, is more receptive—feels more receptive toward Europe. We may, at some point, achieve a mutuality of reciprocal respect.

What struck me in your memoir was your speaking of the rather special autobiographical form that combines the I and the we, the first-person singular and plural. It was so problematic and paradigmatic, your personal story and also the story . . .

Of the Tel Quel group.

Of the Tel Quel group. I was wondering whether you thought you would perhaps some day write about . . .

Yes, the whole story.

And if so, if you would write something novelistic, or would it be more of a documentary account. What form would it take, and in what style and language?

I don't know! I am, indeed, asked that question because of the text called "Memoir,"[5] and because one-half of "L'Hérétique de l'amour" is a text on maternity that contains a rather poetic and subjective section.[6] Because of that, good friends of mine have suggested that I take up a more fictional kind of writing. I don't know. For the moment, I think that psychoanalytic interpretation, which is very close to the economy of fiction, completely absorbs that kind of desire. I don't really need to produce an object, detached from myself, based on my life story, because I feel that in psychoanalytic interpretation there is a discourse that, while more or less detached from direct reference to biography, does go, nevertheless, by way of my own life story to meet the life story of the other person. There is a back-and-forth movement there that spares me the need for novelistic writing.

At times, I think the important thing would be to write if not a novel then at least an account of those years of personal theoretical work that marks French culture of the sixties and seventies and continues to mark it in a certain way that will make it a part of literary history—there should be an assessment of that period. But I think that the period has not yet come to a close and that we don't have enough distance from it yet. Maybe someday it should be done, but not now. In any case, when the question comes up of whether I can see myself as a writer of fiction, I can see myself as one later on—if life goes on! That would be an activity for one who had emerged somewhat from the action. I see it a bit like the characters of Ronsard—in the evening by the fireside, after the story proper. For the moment I feel too involved in the story in question to take stock of it. One could answer that novelistic writing does not assume any distance, and that to write a novel means by definition to remain immersed in the action. But for now, again, psychoanalytic interpretation takes the place of that; I must add, moreover, that theoretical writing, along with psychoanalysis and literary criticism, absorbs certain subjective elements, and for the moment this gives me enough balance without my needing to move into fiction. There is also the fact that to the extent that French is still, after all, a foreign language for me, I feel a certain reticence about writing anything in French; I think it is perhaps not well enough connected, organically, with my unconscious for me to produce valid creative work.

Whereas you were saying yesterday, of Beckett, that after his mother's death he wrote in French. So it was possible for him to write in two languages.

Yes—but a rather special kind of writing, and one that may correspond to some deep rupture or distress in Beckett's personality, something that makes it necessary for writing—which, in any case, is translation—in his case to be explicitly translation on a direct level, between two languages, and not merely between an affective life and a personal language. Beckett's is a rather special psychic life, and my distress is not of that order.[7]

One last question: you said that your work in psychoanalysis and literary criticism absorbs, so to speak . . .

A certain need for fiction.

Yes. And that your choosing to be a literary critic has something to do with your personal history. Your choice of texts, I would say, is also a very personal choice.

Yes, of course.

So why certain texts and not others? You work on all different kinds of texts. What ties them all together?

Maybe I am an intertextual personality. I have a lot of facets, like a diamond. I really think that if there is a "pattern," it is the borderline between sense and nonsense, between the semiotic and the symbolic. Obviously it takes different forms in different centuries for various people. But what interests me is the dividing line. I sometimes have the feeling that the human condition, insofar as it involves the use of speech, is very fragile, and that writing explores that fragility. I try to find examples of literary texts where this fragility appears to have maximum visibility.

And in your psychoanalytic practice, too . . .

Well, there it depends rather on the people who present themselves, but I find this stage appearing there, too, in a very flagrant way, and times of crisis, whether hysterical or depressive, touch on this same subject of borders. So I am fairly sensitive to this fragility; I believe I'm trying to help people cope with it.

18

Reading and Writing

Serge Gavronsky conducted this interview with Kristeva at the Hotel Lutetia bar in Paris in 1987. The translation is his own. The interview focuses on *écriture* as defined in Jacques Derrida's *Of Grammatology*. Kristeva first addresses the development of her own *écriture*, tracing it from the "rational power" that marked *Séméiotiké* through the textual analysis informed by the crisis in subjectivity and on to a "connivance with the text" resembling the early empathetic stages of an analysis. Kristeva then goes on to juxtapose two "ethics of aesthetics" manifested in interpretation: a "rationalist" ethics that resists the "pleasure of regression" in a text and an ethics of "crisis" that entails an embracement of pleasure and regression. Favoring the second mode, she suggests that the reader should carry out "a true resurrection of the critical body based on experiencing the writing of the Other." In this sense, she says, literary interpretation is similar to psychoanalysis. In the next part of the interview, Kristeva's claims that the distinguishing feature of French literature is its search for "jouissance" and its penchant for combining Descartes and *divertissement*. She also argues that in the famous salons of the French Enlightenment, the art of conversation was "the essence of one's relation to the Other," even in the face of melancholia or death. Finally, Kristeva resists the notion that "feminine discourse" exists on the level of the signifier, claiming that femininity in literature may be less a matter of *écriture* than of the avant-garde (and sexually ambiguous) thematics she has discussed in her theoretical work.

*At least in French, it's a common assumption that style/*écriture *is the man or woman; that is, at any given time, what we do as writers is project our beings-in-the-text and, as such, somehow our own property. Yet reading one author's production over a period of time, or what is generally considered to be a particular style marking a period, quickly demonstrates the interaction between individual and collective enterprises in the field of* écriture. *When you yourself look back on your numerous works, are you aware of changing models of* écritures *that might no longer correspond to your present practice, for example as you've expressed yourself in* Black Sun: Depression and Melancholia?

That's an easy question to answer since I'm now at a certain distance from both what I wrote in the past and what has recently been completed. My first work in French [*Séméiotiké: Recherches pour une sémanalyse*] was written in a structuralist context. It seemed to me to be important, both for myself and within the intellectual debate in France at that time, to render the analysis of a literary text with as much rational power as possible. I wanted to propose models that would most convincingly take into account the polyphonic elements in works of twentieth-century avant-garde writers as well as in Mallarmé, Lautréamont and, going farther back, Dostoevsky and Rabelais. With this in mind, I selected highly controlled forms of discourse at the crossroads of philosophy and linguistics. Of course, this wasn't pure linguistics, and real linguists screamed "Sacrilegious!" But it was, on my part, an effort to rationalize the explanation and to grasp the fleeting meaning that characterizes the literary text. In order to read a text, I think you've got to get into the precise details of signification, rhythm, syntax: everything that structural rhetoric taught us and to which I have contributed. But very early on, I asked myself if that structure—to use a term then fashionable—was not something produced in a vacuum but rather was produced because of a crisis in subjectivity and a crisis in society. Marxist and sociological doctrines addressed the issue of the crisis in society, but the issue of subjectivity remained within the field of textual analysis. I therefore decided to take up that analytical direction and assumed the position of analyst, on the other side of the couch. As of that moment, my relationship to the text was marked less by a mastering *of* the text than by a sort of connivance *with* the text. This connivance represented the first period of analysis: identification, sympathy, and love. Quite clearly, those attitudes influenced my style of writing, which may not be, strictly speaking, "literary," but which is much more liberated from the constraints of concepts and models and attempts, as a result, to penetrate into the meanderings of suffering and pleasure that writers have found.

Doesn't this imply that at one time, and perhaps still today, there has been a particular ethics of aesthetics, a way of approaching and interpreting the literary text through critical writing?

Absolutely. I believe this is understood in different ways, depending on one's own understanding of ethics. There may be a rationalist ethics that struggles against the pleasures of regression evident in the literary text, and thereby tries to extract its quintessence. Something like that happened during the structuralist period. There may also be another way that might consist of placing oneself fully within that pleasure, including its regressive phase, to follow it, to reconstitute it for readers who might not always be able to see it, and perhaps in a second period, to differentiate oneself from it in order to formulate an interpretation of it. But I'm persuaded that interpretation is impossible if one hasn't followed the moment of crisis.

In an unexpected way, this mode of adhering to the subjectivity of the text and exploiting it as one explains it plays on translational metaphor; that is, in order to understand what we hold in our hands, we come within certain limits to associate ourselves with it as we do with the possibility of making errors. However, with the analytical tools you mentioned before, errors are supposedly reduced to a minimum, and we then find ourselves able to render the "original" into our own language, through our own voice.

Without a doubt. Our forms of writing, unquestionably affected by television and music videos, make that moment of connivance with the Other all the more difficult. The mediation on the abyss of the other person is not a contemporary practice. We pass too rapidly over that. We go on to other things. But what, after all, is the role of the critic or the interpreter if not to try to maintain a particular mediation, and mediation presupposes first an intense empathy with the text and, beyond that, with the interior experience of the writer. Contrary to the belief that the critic is a sort of vulture hovering over the writer/cadaver, what actually should occur is a true resurrection of the critical body based on experiencing the writing of the Other. And so, in a certain way, the critic does become a stylist within his own possibilities, within his own field, and he throws himself into a form of writing where he tries to bring forth, in its totality, not only the intellectual aspects of a Mallarmé, a Baudelaire or a Nerval, but his sensitivities as well. Once this happens, and a hyphen has been introduced between a historical epoch and a contemporary sensibility, the critic regains a degree of distance and, eventually, tries to give meaning, an interpretation, a message. That is why I believe that the function of interpretation, as it plays on the literary text, is similar to an analytical situation.

Would you agree that in both situations there exists a sort of atemporality as well as an inscription of oneself as critic within a temporal moment? In fact, aren't we always historicizing our discourse? Isn't it impossible to get out of that bind even though the text itself is fixed in time?

One is constantly situated between numerous temporalities. There is an extratemporal time; Freud says that the unconscious ignores time, that it is a form of eternity. The unconscious is a sort of exit out of chronological lines, and there it is our own regression, our own infantilism, which is called into play. Simply stated, through an adhesion to a cultural ideal, both analyst and critic feel they must transcend the moment, this breakdown in time, this time out of time, in order to return to present history and thus transmit a message.

You allude to "infantilism." In my discussion with a number of writers and critics about the contemporary directions écriture *is taking in France, that subject—in a different light, of course—came up. There is today a strong pull toward childhood (as differentiated from adolescence) as a literary theme in French writing. From your own point of view, to what do you ascribe this return to childhood?*

I believe the distinguishing trait of French literature is its search for a sort of jouissance, of pleasure. It's a literature of *divertissement*, of distraction, which attained its highest level in the eighteenth century. If you assume that the French mind is simultaneously marked by Descartes and distraction, the question that our own century asks is, How, given computer science, customs, the Concorde—all those permanent stresses imposed on the individual—how can one set aside a space for distraction? The answer that most readily comes to mind is that this can occur only by returning to a form of the infantile in us; and I'm not surprised to see, given that situation, writers describing their own childhood. Isn't it a myth? An enigma? After all, who knows what it is to be a child? There are a series of projections that surround the child's image, but what they signify, as Freud called it, is the perverse polymorphous inside them. Furthermore, the examples of contemporary texts that bring childhood back are connected to homosexuality, to perversion, and so on, and all that goes back to the direction I've just indicated. It's one of the directions by which the French mind defines itself.

How does this concept of distraction work within the context of the idea of a written dialogue, the text as an opening, a participation? Is the idea of distraction, by definition, a public event or a private one? Is it centered on the self?

It seems to me that conversation is a very particular form of distraction in the eighteenth century that has not yet been fully studied. When I mention distraction, one thinks essentially of the various pleasures of the body, especially sexual. While that is indeed a component of contemporary French culture, one shouldn't forget that what may be even more interesting is its transposition into a carnal commerce with words, which results in the sparkling dialogue of Diderot's *The Tell-Tale Jewels* as well as of other eighteenth-century texts. Even when melancholia is being sketched out in the background, as is the case with such an extraordinary woman as Madame du Deffand, the art of conversation remains not only the facade but the essence of one's relationship to the other.

When Pascal uses the term "distraction," he means it as that amusement which momentarily distracts us from the confrontation with the essence of our predicament; that is, God and death itself.[1] Do you think conversation might be an eloquent means of sidestepping this confrontation?

I agree. This problem is particularly close to me since my most recent book [*Black Sun: Depression and Melancholia*] is devoted to the inevitability of death and the permanent confrontation with death that is endured by those who are depressives or melancholics. I tend to attribute importance to staring death straight in the face, as opposed to the belief that neither the sun nor death can be looked at directly. Those who do look at them directly are either depressive cases or philosophers. Both exist within the problematics of apprehension, which is obviously not a form of distraction! In the media, distraction is clearly preferred over our state of apprehension, of concern, but I believe that we cannot merely emphasize death, which permanently inhabits us all and is our truth. In my analytical practice today, I am forced to take two things into consideration: on the one hand, that particular truth, and on the other, our ways of surviving. There's really no way out. Survival depends on passing through that artifice, that game of appearances, on the condition that the individual is neither duped nor completely naive and that he carries through the artifice of distraction his understanding of our impossible nature. I am convinced that our contemporaries, and especially the French, are totally impregnated with that difficulty of being.

Do you also believe that this theatricalization, as in the salons of the eighteenth century, and in the effect it has on social behavior, is our particular way of placing a bet on civilization?

Absolutely! It's truly betting on civilization. Both death and depression rely on a feeling of hatred toward oneself as well as toward the Other, which cannot find a means of expression. Conversation assumes that even hatred is mentionable, provided it is based on rhetorical pirouette such as irony. It's a form of forgiveness. I can forgive your hatred on the condition that you express it in an elegant manner. What better antidote to depression! As long as it works, I say, great! Today, the fact is we no longer have much room for conversations and dialogues. We're too much in a hurry. We lead stressful lives, and as a result analysis and monologue become important.

If we assume that in the Other there must be a degree of authenticity in the conversational exchange, both in form and in content, do you think—and this gets back to my general question on écriture*!—that there's such a thing as the sexualization of discourse? Is there, from your point of view, a feminine discourse not just on the level of themes expressed but on the more elusive signifier level?*

I have trouble answering that question. The fact that women can find their way into the world of intelligence seems to me to be great praise for femininity. But I do believe femininity is more a question of themes, of fantasies, imaginary experiences, a relation to the Other, the child, to one's mother and father, than it is a question of *écriture*. The moment there's a stylistic effect there's a clear sexual ambiguity—and Artaud, Mallarmé, or Joyce are as female as Virginia Woolf.

Wouldn't the perfect example of that particular gender distribution in a transcultural manner be the eighteenth century, where women were philosophers and exercised, in their conversational abilities, that very idea of distraction you mentioned before?

That period may have been overly idealized, but it's true that women occupied a position they have never held since! Certainly not in the twentieth century, where the university gives them a very privileged position but not as powerful as they had once held within their own salons. And yet I wonder if, in that world, there wasn't an extraordinary tension on the part of women trying to rival the phallic position with a seduction they weren't allowed to express, with a depression they couldn't formulate. That seems clear to me when I read Madame du Deffand's correspondence. Today a woman may demand the right to express both her power and her depression, and I'm not sure we're able to listen. It may be too much! If we speak of a feminine realization, then it cannot be for militants only, for feminists alone, but for the pain of all women.

19

Avant-Garde Practice

Vassiliki Kolocotroni conducted and translated this interview, which was published in *Textual Practice* in 1991. Framed by well-informed questions, it provides an exceptionally clear exposition of Kristeva's notion of avant-garde practice. Kristeva compares her notion of poetic language with Jakobson's, defining the poetic "text" as the process in which "the semiotic enters the symbolic" and in which "drives are codified within the language of communication." Poetic language is thus a "subjective crisis" and an "amplification of the register of expression." Kristeva also calls poetic language a "return," a "repetition," and a "regression" and yet a "transformation [. . .] of the unconscious, of the most archaic elements: fear, passion, abjection—themes that are worked through in literature. It is also the elaboration of the archaic material in an outlook of revolt, insubmission, and defiance." She expresses reservations about the idea of art as salvation, though she endorses its therapeutic potential. She nuances, moreover, the notion that artistic revolutions are tantamount to social revolutions, suggesting that the surrealists' and symbolists' hopes for revolution are no longer possible in today's "society of the spectacle." At the same time, she claims, artistic practice can still help counteract the effects of the repressive state. Kristeva also displays what she calls her "polyvalent" side as she responds to questions about her novels, other theoretical writings, and political views.

In La Révolution du langage poétique, *you seem to discuss poetic language in the Jakobsonian sense of the term,*[1] *although with your model of different signifying practices and, especially, the text, you introduce a new understanding of the language of art: "The drive process cannot be released and carried out in narrative, much less in metalanguage or theoretical drifting. It needs a text: a destruction of the sign and representation, and hence of narrative and metalanguage, with all their lock-step, universal seriousness. To do this, however, the text must move through them; it cannot remain unaware of them but must instead seep into them, its violent rhythm unleashing them by alternating rejection and imposition."*[2] *Can "the poetic" as a term be replaced by "the textual," or is the former still to be understood as a heightened, more specifically realized version of the latter? To what extent does the reactivation of the semiotic within the symbolic bring down genre barriers or bring about changes in the artistic practices of the past?*

I began by using the term "poetic" in the sense used by Jakobson, that is, of poetic language that consists of poetry but also of prose, to the extent that it is a reordering of everyday communication. I tried to enlarge the Jakobsonian notion by understanding poetic language as the inclusion of the semiotic within the symbolic. In other words, I call semiotic the rhythms, the alliterations, the primary processes that, according to Freud, are represented in the oneiric scene—the psychic function closer to the unconscious. Charged by drives, of life and of death, this scene can pass over, can be codified within the language of communication, the language of signs constructed in grammar and logic. Once this passage is effected, once the semiotic enters the symbolic, we reach a moment of distortion, a moment of rhetorical figures, rhythms, and alliterations, what is in fact poetic language in all its particularities. This is for me an instance of both a subjective crisis and an amplification of the register of expression, since repression is overcome and the individual is exposed to his passions, while, at the same time, he becomes able to formulate them and to communicate with others. This is what I call "text." It resembles the "poetic" in the Jakobsonian sense, but my formulation includes the psychoanalytic aspect of the phenomenon, that is, the unconscious and the drives.

"The always renewed returned (which is not in the least a merely mechanical repetition) of 'materiality' in 'logic' ensures negativity a permanence

that can never be erased by the theses of a subjective and blocking desire. Thus hetereogeneity is not sublimated but is instead opened up with the symbolic that it puts in process/on trial. There it meets the historical process under way in society, brought to light by historical materialism."[3] *Am I right in reading "revolution" as both revolution and renewed returned— that is, etymologically—in which case the title of your thesis could be translated in English as* Revolution (= Return) of Poetic Language?

Yes, it is also a "return." The way in which the semiotic enters the symbolic constitutes a return, a repetition of language in its origins, in its past, and thus a regression. At the same time, it is a transformation, revolution, then, in the sense of repetition of children's language, of the repetition of oneiric regression, of the unconscious, of the most archaic elements: fear, passion, abjection—themes that are worked through in literature. It is also the elaboration of the archaic material in an outlook of revolt, insubmission, and defiance.

It seems to me that your concept of revolution, in both its connotations, can also be read intertextually with other theoretical formulations. I am thinking, for instance, of the notion of the return of the memory and of nature discussed by Adorno and Horkheimer in Dialectic of Enlightenment.[4]

Certainly, it is a Hegelian, Freudian, dialectical, and Nietzschean idea that reappears in various forms.

> The problem of art in the twentieth century is a continual confrontation with psychosis. It's necessary to see how all the great works of art—one thinks of Mallarmé, of Joyce, of Artaud, to mention only literature— are, to be brief, masterful sublimations of those crises of subjectivity which are known, in another connection, as psychotic crises. That has nothing to do with the freedom of expression of some vague kind of subjectivity which would have been there beforehand. It is, very simply, through the work and the play of signs, a crisis of subjectivity which is the basis for all creation, one which takes as its very precondition the possibility of survival.[5]

In La Révolution du langage poétique, *you define art as "the semiotization of the symbolic," and in the preceding passage you discuss creation as primarily "a crisis of subjectivity." You also define "great works of art" as "masterful" sublimations of those psychotic crises that a process of creation entails for the subject* [le sujet-en-procès]. *Does that mean that artistic practices can save or destroy? Where and how would one draw the line between the two possibilities? Is this definition of art particularly pertinent to the problem of art in the twentieth century, and if so, why?*

I would not employ the phrases "being saved" or "destroyed" by art, because that is not exactly my metaphysical conception of aesthetic practice. That said, for many writers, the experience of art was lived as a salvation. I am thinking of someone like Dostoevsky or Kafka, in particular. One can, however, give counterexamples to this; I am thinking of Nerval—whom I discuss in my book on melancholy [*Black Sun*]— who was not saved by art; that is, art did not stop him from committing suicide. We can say the same about certain great women writers, like Virginia Woolf or Sylvia Plath. More specifically, then, I think that the aesthetic process, which for psychoanalysis is a process of sublimation, consists in finding a certain harmony of the most violent drives, the life drive and the death drive. This harmony is obtained through the powers of language; an everyday language that, in the case of literature and poetry, is modified through music, through the rhythms and rhetorical figures, through pleasure, is introduced into signification that then brings about a sense of stability within (and with) the crisis. By these means, the artist prolongs the conflict and is able to live with it, but alternatively, such a harmonization can be very fragile, and when it is not accompanied by what psychoanalysis would call a "favorable transference," destruction is inevitable. This favorable transference can be a person, a group, or a society that favorably accepts with confidence and understanding. Once that is lacking, the fragility is such that very quickly this provisional harmony is swept away and with it the individual himself. In other words, this is a question that I am frequently asked in the context of psychoanalysis: do I see art as a means not of salvation, as you say, but at least of therapy? The answer is provisionally yes. But never absolutely, because as a means it is insufficient. It may help the therapeutic process, it may lead to a truth of self and to knowledge, it may even be the only possible truth, since for a lot of people there is no question of going through analysis (the analytical process is extremely demanding and to a certain extent violent), but we need to understand that it is an extremely fragile and relative medium.

Is it a problem of the twentieth century? I do not think so; I believe that it has always been a problem. Art has always been a response of harmonization of the crisis—a relative response—and the events of which I speak, the cases of Kafka, Dostoevsky, Nerval, and Virginia Woolf, are there in other centuries, in other individuals. What is perhaps different is that in our century, this problematic of individual crisis becomes more explicit; perhaps we live in a society where individual values, or individual and familial identities, are displaced irreparably and more than ever. Heidegger would say that "only a God can save us," and that is certainly a temptation or an escape/attempt. I think this is a reactive, if not reactionary, attempt and temptation. The situation is rather one of trying to live without an absolute shelter and, at the present moment, to live in a permanent crisis. In this context of permanent crisis, art is an extremely important companion, but not the only one; we must not think of it as absolute, we must make it into the God of modern times.

"The sadistic negativity of the avant-garde meets and joins forces with the 'collective furies' in the eras of the great social and artistic revolutions—and that divided junction is the condition for the great artistic realization. [. . .] A question, among others, persists: if there are moments where self-protection is the only thing possible, there are maybe others when that is not enough. Will the artist be able to be heard, and how, by those subjects that transform the process of history?"[6] *As in the third part of* La Révolution du langage poétique, *you seem to be stressing here the correlation between artistic and social revolutions. Is there any room for assuming that artistic practices can serve more than the purpose of individual well-being? Do you see any possibilities or ways in which artistic practice could have subversive or transformative effects on sociopolitical structures? Is the question you asked at the end of the 1973 article on Artaud still a valid question for you?*

Yes and no. I think that it is always valid in a totalitarian context and in the context of restrictive societies, even if they are not totalitarian— bourgeois democracies have their restrictive aspects. In this context, the calling into question of language and of the individual, which represents a microrevolution, is something that affects the social fabric and can potentially challenge to the entire social framework. We can see that in what the romantics did, in the anarchistic elements in the work of Mallarmé and the symbolists, who were linked with the political "tremors" that shook French society during and after the Commune; it is also evident in surrealism. Furthermore, it is the case of the postwar avant-garde, particularly in France, but also in the United States, where the problematics of the individual and sexual freedom was carried out in aesthetic experiences. One can even say that, closer to us, what is currently happening in Eastern European countries—the major event of last year—was caused, on the one hand, by an enormous economic crisis and the inability of the Communist party to respond to the technical developments of modern society, and, on the other hand, by the revolt of artists—from Sinyavsky to Solzhenitsyn, from Josef Brodsky to Václav Havel. Of those who were persecuted, who had challenged the regime, the majority were artists—and, of course, scientists; the one does not exclude the other. What I mean by this is that certainly the intellectual and scientific experience is incompatible with totalitarianism, but this incompatibility is perhaps greater in the intensity of the aesthetic experience that demands an extreme freedom, against all forms of convention. Consequently, all those artists were immediately positioned at the fringe of society and were among the first to question it. Therefore the fact that they are now to be found amid the democratic "figures" of the opposition, if not among the leader of democracies, like Havel, should not surprise us. That, I think, is inscribed within the lineage of the avant-garde, which is simultaneously aesthetic and political.

There is, however, a note of qualification to be added here: we live in a society today, we are in the West, I mean, which is a society of the media, a "mediatic" society, which some have called the "society of the spectacle." It is an extremely permissive society and, in a sense, pleasant and exciting; even though we are faced with enormous crises, unemployment, and so on, compared to countries of the third world or Eastern Europe we live in harmonized societies. The price to be paid for this harmony, however, is exorbitant: it is a leveling, the uniformization and elision of all differences. In such a framework, the aesthetic revolt is immediately clouded and confused. You can have your own little revolt, but it doesn't sell; nobody buys your books because nobody will publish them. Even if you do get them published, they will sell two thousand copies, they will not be a success, they will not reach the public. The symbolists' and surrealists' hopes for a new society of change that would allow the forgotten of today to be rediscovered in ten or twenty years are a thing of the past. If you are not ready today you are dead forever. Alternatively, you are taken over by the mediatic society, you are "recognized," you appear on television, but what remains are the most consensual, flat, and general elements, the least interesting, least acute and "biting" aspects of your work. In this context, then, the space is very narrow, and it is the one to which intellectuals are reduced at the moment. This does not mean, however, that one should refuse to play the game, enclosed in the ivory tower of the university, but rather that one should assume the challenge to the mediatic society and try, despite everything, to pass on a message, hoping that with time there will be an amplification of understanding in the process of reading. If, in the beginning, there is only a portion of one's work there, the intimacy of the process of reading may bring about a different and more intense discovery. That is, after all, what writing is about, an appeal to intimacy, and it is something that particularly interests me. As we have seen, this may appear to reduce the hope—too enthusiastic and too optimistic, perhaps—of the avant-garde; but in a different context, that of the society of the spectacle, one should try to modify conditions and limitations.

Your analysis of the limitations and marginalizations imposed on intellectual activity by the Western "mediatic" societies is in a sense reminiscent of the critique of the "culture industry" in the work of Adorno and Horkheimer.[7] Their formulation has been regarded as a deeply pessimistic view of the role of cultural production in Western societies. Do you share that view? Have you been at all influenced by their work?

It is true that, as intellectuals, we live in a kind of cosmopolitanism, a Babel of works; and in this sense I think there has been a reciprocal reading. I am familiar with what they have written, and in what concerns the "cultural industry" they are absolutely right, although in the analysis of aesthetic products I use different terms, I stand closer to psychoanalysis and rhetoric. Your question seems to me more useful not so much as an attempt to establish connivance among different theories in looking for what they have in common, but because it poses questions about the pertinence of aesthetic revolt. In fact, you mention that they have been regarded as extremely pessimistic in that context, and I suppose you are asking whether I hold a more optimistic view. Answering that, I would say that I *try* to be optimistic. It might be a center of illusions, but it is the position that I am obliged to take, maybe because of my experience as a therapist. When I am faced with situations of a truly human, psychic, and social misery with which I am confided, I cannot approach that with pessimism. I am committed to a possibility of change. It may not finally come about—we are often faced with failure—but nothing will be obtained if we posit that failure at the very beginning. Perhaps it is a professional conditioning to start with the idea that not everything is lost.

In what concerns contemporary art, it is evident that it is extremely reduced, that it proceeds by extremely reduced maneuvers. As I just said, it is "mediatized" and also—and this is a trap for plastic art in particular—completely taken over by the stock market and other markets. We have witnessed all the bids currently placed on artists, more notably the impressionists, the van Goghs that cost billions, the Monets, and so on. There is a whole business that flourishes and has very little to do with the aesthetic value of these objects; their value has become a question of cultural refuge, like the ancient stones or the old cathedrals whose aesthetic or subjective aspects are not analyzed but are simply means of historical placement. It is thus not by chance that objects of art are obtained for investment in the market, more so than other things, than toothpaste or even books. Why? Because these artistic objects, in their function as commodities and as what interests the dealers, are easier to shift, but also because they partake of this mystery of psychic experience, as a result of condensation, which fascinates and becomes a new form of the sacred: the sacred in the stock market, in the monetary society, in the society of the spectacle. In this sacred niche, occupied at the same time by television, Sotheby's, and Christie's, the margin for maneuvering is extremely narrow. I do not think, however, that this is a sufficient reason for giving up. I believe that one has to outwit this mechanism, this logic, that one has to accept this challenge, to assume the debate, even to accept being positioned in a minority and to try from there on to give out a message. Again, that can be done by exploring and exploiting that intimacy through which the message can be amplified, since the channels offered by the media allow very little to pass through.

In "My Memory's Hyperbole," you seem to be announcing and analyzing your recent novel Les Samouraïs *in terms of an effort to make and record history.[8] You also give a detailed account of your own development as a scholar, writer, intellectual, and analyst. At the present stage of your career, which of these terms or roles do you feel define your work most accurately?*

It is difficult to answer, because I try to have different activities. I feel very polyvalent, maybe because I am still a foreigner while living in France. I do not live according to the law of dichotomies, I do not make clear-cut choices, I live in a sort of polytopy, of kaleidoscope. I am Bulgarian in Paris, French in the United States, cosmopolitan in a way. What I enjoy more right now is writing novels. I have almost completed a new one. I think, in fact, that I have found there a form of expression that really suits me, for a few years to come, anyway, as I have various projects in mind. My analytic work, however, is very much a parallel commitment; there is no contradiction there for me. I believe that the sort of writer I am—if I am one—is indistinguishable from the analyst. Maybe those who are not analysts would write better, or worse, about the life of the 1968–90 generation, but in any case they would not have the analytical point of view, the gaze that I tried to assume and work through in the book. Currently I am working on a novel about hatred, the sort of hatred that kills people. It concerns the experience of a man in a totalitarian country, but it can also apply to democratic countries, since, in a sense, hatred is eternal. It is not solely my knowledge about life in Eastern European countries that enables me to write this book, but the knowledge of hatred that derives from the experiences of my patients. They are subjected to that hatred, and they live in a country of the West. In other words, there is a kind of permanent connection between the work of the analyst and that of the writer. Despite those points of contact, it is the analytic listening that allows me to look at the world in a specific way— less naively, perhaps, than the way a writer unexposed to that listening would regard it, with fewer illusions, maybe in a less refined manner, less beautiful, more serious, but linked with the Freudian vision.

Still, I continue to pursue my activities as a critic, as a theorist. I am in the process of writing a book on Proust and the relationship between language and sensation, which will be a discussion of Merleau-Ponty's notion of perception.[9] On the whole, this does not seem to me an exceptional phenomenon. There have been intellectuals with a similar variety of concerns—and one does not need to refer solely to the eighteenth century when most philosophers wrote novels. Maybe fewer analysts than philosophers have written novels, but I am certainly not the only one to follow a variety of interests, although I do admit that, for the moment, writing novels gives me more pleasure.

The terms polyvalence and polytopy that you just used to define your own position remind me of the persona of Joëlle Cabarus in Les Samouraïs, *espe-*

*cially in the way her presence seems to complement that of the other two
main female characters, Olga and Carole.*

It is very interesting that you speak of Joëlle, especially because the
French critics read *Les Samouraïs* exclusively in terms of the relationship
between Olga and Hervé, that is, in a very "mediatic" and French way.
They recognized Sollers, they recognized Kristeva, but they almost
completely ignored Cabarus.[10] Not only is there a polyphony of characters, between Olga, Carole, and Cabarus, who form a trio, but the
Cabarus element is for me the most lucid and central. If there are biographical connections to be found, and that particularly interests the
journalists, there is ultimately more that I have in common with Joëlle
than with Olga. We come across the same problem here that was discussed earlier; there is a lot of superficial reading. *Les Samouraïs* was
read by the press in a certain fashion, light and on the surface, but I
hope that people go further in their reading. I was confirmed in that
hope by readers' letters or by contact with people I had never met. We
have to "use" the mediatic society to the extent that it allows our work
to exist but place our confidence in the individuals who are not totally
duped by the media, who can move beyond that.

*You speak of "pleasure," at least in your own experience of writing. What
other power(s) do you ascribe to that experience?*

Primarily, it is cathartic and extremely reconstitutional for the writer. To
the extent that it deals with imagination, the writing of novels leads us
into memory, and memory proceeds from signs to perceptions, from
ideas to the body, which, in turn, allows for a kind of permanent come-
and-go that remakes the personality as a whole. I often cite Mayakovsky's
belief in resurrection—which may sound delirious, since he was an athe-
ist and a Bolshevik; it is not, however, an aberration in thinking about
literature. In the experience of imaginative writing, because of the constant passage between words and perceptions, one encounters the specter
of a bodily restructuring, of a revitalization that is extremely pleasurable
and that opens a space for the illusion of eternal life—the soul of madness. The experience in itself is extraordinary; Joyce speaks of it when he
speaks of transubstantiation. He uses these terms from the Catholic
mass; he is a Catholic himself despite the distance and irony, in the sense
of the writing experience as the passage of words into the body and vice
versa.[11] Again, it is very important for the individual. There is evidence

of that in the therapeutic role of writing and of aesthetics in general, in the use of art as a therapeutic medium in psychoanalysis. It may be a limited use, but it exists and has inspired therapy to a significant degree. I emphasize that it is limited because it is provisional. If the reader enters that alchemy of the word, he is caught up in that force, and the reading consequently becomes more than a process of comprehension and mentalization. It allows the reader to recover his own memory, his own body, and it can be a truly revitalizing experience. In this sense, it is a sort of antidepressant, since depression is a great danger in our world of performance, stress, and images of conformity.

In Les Samouraïs, *Joëlle, as an analyst and in her first-person discourse, speaks of that transformative experience:*

> *That is a miracle of analysis, of which no one ever speaks. You learn to inhabit your past so intensely that it is no longer separated from your present body, and every particle of memory is transformed into a real hallucination, into a crude perception, here and now. The astounding thing is that this quasi-mystical metamorphosis is prolonged through the patients, uniquely, of course, in those analytical moments of grace, when I am so close to them that I reconstitute them, by my speech, by my own memory, that is, my own body, that they discover as their own. For years, I have lived with a multiple body which is not truly my own, but which survives and is even transformed into the rhythm of others. Joëlle the multi-tentacled, proteiform medusa [. . .]*[12]

The preceding, and what you have just said, is also very interesting if one thinks of the prototypical artistic moment as being Dionysian, a dismemberment. Memory, then, as a re-membering reconstitutes the body having first transformed it . . .

Dislocation and reunification at the same time. It is a Dionysian and Apollonian moment, to use the Nietzschean terms, which resembles the analytical process. It is also a "journey" that can be experienced in a comprehensive and complex reading.

This discussion seems to relate to your original project of semanalysis, which was developed in your earlier work, in Séméiotiké *(1969) and in essays of that period. Already semanalysis as a term implies a blending of the semiotic practice with that of psychoanalysis. Although your concerns since then seem to be more firmly linked with psychoanalysis than with semiotics, do you still see your work—theoretical and novelistic—as pertaining to that original project? Are you still within semanalysis?*

Yes, I think so. I may be less patient now in using the same terms—maybe because I am much older—although I do use them in my teaching, when students ask me about the semiotic, the symbolic, the analysis of Mallarmé and other writers. It may assume me less, but I continue to do that patient and pedagogical work. I do think that there is a very clear continuity between this present problematic and my earlier work. If you take the books on horror, on melancholy, or on foreigners, for instance, you will find the themes that are linked to archaisms, to traumatic moments in unconscious life that were already in semiotics and that I approached through Mallarmé and Lautréamont, in a manner that was perhaps more philosophical and rhetorical than psychoanalytic but that are the same themes nevertheless.[13] I even have the impression sometimes of returning to the same subjects, myself, like that "revolution" we discussed, but always modifying them and finding other angles. In considering fiction, the writing of novels, one might think that it is a totally different thing, but for me there are links, there are bridges; it is a more a question of putting something into practice. I am concerned with the same subjects—foreignness, violence, death—but without treating them in a metalinguistic fashion. I have the ambition of looking from within.

You have recently explored the theme of love and its role in a new conception of sexual difference.[14] You have spoken of love as "the only thing that can save us," as "the space of freedom for the individual."[15] In what concerns sexual difference you have stated that "the adventure of ideas should be read against the background of a revolution in the reproduction of the species that attacks the classic conception of the sexual difference, makes women emerge aggressively, and finally leads to erotic ties around a new calm and civilizing secular cult of the child. [. . .] Political demands, of course! But also something beyond demands with their explosiveness integrated into the fabric of time, of ethics."[16] Do you see an agent of change in this hopeful redirection of concerns? What is the role of women in this context?

What I emphasized through the theme of love, of sexual difference and of the role of women, was the singularity of individuals, which seems to me to be the only interesting struggle, especially in relation to this society that stifles, that uniformizes, represented by the spectacle or the stock market. I do not imply by this a romantic cult of love, or a feminist cult of woman as the only solution. It is an insistence on difference, on singularity—an insistence on love in its specificity in the context of a society governed by professional demands and the market. It is an insistence on the women's struggle in the sense that it carries a voice of irony and defiance of the consensus, but not in the sense that it becomes a religion in itself. What interests me is love and women as voices of difference.

Speaking to Elaine Hoffman Baruch in 1984, you discussed—prophetically, it now seems—the future tendencies in European societies, in view of the threat of an "economic crisis affecting the whole world." You go on to argue that

> *there are two solutions to this. I think that this threat of a crisis, which is real, stems from the entrance of the third world on the scene, from the lack of resources, and, of course, from the way these problems are handled. Either, then, this crisis will be resolved through a war of extermination, or—and I am inclined personally to believe the second alternative—it will find a solution in, to put it brutally, sovietization. If we are lucky, our ruling groups will find reformist solutions to the internal conflicts of the Western countries, which will move the Western world in a social-democratic direction. This sort of society, at first, will have to maintain itself by relying on certain conservative forces in the domain of morality, of sex, of the relations of individuals to each other. It will have to avoid having too many explosions, too much violence, too much free acting our of desires.*[17]

Do you see anything working against this conservative tendency at the present moment? Is there a space for resistance in this framework? Is it an individual or a collective space?

This is very interesting. I forgot that I had said all this; it is indeed prophetic. . . . For the moment, I don't think there are collective forces. I believe that all the collective movements that we now see in Eastern European countries or in the third world are conservative movements. In the former, for example, there is an effort to remedy the economic misery and spiritual crisis—created in a sense by the loss of confidence in Marxism, by a return to dogmatic and archaic forms; a return to ideologies such as nationalism, a return to anti-Semitism, xenophobia, and extremely retrogressive forms of religion. In the third world, there is a revolt against the unresolved crisis, the differences between the north and the south, between the rich and the poor, but it is a revolt that has taken barbaric forms: fundamentalism, a return to the most dogmatic and deadly aspects of Islam. In this context, then, collective ideologies are reactionary and totalitarian ideologies; in the place of Marxism, ideologies in conservative and archaic forms. What collective ideology would stand against this? We have the French Revolution, we have the Rights of Man. Again, we need to explain and modify them, not make them into a religion. Often, for instance, the Rights of Man, in the name of secularity, have underestimated the difference of others. France, as a secular country, has gone to the extreme of denigrating the belief of believers. We cannot dispose of them, we need to be more subtle. We need to adapt those rights to our present situation and, even though I stand firm and convinced in my commitment to secularity, I think that we need to take into account the difference of others.

In my view, the elaboration of a collective discourse is a great project to which intellectuals, and in our case French intellectuals, can contribute by taking up the legacy of the Enlightenment, most notably of thinkers as free as Montesquieu, Voltaire, and Diderot. This would not be a repetition but an adaptation in the context of contemporary crises. We should address the theme of nationhood, of tolerance, of difference, of intransigence in the face of religion but also of comprehension of religious belief. That remains to be done. I am personally interested in the theme of nationhood and foreignness; it seems to me that the intellectuals of the left have committed a crime in totally rejecting that theme. It is certainly reactionary, but in view of the coming century we cannot leave that theme in the hands of the right, of people such as Le Pen or the fundamentalists. We need to develop a different conception of the nation in which foreigners will find a polyvalent home.[18]

In the context of art and literature, I think that they remain individual responses. The struggle there will be fought in the media, which uniformize all differences; we need to fight for these differences. How? By writing works that are accessible to the public but that will also pass messages on different levels: political, social, and moral. We also need to try to develop means of communication, through publications, television channels, or universities, which will be the forum for that work.

What do you think is the future of literary "movements" in this context? I am thinking of postmodernism, both in its claim to be the voice that disseminates difference and its function as a marketed product par excellence. Is this another example of conservative regression, positing an after-the-modern in an attempt to defuse it?

That is another mediatic notion, putting labels and announcing movements. It is inevitable in a way, you put three or four individuals in a group and you come up with a schema that simplifies the world. . . . I believe, however, that we have arrived at a period of singularity; and in that sense postmodernism allows for a diversity of concerns. It is still a label that conceals a variety of experiences that remain irreducible to the term. This is also an aspect of its marketability. Take *Les Samouraïs*, for instance: it was a best-seller, and it was received by the journalists as a postmodern project; mainly because it is not a *nouveau roman*, it is more accessible, while at the same time it tries to take into account certain modernist experiences. I do not mind that, as long as people read my work in its specificity and singularity. That said, there seems to be a conservative reaction in what concerns the—literary and theoretical—modernist experience. The recent publication of a biography of Roland Barthes, for example,[19] was used by journalists as an opportunity to put forth all the negative views of modernism that the media hold: this is a defensive and retrogressive reaction and, perhaps, an aspect of the term *postmodernism* itself. This is an attempt to reject the achievements of modernism. It may have moved too far into abstraction, it may have been at times inaccessible and too rigid, but it is impossible to analyze a text today without looking at its form in the way that structuralism and psychoanalysis did. We may need to move *beyond* that work, but in doing so we have to pass *through* it.

LITERATURE

20

On Céline: Music and the "Blunder"

This interview with Jacques Henric was published in 1976 in *Art Press International*. It provides a glimpse of Kristeva's gifts as a literary critic and complements her extensive stylistic and psychoanalytic commentary on Céline in *Powers of Horror: An Essay on Abjection*. The translation is by Ross Guberman. For Kristeva, the experience of Céline is an exemplary modern "crisis." She praises his implicit critique of formalism and rationalism as well as his ability to introduce the "maternal continent" into his writings through rhythm, music, and an emphasis on drives and the body. At the same time, she warns that a total rejection of the paternal function may result in psychosis and claims that Céline failed to recognize the positive potential of the symbolic function and of the "law" that he so harshly criticized. This "failure," as she puts it, may help explain Céline's anti-Semitic and fascist tendencies. What is needed, Kristeva believes, is a discourse that "retains what Céline has revealed to us (the repressed being of rationalism) yet acknowledges the potential of the symbolic function."

Julia Kristeva, why study Céline?
To show that our contemporaries are "deaf" and "dumb," as he put it! In other words, it seems to me that Céline's writings and experience are the only ones that portray a true *crisis*—an identity crisis, a structural

crisis, and an institutional crisis—and that is what makes them modern. Let me give another reason: despite the populist veneer of Céline's work, his writings are difficult precisely because his experience catches logic and reason off guard. This experience is Céline's, yet it is also that of the twentieth century in general because our era has put rationality into question. Céline throws us a challenge, and facing up to it entails some risk. I should also add that Céline assails all brands of formalism. It is time for us to strip the academy of any trace of the formalism that reigned supreme in the 1930s and even 1960s; formalism has become a scar of sorts because it is a contrivance aimed at explaining the experience of literature while disregarding both its subject, who lives through a horrible tragedy, and its political and social context. Finally, we should keep in mind that Céline was vehemently opposed to all sorts of Mafiosi, professions, and professionals—and these days, such opposition is extremely healthy. Céline is clearly our contemporary.

How do you view Céline's decision to use his mother's first name as a pseudonym?

I will give a two-part answer. We should remember that the person walking in the street with a driver's license in his pocket is different from the person doing the writing. For Céline, moreover, there is a clear split between the ideologue and the writer. Thus the experience of the writer is not necessarily connected to his daily life, opinions, and political views, and this split is reflected in Céline's use of a pseudonym.

So why did Céline use his mother's name? It is a difficult question to answer, but I will venture a guess. Perhaps every writer experiences writing as a sort of battle or eternal struggle with the symbolic function, a function represented by the father and by the Name of the Father. The first stage of this battle would involve the return of the repressed, itself suppressed by the symbolic function and located alongside what the mother can represent and visualize. Another stage would entail a refusal to behave like a repressed being or to assume the role of slave to a desired master, choosing instead to reappropriate the symbolic function. This second stage resembles the moment of writing that inscribes and posits the new device behind the written word. So writers find themselves wavering between a first stage, in which they identify with the maternal continent, and a second stage, in which they reappropriate the paternal function by playing the role of a son adopting a proper name. Céline's work seems to favor the first of these two stages in the writing process, which lends an intriguing touch to the portrait of his experience. On the one hand, Céline depicts brilliantly what is repressed and what is primary (music, drives, the body, and so forth). Yet on the other hand, he could be accused of "failing" (although it is only a relative failure, since I have great respect for the risks of this experience) to reappropriate the paternal function. Céline's "failure" may help explain two things that pose a problem for me: his ideological viewpoints, of course (his anti-Semitism and fascism), and his difficulty in being "positive." Céline is an apocalyptic writer, but he is less strong when he tries to be affirmative.

How is this "maternal continent" reflected in Céline's writing?

Through his insertion of rhythm and music into the discourse of everyday communication. This rhythmic element extends to the assonance of the words he uses, especially to the specific syntactic patterns of his texts. This effect is most obvious in his unduly neglected later novels *Nord* and *Rigodon,* which exhibit an uneven syntax and a reliance on ellipses that serve not to adorn the text but to show actual breaks in thought. . . . The role of slang could be interpreted in a similar fashion. I would also note how much Céline celebrates music, which is reflected in the theme of vocal phenomena. Céline's text is split apart by this vocal theme and by the themes of orientalism and drugs (in *Pont de Londres* and especially in *Guignol's Band*), all of which point to a break in the symbolic function that could ultimately result in psychosis. The text, however, is able to master this latent psychotic state through its literary devices and writing style.

You have spoken recently about the psychotic and fetishist elements that threaten the subject of poetic writing.[1]

This phenomenon has been with us for a long time. It used to be considered "mystical," "mad," or "sacred," but the increasingly secular and rationalist era of modernity has no particular code, religious or otherwise. Modern literature (and this is why it has so affected the imaginary even though we have tried to restrict it to the confines of the avant-garde) is pregnant with meaning because it puts into words what we place under the rubric of the *body.* Being a doctor, Céline was well suited to speak about the body. More important, though, he was one of the first people to understand that the body is not only a substance he could know well and examine with a doctor's eye but a signifier that holds a signified in check. I mean "check" in both senses of the word: the body as a signifier that eliminates a signified, and the body as a signifier that brings the signified into play. Therein lies the gambit of Céline's writing: will the signified be brought into play to create a plurality of meaning, an abundance of messages, a series of plots, and a symphony of significations, or will it be held in check, eliminated, and emptied? Céline's experience risks the loss of identity, which is why I mention psychosis. Yet this aesthetic experience, which occurred in a specific social context familiar with the crises I mentioned before (structural, religious, identificatory, and the like), faced a stopgap measure in what the twentieth century has put in its place and in the decline of religions: in the totalitarian systems that present themselves as orderly phenomena when they are fascist and stem from the failure of a revolution when they are Stalinist. So despite the risks I just mentioned, when such aesthetic experiences are faced with a political landscape, they often grab hold of it as if it were a life preserver, which guides them in turn toward historical notions of the past.

This provides a context for the ticklish fight between Céline and what he considered (correctly, I might add) to be the modern mainstays of symbolism: monotheism, which is rooted in Judaism, and Masonic rule. Either we address Céline's confrontation with these symbolic mainstays, or we ignore the issues at hand and let the question go unanswered. What we *should* do, however, is take the matter seriously and acknowledge first that Céline had the right to be angry about the aspects of symbolic institutions that are unjust, repressive, and arbitrary in the name of universalism, goodness, and tolerance and second that Céline's aesthetic experience failed to appreciate the essential and indispensable features of the symbolic function, which is incarnated in an archaic manner by institutions but must be renewed and adapted to our time.

Regarding Céline's anti-Semitism, his popularity offers a way to return incessantly to the problem, since as easy as it may be to say that Céline is anti-Semitic, we must realize that *everyone* is anti-Semitic. As soon as you speak about "everyone," there is anti-Semitism. I'm not implying that we should exonerate Céline, but nor do I condone the self-righteous practice of those on the left that consists in believing that touching opprobrium will make their own hands dirty.

I would say that Judaism is a discourse that emphasizes both the importance of the paternal function for the speaking being and the right to be *different*. The exodus and hardships of the Jews helped them incarnate, in other people's eyes, both this very risky right to be different and the law. One could ask if the modern symbolic experience measures up to Judaic discourse, for rationalism has not yet absorbed it. In an incisive article published in *Les Temps Modernes*, Scholem has shown that the growth of anti-Semitism in Germany has been commensurate with the growth of universalist, humanist rationality.[2] Universalist thought has denied the Jews their right to be different, and it has encouraged, at first in the name of tolerance (but only at first), the abdication of their right to be specific and unique. Since aesthetic discourse repudiates the paternal function and partakes in the illusions of socialist communities, it also ignores this truth of Judaism. So we find ourselves today needing a third stage, one that retains what Céline has revealed to us (the repressed being of rationalism) yet acknowledges the potential of the symbolic function.

Such is the problem of our modern, and decidedly post-Célinian, era. Céline is our contemporary because he makes us confront his music and his solitude. Since the discourse of Judaism assumes the right to be different and sustains the paternal function, I would say that the Jew is someone who speaks a *foreign* language and who creates meaning differently from other people, someone whose very exclusion allows a community to develop without him. Céline said these things without intending to. The music and structure of Céline's texts speak about the right to be different, but Céline didn't know it. When he failed to know this, other people knew it for him, and he sometimes appropriated their discourse. That is what he called his "blunder." Still, the internal economy of his writing runs parallel to his experience of exile and of singular negativity, *which is also the experience of the Jews in the Bible*. Regarding what I have called "socialist illusions," I must add that Céline's populist allure makes him readable and thus saves him from the trap of elitism that has hindered so many ambitious efforts in the past. At the same time, his populism is a fantasy suggesting that there is a universal of the unconscious or a community of different unconsciouses—yet a community of different unconsciouses is another way of describing a concentration camp. That is the post-Célinian message communicated to us in the aftermath of the Second World War.

When Arletty was asked to give her opinion on Céline, she answered that "since women have nothing to say about Céline, I shall remain silent."

It was once considered very important to speak as a woman. Yet I believe that when we use the word *say*, as in "I have nothing to *say*," it means that the "I" has nothing to say as a speaking being. The notion that you are speaking "as a woman" is perhaps a way to give yourself an excuse. My view of Céline's relationship to women is that he saw women as a mirage and an element of fascination. I prefer to see the woman (or the feminine element) in Céline through the rhythm and music of his writing rather than through his fantasies.[3]

21

Proust: "A Search for Our Time"

This interview was conducted by Alain Nicolas and published in *L'Humanité* in 1994. The translation is by Ross Guberman. The interview serves as a useful introduction to *Time and Sense: Proust and the Experience of Literature*, highlighting Proust's "timeliness" while emphasizing that he continues to disturb "committed intellectuals," "formalists," "conformists," and "clans and sects." Kristeva touches on some of the major themes of her book, including Proust's visionary style, unprecedented syntactic patterns, and sensorial approach to metaphor. She explains that Proust's characters are rooted in the Age of Reason and argues that psychology is not at the heart of Proust's project. She also denounces the "clannishness" of the contemporary French literary establishment and bemoans the "death of literary criticism." At the end of the interview, Kristeva suggests that Proust's "synthesis of formal study and social or metaphysical preoccupations" may offer the most promising direction for the future of the novel.

We do not talk about Proust very much these days. Is he a difficult author?
Proust is read passionately all over the world, especially by young people, who find that his texts offer a resounding response to the most pressing problems of the day, including sensuality, pain, intimacy as a privileged experience, female and male homosexuality, Catholicism,

Judaism, anti-Semitism, assimilation, our dispersal into disparate time frames, and so on. I have become aware of Proust's timeliness through personal experience: I wrote *Time and Sense* after teaching for several years in Paris, New York, Toronto, Kent, and in other universities—and Proust continues to be disturbing. He disturbs "committed intellectuals" because he pokes fun at those who want "to be one of them." He disturbs formalists because his work contains too many characters, ideas, and erotic and metaphysical debates. He also disturbs conformists, since, as one man told me after I gave a talk on my book, "Proust sees evil everywhere!" And thank God for that! And he does so with such sarcasm, but also such grace!

Finally, Proust disturbs sects. Contemporary media life in France, perhaps more than in other places, is a kaleidoscope of sects. Lacking a political, ideological, and aesthetic project and living in an environment where people enjoy disparaging the critical philosophy that has taken shape for the past few years, we are witnessing the death of literary criticism. Can you tell me the name of a single literary critic? Instead, we have seen a remarkable outbreak of groveling, reciprocation, and favors that become narcissistic and overtly sexual. We place too much stock in the confidence of our friends in order to compensate for the weakness of their work, which we nevertheless encourage. We glorify the minimalist feats of these cherished few; we are as proud of their loves, which in the end are not so secret, as we are indifferent to ideas and the world. Each little enclave has its "faithful members" who gravitate toward a Madame (or Monsieur) Verdurin, a governess or governor of arts, literature, and the sexes, because they are unable to interpret or to inspire styles and ideas. Clannishness is the childish illness of the French literary world, and even though this compartmentalization may have created and protected innovative stylistic experiences in the past, it is now hindering the development of the novel. So how could you expect this circle to be interested in Proust, who spent all his energy trying to be accepted by it, but only to poke fun at it more effectively?

And then there is psychoanalysis. Psychoanalysis is not my only means of access to the immense cathedral of Proust's work, but it guides my reading, and, after all, I am considered to be a "psychoanalyst." The clans of the literary establishment loathe the culture rebellion inspired by the psychoanalytic experience. They want to amuse and gratify one another, and they have no need for knowledge. They naturally prefer to sell "mystery," "charm," "taste, "tradition," or what have you, provided that their client remains asleep. The literary marketplace, along with the way it is overseen by the publishing industry, has become a prime fixture in the normalizing and corruptible order in which we live today. Proust was obviously poles apart from it.

Your book begins with episodes and characters familiar even to those who have never read Proust.

I use the episode of the famous "little madeleine" to offer readers a concrete entrée into Proust's work, and I then move on to the characters and their psychological complexity and social role. We see them in their relationships with the nation, with sexual problems, with religion, with the Dreyfus affair—in a word, we see them in Proust's frame of reference and in the society in which he lived. My book is addressed to those who have never read Proust, who have not read him in a long time, or who read him poorly, forgot him, and, after reading the first part of my book, may get a taste of his magic.

Nowadays, it seems that images are more attractive than books . . .

I believe that we are losing our interest in reading and that many people no longer have time for the isolation and concentration that preserve the personal space surrounding the act of reading.

I have patients who have been complaining for several years that they are unable to read. Their inability stems no doubt from their exhausting social and professional activities as well as from the hardships of life, unemployment, and other personal problems. Yet I believe that their symptom goes deeper than that, for we are witnessing a destruction of the psychic space that defines our civilization and that registers like darkroom impressions taken in from printed paper and connected with memories and sensations to create meaning.

As a result, the reader almost needs to be taken by the hand and guided into the side of Proust that is the most direct, the most accessible, and perhaps the most familiar.

The character is also a sign of recognition; it bears the connivance of the "Proustian" clan.

The construction of the character, which is no doubt underestimated by modern criticism, is also the building block of novel writing. Is it not a wonderful thing to create living beings out of words, metaphor, metonymy, syntax, meditations, and dreams? Proust sought what he called "embodied time" and transubstantiation. These terms are rooted in Catholic theology, but in his novel they point directly to the ability to use the abstract entity of language to give life to psychological or social realities.

Going beyond what he called the "descriptive literature" of the nineteenth-century realist novel, Proust wanted to return to the tradition of Characters, to the legacy of La Bruyère, Madame de Sévigné, and Saint-Simon, and to take it with him into modern-day life. His characters are both compact and inconsistent, statues and reverberations, for the narrator is both inside and outside—he "is one of them," and he pokes fun at them. These characters are caught in a whirlwind of mirth, horror, and grace.

You restore the reputation of characters thought to be unappealing or even abhorrent, such as Bloch . . .

That aspect of my book is particularly dear to me, and it is rooted in my highly personal reading of the characters. I wanted to bring to light the way Proust constructed his characters through the many drafts he completed, but I also wanted to reveal my own attitude, which ranges from love to irony.

My book is a scholarly book, a book of ideas, and a book of discussions with Proust and about literary theory, yet it is also a personal book. It takes place in the present, in French society today. Take the example of Bloch. On the one hand, even though he is clearly crude, tainted with the absurdities of the assimilated Jew in Proust's eyes, and unable to see the blunders he makes or to recognize the scorn directed at him, he succeeds despite it all.

Yet I would claim that Bloch also enjoys Proust's sympathy. A member of a rather poor Jewish family, Bloch starts off with an enormous social handicap for which he tries to compensate by becoming a staunch advocate of what he believes to be the aesthetic project of the day: "neo-Homeric language" and the Parnassian poets. His imitations of these fashions are ridiculous, but they may also show that he knows that a foreigner has little chance of being assimilated into French culture, which has no room for newcomers. Bloch finds the only available "slot"—modernity. Since trends are only temporary, the gatekeepers of literary and intellectual legitimacy feel reassured and can engage in a certain apathy or indulgence. Yet if the success of modernism ever went beyond the ephemeral and the superficial, a literary police would be brought in to keep an eye on it.

Proust's sympathy for Bloch is particularly pronounced in the salon scene in which Bloch is made to understand that he is undesirable because of the Dreyfus affair. The noble members of the salon, the troubled author tells us, speak to Bloch "as though he had been the son of a convict."[1] In the drafts, moreover, the traits that will be attributed to Bloch belong first to Swann, that is, to the beloved character, the refined aesthete, the sublime man, the narrator's alter ego. So Bloch's negative traits were initially those of a positive character, which lends them an ambiguous quality. All the characters share this polyphonic aspect, and Bloch more than the others.

With Proust, we are in the realm of a psychology that is quite "classical." What sort of reading does psychoanalysis permit?

Proust excels at exploring psychic life, and his interpretations of some dreams that I take up myself often go beyond the realm of psychoanalysis. Yet contrary to what one might think, psychology is not at the heart of Proust's novelistic investigation. Proust became very angry when people told him he was engaging in psychology; he said that his work was not "microscopic" but "telescopic." For Proust, psychology was a sure way to X-ray human beings and to go beyond appearances, roles, and masks. He compared the novelist to the X-ray operator and the geometrician because he sought to grasp the essentials, a gesture that in a philosophic sense is tantamount to the notion of Being. In my view, the experience of the novel is the only thing that can reveal the truth of meaning and the senses by discovering that the Absolute subsumes the interplay of plots, the ambiguity of characters, and the immersion of signs in sensations. Such is the dynamic of Proustian transubstantiation, which he grounds in a wonderful art of metaphor and syntax.

Metaphor is the best-known figure of Proust's style.

To the classical metaphor, usually defined as a telescoping of two different terms (for example, "the earth is blue like an orange" or "man is a reed"), Proust adds a layer of sensation. That is what he views as the ultimate "impression" that can be attained introspectively by relying on memory, by joining two moments separated in time and space, and by reuniting them in the "rings" of his hyperbolic syntax. Proust's words come in pairs (Mamma's madeleine and Aunt Léonie's madeleine, the paving-stones at Saint Mark's cathedral and the paving-stones in the Guermantes courtyard), and each of them contains at least three layers: sounds, meaning, and sensation. This formed a style that Proust called a "vision," a style in which verbal abstraction joins flesh, incarnation, and sensory and emotional experiences.

My goal is to draw the reader into the same alchemy. The world of reading, particularly where Proust is concerned, can inspire us to resuscitate this sensory experience: the smell of the hawthorns, the taste of the madeleine, the sound of Saint Mark's paving-stones or the spoons at the Guermantes home—all the little details of daily life that make up the richness of psychic life, as well as life itself.

We are also familiar with the "Proustian phrase."

The other process to which my psychoanalytic and linguistic interest in language has led me is indeed the subtlety of syntax. Everyone talks about the virtuosity of the Proustian sentence, but few have wanted to study it closely. In fact, the Proustian sentence is so rich that the syntactic theories of today, as complex as they may be, cannot account for it. I myself had to contort classical theories, including the most recent ones, before I could describe the infinite interlacings that enable the Proustian sentence to escape from the linearity of passing time and to create the highly specific temporal weaving, a weaving that makes us think of Heidegger's temporality but is deeply different from it because it goes beyond concern and into joy.

Because of this complexity, these sentences sometimes had to be put together by the editors.

Proust's early editors had a great deal of trouble, particularly with the later volumes, and they settled on a possible variation that they believed to be the most coherent. If we refer to the manuscripts, however, we see that the matter is much more complicated. We see, for instance, that the dying Proust remained vigilant until he wrote the final phrase of the novel, returning to his central themes and gradually absorbing more moving ones that he found anguishing at first. He thus managed to summarize what is essential, that is, the insertion of time into the interior of the human being. Proust's act of bringing together this train of extremely complex thoughts inside a single sentence and with a shaking, pained hand is brilliant, rare, and unique. And his ability to forgo the weakness of self-pity about his impending death is the work of a genius.

At the end of your study, are you laying out a program for the French novel and for the novelist that you are?

I liken the era in which we live to the fall of the Roman Empire, but without the promise of a new religion. I look to the novel to offer an imaginary that might correspond to this reality without accommodating the culture of the spectacle. This brings up a question: how can we write a critical, incarnate, sensory narrative that could be transmitted to the masses, a goal that has been the traditional vocation of novel?

Although I do not really establish a program, I believe that Proust's experience (which can be opposed to Mallarmé's but does not neglect the musical ambition of the avant-garde) goes in the direction of a resumption, a synthesis of formal study and social or metaphysical preoccupations. Proust's cathedral is more timely than ever.

Even though I may appear to be assimilated, my experience of the present is an experience of suffering. I feel foreign in France, and I am very sensitive to pain—in myself and in other people. This experience is reflected in my latest novel, *The Old Man and the Wolves*. I plan to undertake this writing by focusing on the "detective novel" traits of my book. The advantage of the detective novel is that it allows you to confront violence, pain, and suffering in a direct and flexible way that reaches the maximum number of people while preserving a strange world for language and reflection. My novel will be a metaphysical detective story . . .

22

On The Samurai

In this interview, Kristeva speaks candidly and at length about *The Samurai*, her first novel. The interview was published in a 1990 issue of *L'Infini*, and the translation is by Ross Guberman.[1] Kristeva explains why she wrote *The Samurai* and describes it as "popular" and "polyphonic." She also discusses some of its formal and stylistic features as well as its significance for her theoretical and psychoanalytic work, claiming that writing fiction allowed her to "compromise herself" and thus to be more attentive to her patients. Finally, she challenges the notion that her novel is similar to Simone de Beauvoir's *The Mandarins* even though she criticizes implicitly the "lukewarm" media response that both novels received. Kristeva states in conclusion that she feels closer to the "populism and religious wanderings" of a Simone Weil than to the existential "rationalism" of a Simone de Beauvoir.

With The Samurai, *your first novel, you set aside theoretical writing and turned to fiction. How do you account for this shift from theory to the novel?*
I was recently reading the manuscripts of Proust's notebooks, and I came across a question he asks in one of his drafts: "Should I make this into a novel or into a philosophical study?" People have always wondered if they should treat a subject that interests them through theory or through fiction. Is there really a choice to be made? Must we prefer one form of discourse to the other? If we think of more recent writers, we realize that *Being and Nothingness* did not prevent Sartre from writ-

ing *Nausea*. And Merleau-Ponty, who was less committed than Sartre or perhaps committed in a different way, planned to write a novel although he never did so. The imaginary could be understood to be the deep structure of concepts along with their underlying systems. The core of the symbolic lies in the fundamental drives of the signifier, that is, in sensations, perceptions, and emotions. When we translate them, we leave the realm of ideas and enter the world of fiction, which is why I sought to describe the emotional lives of intellectuals.

You will forgive me, moreover, for believing that the genius of the French people is rooted in the links they make between popular passions and the dynamics of intellectual tensions. This close relationship exists nowhere else, yet certain time periods, particularly those plagued by national depression, such as our own, place a greater distance between intellectuals and the rest of the world. I thus tried to give nonspecialists a taste of what intellectuals do and what they are like. Finally, the lewd and pervasive influence of television has forced literature to go back and forth between documentation and invention and between autobiography and fiction. Yet because the whole truth can never be known—at least, this is what psychoanalysis along with other disciplines has taught us—inserting a bit of autobiography into a narrative guarantees a grounding in reality. At the same time, another piece, a fictional one, serves as a magnet for the intense subjective bonds that connect the narrator to other people as well as to himself. As opposed to the autobiographical piece, this fictional piece releases a certain discretion and modesty while transforming real-life characters into literary models.

Why did you wait so long to shift the focus of your work to fiction?

When I finished writing my book, I realized that I had needed to acquire enough distance from myself to become a "character" before I could become an "author." And my experience with psychoanalysis may have made me aware of the banality of life and the insipid richness of everyday language, which may have enabled me to take a step back from the symbolic asceticism of theory—for the time being, that is.

In which fictional genre would you place The Samurai?

I wanted to write a *popular novel.* This may come as a surprise, especially because I wrote a story about intellectual circles. Let me explain what I mean.

For me, a popular novel is a sensual and metaphysical narrative. I mean "popular" in the sense of Victor Hugo's phrase, "That enormous crowd eager for the pure sensations of art." Today, the crowds seem to be even more enormous and eager because they are so overtly targeted by the mass media. I mean "popular" in the sense of Mallarmé's concern for the "necessary anecdote demanded by the public." I mean "popular" in the sense of Céline's claim that "in the beginning was emotion."

I wanted to rely on language to reach an infralinguistic and infra-conceptual experience consisting of emotion, sensation, and perception, an experience that could correspond to the conventions of the avant-garde and that could take shape as a source of jouissance that often remains hidden although it is occasionally acknowledged. I thus took note of Mallarmé's declaration of his aesthetic project: "In fact, it is to prolong, *joyfully if possible*, something for eternity. Let it be!" When a state of enthusiasm is attained through immediate access to an undecidable experience that appears to be less concerned with formal problems, it serves as a magnet of joy, anguish, and pain. In sum, such a state is a fusion of Eros and Thanatos seeking to create what is traditionally known as a "catharsis" for the reader as well as for the author. To put it another way, I wanted to reach the sensory core of language by sifting through a network of memories and fantasies. While I was writing my novel, I gave a course on Merleau-Ponty's *Phenomenology of Perception* and on Proust. I had the feeling that *The Samurai* offered me a way to put into practice what I was trying to communicate theoretically to my students: the connivance between words and sensory rapture.[2]

So I wrote a story about intellectual creation, the conflicts that marked the years between 1965 and 1990, and the rise and fall of different theories and intellectual preoccupations: structuralism, psycho-analysis, political positions and experiments, religions, ecology (immersion in the mother-of-pearl reflection of a salty marsh or in the beautiful birds inhabiting an island), but also feminism, motherhood, an often burning or obscene intimacy. . . . The theoretical project, the "novel of ideas," never truly disappears from the novel, but it becomes increasingly intimate and personal as the novel goes along. The story becomes simply subjective, microscopic—and ethical.

Does the story become incarnate?

Yes, particularly in the experience of motherhood, which is rejected by Carole and chosen by Olga, who views it as a quasi-pantheistic accomplishment . . .

My desire to reconstruct the sensory basis of language made me a great admirer of Colette. As to the theme of intellectual maturation, I was moved by the reflections on the body depicted in Thomas Mann's *The Magic Mountain*. Mann's novel is not very well known to French readers, who fear the weightiness of German literature, but the character of Hans Castorp is confronted with an ill body just as the Samurai contemplate erotic bodies. That said (am I simply echoing avant-garde thought here?), I sought not to build a mountain but to construct fragments, discontinuities, unexpected links, and reciprocal relationships among characters, places, and discourses. I wanted the emblem of my book to be not a mountain but an *island*, a secret island where characters could meet, an island open to all winds, the winds of other chapters as well as the winds of the interpretations that readers would use to fill the empty space between narrative sequences.

How do you think your writing compares with the "neutral writing" [écriture blanche] that Blanchot and Barthes discuss?

Roland Barthes's *Writing Degree Zero*, a book I have discussed at length and continue to admire, successfully delineates the most rigorous currents of postwar literature. With "neutral writing," the writer acts as a technician of words, a sort of Orpheus (as Blanchot says)[3] who crosses the river Styx into Hades, the hell of daily life. Along the way, he collects a few rare trophies that he transposes onto a sparse poetic text through ellipses and litotes. This sort of writing condenses impossibilities; according to Barthes, it "outlines in detail the breakup of bourgeois consciousness." I would add that it outlines in detail the breakup of all consciousness by collecting the fragments that remain and by extracting minute, modest, and extremely sparse traces. Our silent anguish latches onto these traces, and when we experience psychic catastrophes, evidence that they exist is what enables us to survive. We see this process at work, for instance, in the writings of Samuel Beckett.

An entirely different trajectory could be mapped out, one in which it is not Orpheus who descends into hell but someone such as Pluto, who lives in the underworld and returns to the surface. I think of Eurydice: rather than founder again in hell because Orpheus turned to look at her, if no one cared about her adventure and her solitude freed her from her painful experience, she would have no need to express herself in a sparse poetic discourse. Instead, she could release a plethora of sensations, an excess of sorrow as well as joy. Colette depicts a solar version of such an experience, whereas Céline paints a full-bodied portrait of horror and abjection. Finally, Varlam Shalamov, a modern Soviet writer, describes the Gulags in a dry, drab language that is technical and dull yet full and continuous—a style resembling live coverage of an event. His work focuses on commonplace anecdotes and reflects a vision saturated by evil, a vision I consider to be more "Plutonian" than "Orphic."[4]

These two forms of writing do not entail the same relationship to meaning . . .

The version I call "Plutonian" is more similar to *contagious writing,* the postmodern, communicable writing I mentioned earlier while discussing the "popular" novel. What is more, the fusion between Eros and Thanatos that inspired *The Samurai* clearly stems from Freud's conception of the psyche, a conception that precludes any idea of a rational power rooted in an existential demand. None of the characters in *The Samurai* could say that "hell is other people," for hell is inside us. Similarly, no one can ask, "Should we burn Sade?" because Sade burns inside us. Acknowledging such cruel truths may open a path to "neutral" writing, but striving for a more immediate and cathartic contagiousness and communicability can also pave the way for a writing marked by the plenitude and abundance of joy and suffering. Childlike and infantile, this sort of writing may respond to the eternal childhood lurking inside us and to our need for ghost stories and fairy tales. In *The Samurai,* Olga writes a children's book called *The Samurai.*

What role does the impossible play in your project?

The "impossible" is reflected in my book through its discontinuous composition, fragmentation, polyphony, breaks, blank spaces, and the heterogeneity that unites them all.

On pp. 214–15, you write, "The advantage of life (or a story) in the shape of a star—in which things may move without necessarily intersecting and advance without necessarily meeting, and where every day (or chapter) is a different world pretending to forget the one before—is that it corresponds to what seems to be an essential tendency in the world itself: its tendency to expand, to dilate. The big bang, which has made us what we are and will destroy us in order to write a new chapter, remembering very little of our own, is never seen more closely than in the countless rays spreading outward in a biography full of new departures. The same movement is reflected in a story that keeps making new starts, leaving the reader half disappointed, half eager: he may never find what he's looking for, but as long as progress is being made." Could this excerpt be seen as an image of the composition of your book?

Yes. At any rate, that is one way to interpret it. I wanted my *sentences* to resemble a spoken, even dreamy, breath. . . . On the other hand, I wanted the *narrative* to be composed with great care. I began by working with short and rapid sequences; I compressed the descriptions to make them appear lively and spontaneous. For example, in less than half a page, the first sentence of the novel describes Olga's leaving her country, her separation from her parents and her lover, her check-in at the airport, the flight of the Tupolev jet, her three hours of intolerable boredom, her desire for tea when she is upset, her arrival during a Parisian snowstorm, her discovery that the City of Lights doesn't exist, and her confusion upon arriving. Everything occurs in a few lines— and in one continuous breath. One might imagine a different narration in which a novelist would take fifteen pages to describe a Christmas party . . .

You wanted both to condense and to diffract?

Yes, the sequences are rapid yet dense, as if posing a challenge to the commercial spots that have familiarized us with quicker and more fragmented mental processes. I wanted to make this book into an object that was mobile, alive, and alert.

What about your unorthodox use of parentheses?

The parentheses insert and interject logical references or items left in suspense. In the dialogues, such remarks do not introduce such interpolations as "he said," "he thought," or "she answered," but encircle the name of the character who is speaking and accelerate the rhythm.

Do they also serve to revive your rhythm?

It is rather the rhythm of our time, of an age in which we live with stress and exploit it. Also, the speed at which information can be transmitted through the image has required other modes of communication to conform to cut-ins and sequential editing of this kind.

Does this offer an aesthetic advantage?

That is the challenge we face. My approach to rhythm may provide an aesthetic advantage, but it needs to be complemented by something that can be experienced only through language: meditation. Carole's letters, and particularly the diary of the psychoanalyst Joëlle Cabarus, stake out a path toward this time of reflection and interiorization. Such time moves more slowly and intimately; it characterizes the moments when Joëlle participates in her own observations, in her sessions with Carole, her patient, and even in her reading of the Stoics. This pensive time serves as a counterpoint to rapid and sequential time.

Does her diary offer an antidote to alienation?

The diary counterbalances the social world—its rhythm and its meaning.

At the same time, you paint a detailed picture of the social world.

Through speed and sequentiality, I wanted to condense a large amount of assorted information. I sought to open up the records of the theoretical debates among intellectuals and discuss certain aspects of society that continue to intrigue us, but only allusively and without falling prey to didacticism. I wanted to avoid writing a conventional novel with a linear plot, a disciplined and streamlined structure, a catchy tune . . .

You focus on a specific moment, yet you also rely on temporal duration. In fact, the condensed information you provide covers nearly twenty years of intellectual events and movements. Yet your novel exhibits still another modern device: polyphonic construction. Could you elaborate on that point?

The characters, who are modeled after real people whom the critics have had no trouble identifying,[5] turn out to be nothing more than signposts placed along a polyphonic narration. This polyphonic structure scrambles them up and rearranges them into three interwoven narrative threads, each of which pertains to one of three embroiled couples: Olga and Hervé, Carole and Martin, and Joëlle and her entourage. Olga and Hervé represent the social side of this intellectual adventure, the side that is the most bold, greedy, aggressive, and under attack, and the side that the narrator occasionally mocks. Martin and Carole represent the segment of our generation that is the most exposed and the most deeply inscribed inside the sexual and political adventure, Carole through her depression and Martin through his abandonment of anthropology for painting and his participation in sexual escapades that culminate in his death. Carole and Martin are at once polar opposites and nocturnal twins; they are the first couple's dark doubles. Finally, Joëlle and her set illustrate that polyphony is intrinsically reflexive. With her sarcastic and cynical tone, she may be the character who most closely resembles the narrator. Indeed, there is a similarity between the narrator's voice when she speaks of the Montlaurs and Joëlle's voice when she speaks of the spectacle surrounding her. Cabarus is a Freudian, but she is also a Stoic who reads Marcus Aurelius and Epictetus. She lives in a world of psychological collapse, depression, and anxiety; she is familiar with the threat of suicide and with its Stoic value. For Joëlle, knowledge may coincide with the end of the world ("if I already understand everything, I have no reason to go on, for I have reached eternity"), yet she rejects the comfort of knowledge and ventures into care—as well as pleasure. Joëlle is someone who gets through her crises and who lives more convincingly than the others in a state of sparkle and grace. At the same time, however, she experiences the discomfort that such a state can entail. She provides the link between the other two couples, whom she keeps together even as she distances herself from their emotional lives. The couples are thus granted a certain depth and an ability to go on—indefinitely. Bakhtin would say that these three couples are characterized by "dialogism."[6]

Isn't the character named Edward Dalloway also dialogic?

He has the same name as the well-known heroine of Virginia Woolf's *Mrs Dalloway*, but he displays the typical characteristics of a modern politician. At the same time, he is aware of women's fragility and has a beatnik past reflected in his fascination with Céline. Yet Edward Dalloway is himself a polyphonic character from the inside out, for he represents an element of the dialogue between the American world and the Israeli world that has captured the attention of our generation, and then introduces into the novel the complex but unavoidable relationship between modernity and Judaism. Ruth Dalloway-Goldenberg is the nomadic figure who has chosen the Law and who intrigues Olga almost as much as the figure of Dalloway does.

The United States and Israel, the polyphony of places, Paris, China . . .

The Atlantic coast, intellectual Paris, childlike and charming Paris, day-to-day life in the Luxembourg gardens: all these places make the space of the novel into kaleidoscopic images that cannot be unified and whose elements resonate with—and contaminate—one another.

Throughout your narration, the reader perceives another ambivalence, one that is rooted in tragedy and irony. Why did you include this tension in your novel?

The characters' self-irony and the narrator's ironic view of such characters as Olga, Hervé, Bréhal, Scherner, and Lauzun create a corrosive force, but also a deliberate form of sympathy and affection. At the same time, death keeps the lightness of this irony in check. A significant number of indispensable and noteworthy characters who are the true keys to the action die during the novel. In Meister Eckhart's sermon, which Sinteuil reads at Jean de Montlaur's funeral, the believer asks God that he "no longer be considered in His debt" . . . such subtle atheism at the very heart of the mystical! This sermon lends a seriousness of purpose to a narrative that I wanted to be ironic, fast-paced, and aggressive—as my life was then, and still is today.

In that context, does the experience of motherhood take on a graver hue?

The theme of motherhood can be juxtaposed with the relationship between father and son. The title of *The Samurai* refers primarily to a game that Hervé Sinteuil plays with his son, Alex. I wanted to describe fatherhood as play: not a rigid law, but a way of playing that respects the constraints of the martial arts, particularly their simulation.

Doesn't the title of the book also reflect a give-and-take relationship between the French tradition (Olga's desired and achieved assimilation) and the Far East?

Olga lays claim to this relationship with French tradition through the mere act of settling in France. She has a deep affection for the scenery of Paris and the Atlantic coast, and she is playfully fond of her in-laws. At the same time, the French tradition is eclipsed by the image of the

Far East, of China and Japan, if only because of the title of the novel and of the martial arts games that the protagonists play whether they know it or not. By juxtaposing these two civilizations, I wanted to suggest that the vitality of a culture perhaps depends on its capacity for interaction with its own memory as well as with the memory of other civilizations.

How do you reconcile psychoanalysis and literature? Therapy and fiction?

We often wonder what analysts work with and what quality or instrument destines them to become analysts. Some say that it is their ability to listen, and others say that their erogenous zones are what enable them to identify with their patients. Still others believe that analysts must open themselves up to the unconscious. All these hypotheses are probably valid, as long as the three views are combined into one; yet one could also say that analysis occurs when we are willing to compromise ourselves. Freud compromised himself to some extent by removing himself from psychiatric society and by showing an interest in sex, which was not on the list of objects deemed worthy of medical attention. All the great psychoanalytic innovators did something controversial: Lacan is well known for his surrealist and scandalous histrionics, which he introduced into analysis despite the rigidity that characterized his teaching; and Winnicott, Bion, and Klein were all iconoclastic. In different ways, they challenged the establishment through their theoretical writings, of course, but also through the lives they led, which distinguished them from those who simply repeat the orthodoxy of the moment.

I believed that I could no longer listen to the fresh perspectives and violence my patients brought to me without reducing them to what I already know or to what books written before my time had to say about them. I failed to do so at my own peril. One way to compromise yourself is to reveal yourself through a work of fiction that uncovers the different parts of the intimacy that allows you to understand other people, their pain, their perversity, and their desire to die, all of which resonate with your own. When I wrote *The Samurai*, I believed that working on the novel would allow me to continue listening to my patients in a way that was attentive, inventive, and receptive to them and to their symptoms. This type of fiction eases the rebirth of the analyst and an awakening of the unconscious that ventures beyond sublimation and revitalizes the potential of interpretation. Of course, fiction also establishes a new link with the patient, one that is endowed with both seduction and inhibition and that wagers on the patient's ability to tolerate the intense experience of transference and countertransference. Exposing ourselves when we feel the most vulnerable is a way of relying on the greatest force of this transferential relationship, on the possibility that it will be mastered and thus beneficial to the therapy.

Anne Dubreuil was an analyst, but what you have said here bears little resemblance to Simone de Beauvoir's The Mandarins, *a work to which you nevertheless refer.*

I do allude to *The Mandarins*, but also to Virginia Woolf, since Olga's lover is named Dalloway (after the novel *Mrs Dalloway*) and since Olga's musings (on Heraclitus's notion of time or on the grief that underlies our speech from childhood on) open onto a fragile and elusive territory. I must admit that on a deeper level, I feel closer to another Simone, the mystical Simone Weil, whose populism and religious wanderings are closer to my heart than is the rationalism of Simone de Beauvoir. In my view, the notion that there is some similarity between my novel and *The Mandarins* is pretentious and above all illogical, since for Joëlle Cabarus, a psychoanalyst and a Stoic, a logical error is the equivalent of a moral flaw. That said, *The Second Sex* represents for me as for many people an unforgettable lesson of feminine dignity. And Sartre's and de Beauvoir's conviction that a couple has enough room for two people still causes a scandal and poses a problem. Yet that is where the similarities end and the differences begin.

I do not believe that a rational system grounded in conscious assumptions can respond to the evils and horrors of the world. If hell is inside us, the problem is not "to avoid driving the auto workers of Billancourt to despair" but to confront the despair of depression with those who are still able to ask for help. At the same time, we must consider broad solutions to the social hierarchy, though perhaps on a more modest scale, since trying to do too much can often lead us down the wrong path. The generation of *The Samurai* was more interested in sexual difference than in equality. Motherhood is not necessarily a matter of fate, for it can also be a free choice and a source of personal and social fulfillment for the woman as well as for the couple and the child— regardless of any difficulties it may entail. Finally, such concepts as the nation, religion, and the family have mobilized the anarchist aggressiveness of the existentialists, who responded by clearing some ground for us. Yet when these concepts are analyzed and modified, they can create a barrier to barbaric behavior.

At the same time, *The Samurai* and *The Mandarins* are similar from a social perspective, starting from the lukewarm response of the media. Even though de Beauvoir's novel was awarded the Prix Goncourt, people wrote that Beauvoir was "the duchess of Beauvoir," "Sartre's muse," and the "busy-bee of existentialism." Her writing was accused of being "lax" and "haphazard" and of being tainted with "dialogues we've heard a thousand times at the Café du Commerce," "appalling syntax errors," "a language one hears in military quarters," "a style of speaking about a tired subject with your hands in pockets and a cigarette hanging out of your mouth," the work of a woman frustrated both by her belonging to her gender and her belonging to the mandarins, and so forth. The language we use today is different, of course, but the hostility and mistrust have remained and are even better organized than before. The Mandarins were men and women who were both fearful and feared. The Samurai go forward without any protection, vulnerable to myth, but also to aggression, paternalism, and disavowal. That is, unless it were merely to what Mallarmé called a "large-scale human misunderstanding," to a phenomenon at once immemorial and eternal.

PERSPECTIVES

23

Julia Kristeva Speaks Out

I wanted to give Julia Kristeva an opportunity to synthesize some of the ideas she has raised in our personal conversations and in her other interviews. We agreed that I would submit the following questions in writing so she would have ample time to compose her answers. The translation is my own. The resulting "interview" is far-reaching in scope, combining a rich reflection on "poststructuralism" and a highly personal, often biting critique of the American academy and of today's "mediatic" culture. Kristeva also offers her perspective on her work to date and a look ahead to her future projects. Of particular note are her lucid exposition of poststructuralist thought as "anti-identificatory," her claim that this "nonidentificatory" focus is more disturbing than the poststructuralists' use of esoteric language, and her description of the poststructuralist age as "an era that I would willingly describe as a time of serene enthusiasm, a time when I believed we were making a clean break from the archival culture that houses the best of contemporary knowledge and were developing an alchemy of the passions and a radiography of significations." Readers will also note her indictment of the American penchant for "political correctness" and "ultrasubjective thinking," her definition of her project as "contemplating instability, movement, and rebirth," and her remarks on the "semiotic," "female genius" and French feminism. Looking toward the next century, Kristeva remains optimistic that "transidentificatory tendencies" will be developed into a "new humanity" and into "another language, another mentality, another being—a genuine 'revolution' in mentalities and in interpretive methods comparable to the 'revolution in poetic language' I once described."

Which of your books has given you the greatest intellectual or personal pleasure?

It is impossible for me to compare the pleasures I've had in writing my books. In each case I have felt propelled by an absolute and inescapable truth, so much so that even though I was doing a million other things at the time, my life revolved around the *book I was writing*. Still, I believe that *Time and Sense* gave me a feeling of accomplishment because I was able to refine ideas about literary experience that I have been formulating for many years. I also found a sensory discourse for these ideas, no doubt because of the infectious quality of Proust's presence. In a completely different way, *The Old Man and the Wolves* left a deep impression on me because it enabled me to reveal a part of the secret of my profound debt to my father and to suffering in Bulgaria. I also realized how much this universe remains and will remain unfamiliar to French culture. For the most part and despite some notable exceptions, French culture closes its eyes to the ordeal of the former communist empire and fails to appreciate literature about pain, preferring minimalism or indifference instead. I had thought that I was "well assimilated" and almost "French," so this experience was very beneficial for me. I have since clung to the space of margin and rebellion, which at any rate is where I feel most at home.

Along with Lacan, Foucault, Derrida, and others, you are considered to be a prominent member of the "poststructuralist" group. Would you agree that this group shared a belief or a conviction that has since been put into question? If so, will it be replaced by another set of core beliefs, or is French intellectual life on the decline?

The writings of the authors you mention are unique to them alone, and they do not, in my opinion, form a group. Even so, it is extremely important to emphasize that these authors participated in a profound upheaval of mentalities and theories concentrated in France between the 1960s and the 1980s. This upheaval was unprecedented and met with great resistance—a resistance that lends these writings their apparent cohesiveness and perhaps justifies the notion of a "poststructuralist group." What was the nature of this upheaval?

In the wake of Freud, who mobilized to a varying degree the authors you mention, we took issue with the structuralist assumption that "meaning is a structure." We believed instead that meaning was a process of heterogeneous logics, a polyphony of representations, a "trial," a "dissemination," a "revolt," a "jouissance," and a "pleasure"— but also a "violence," an "abjection," and a "horror." In different ways, we tried to highlight the heterogeneous, contradictory, and multifaceted nature of the psychic apparatus, and thus of human experience itself. Our work produced a conception that broke free from what could properly be termed *identificatory thinking*. Identificatory thinking accepts the unity of man reduced to his consciousness and so enjoys dissecting human practices into psychological or sociohistorical categories that closer analysis reveals to be recapitulations of the Aristotelian categories and the theological virtues.

Our work fought against these tendencies, producing instead a vision of man and his discourse that is not "antihumanist" in the simplistic amoral sense that people have attributed to it, but it is clearly anti-identificatory. This new conception unveiled the hidden part of the iceberg, a part that proved to be quite active: a network made up of contradictions, of endless questioning, of shifts from one level of representation to another, and the like. By focusing on excesses—avant-garde writing, psychotic states, hallucinatory or oneiric states, sexualities, marginal or rebellious groups—we made passion into the unexpressed side of normalcy. We also began to reflect on the critical states of the human condition that have exploded in the crimes of our century while hiding endemically in the absurdity of everyday life and radiating sublimely in great art. Because of the work we did, moreover, an earlier vision of the world (supported by "common sense" and by a scholarly discourse limited to describing appearances, phenomena, and their relationships) consisting of psychological and sociological compartments became obsolete. We can no longer be satisfied with saying such things as, "The foreigner must become reasonably assimilated in the following ways," or "Women are human beings in equal numbers to men and must obtain the following rights." That is what is posited by the best varieties of psychosociology and the other human sciences rooted in classical reasoning. By questioning the identity of "the foreigner" or "the woman," we virtually dissolved these metaphysical notions in a series of representations, conflicts, and strategies. As a result, such ideas as the foreignness of the unconscious, the foreignness intrinsic to each of us, or the repulsion we feel toward this inherent foreignness may constitute an approach preceding any prefabricated sociohistorical analysis. Similarly, such categories as femininity and motherhood, the feminine and prelinguistic representation, the feminine and the biological, or the feminine and power may lay a foundation for a new perspective on matters that seem obvious to those who believe they know what a woman is and who hasten to offer solutions. . . . Our disintegration of metaphysical assumptions obviously required new languages that were technical at first, but they were eventually simplified and made more accessible. Although the language we used could be excessively technical at times, that is not what disturbed those who adhere to classical forms of thought. Instead, what bothered them was precisely what I have called our "nonidentificatory" approach to problems.

This approach is a mutation that went straight to the heart of the Unity that became the focal point of our culture and that we celebrate through Monotheism (the Uniqueness of the divine) and Nationalism (the unity of protection offered by national identity: "I don't know if I am, but I am one of them"). We are familiar with the fundamentalist tensions that these constructs can bring about. When the "esotericism" of our poststructuralist work is examined more closely, it proves to be an important movement that our civilization created unwittingly to counteract the identificatory tendencies that have always threatened it and that have become a visible affliction today. Those who chastise what they consider to be the excesses of modernity are not only defending corporatist privileges or protecting the elegance of an accessible rationalism from an obscure theoreticism, for they are also engaging in an identificatory defense that rejects the movement of the *analytic* thought (in the purest sense of the word connoting a "dissolution" of assumptions—"analysis" in Greek means dissolution) we are discussing here, even if not all the proponents of this way of thinking are aware of their deeper motivations.

Yet some concerned people are clearly mindful of the transidentificatory tendencies shaking up our world from biology to migration. Such people will support these tendencies despite the protectionist and fundamentalist quality of the end of this century; they are the same people who are sensitive to the modality of critical thought that has characterized the French scene in the second half of our century. I myself have experienced this break in a radical way: I feel as if a new humanity were being instituted—or unearthed. I'm speaking of another language, another mentality, another being—a genuine "revolution" in mentalities and in interpretive methods comparable to the "revolution in poetic language" I once described. This revolution is so dramatic that those who try, and are trying today, to carry it out assume a great risk to their body and spirit: they are "samurai."

I would add that it was because I believed I was participating in the emergence of a new subjectivity that I became interested in anthropology and in non-European civilizations. That is why I learned Chinese (though not well enough . . .) and participated in a certain French Maoism. During the trip to China,[1] I learned of the crimes of Chinese communism, but I saw another cultural tradition lurking beneath them (characterized by Taoism and Confucianism, by writing and gestures constituting meaning as much as if not more than the voice, by the transfusion of the self into the group and the cosmos, and so forth). This tradition resists metaphysics. I also saw a humanity that asks not to be included or excluded from universalism, but encourages us to consider different ways to be or to signify. We will speak about these alternatives again—at the end of the twenty-first century.

You know how little we remember from a book we have read, and we remember even less from an interview. If people retain one thing from our interview, I would like it to be the following: this was an era that I would willingly describe as a time of serene enthusiasm, a time when I believed we were making a clean break from the archival culture that houses the best of contemporary knowledge and were developing an alchemy of the passions and a radiography of significations. What some people believed or still believe to be gratuitous esotericism was merely a terminological principle of loyalty to the critical states we found in an individual, a society, or a text.

These premises should be developed. And they are being developed—eclectically, less visibly than before, and more cautiously. Will this decrease in enthusiasm and visibility pay off with a greater depth? We hear much about the decline of French thought, often in areas where there is no risk of falling because there never was a rise. I do not have the feeling that I am declining—and yet I live in France and even happen to be French.

It is true that we are now living in what could properly be called a Restoration. I am referring to the French regime in the first half of the nineteenth century that followed the revolutionary upsurge and Napoleonic conquests, an era marked by a social and ideological conservatism under the pretense of economic development. The contemporary Restoration we are experiencing here in France is not simply a shift from the left to the right but a general conservative tide affecting all Western democracies, and, to some extent, all forms of government. In the cultural sphere, and particularly in French culture, this Restoration has manifested itself as a return to traditional values, which feeds into nationalism, but also as a fear of critical thought, which, as we realized after the fact, truly terrorized the academic, publishing, and media establishment between the 1960s and the 1980s. In the domain that interests us, moreover, this Restoration has been manifested as a devotion to archives and museums as well as to the "good taste" and "pleasing style" that enshroud the needs of an identificatory mirror.

It is also true that the French excel at self-hatred and are the first ones to attack their own kind, beginning with those who distinguish themselves from the masses or from tradition and those who claim "not to be one of them." The good taste of the French wants to know "how can it be possible?" and banishes dissidents before it may one day banish the foreigner. Yet as I have said in another context, "Nowhere is one *more* a foreigner than in France [. . .] yet one is nowhere *better* as a foreigner than in France."[2] New ideas and various oddities are persecuted and resisted here, but that is because they are noticed, which implies that they are taken seriously. Through resistance and debate, something unacceptable can make its way in France more easily than it could in an atmosphere of apathy and indifference. Some of us have been trying, for example, to buttress the poststructuralist tenets I have outlined with an inquiry into the relationship between biology and the psyche, and, more ideologically, with an investigation of the religious bond, including the possibility—or lack thereof—of atheism. It may not be much, but I find it to be a worthy addition to today's cultural landscape, one that is divided between an extreme elevation of technique (reflected most notably in the dominance of cognitivism), a nostalgic devotion to the past (we consult archives, and scholars resuscitate philosophical masters from past centuries), and the media-driven penchant for entertainment and the spectacle.

You and I have spoken before about literary studies in the United States. What are your impressions of the American academy today, and what recommendations would you make for its future?

My image of America is twofold: it is the land of freedoms on the one hand, and the triumph of technique on the other. Since these opposites nullify one another, your country gives me the same uneasy feeling one gets from talented, awkward, and troubled adolescents: a feeling of deep familiarity and uncanniness, of confidence and fear. I appreciate the warmth and curiosity of American students, and I enjoy the periodic exchanges afforded by my status as a permanent visiting professor at Columbia University. Faced with a fresh, naive line of inquiry that is free from the pedantry of the European tradition yet full of sincere and timely concerns, I feel inspired to refine and to modify my positions. The time I spend in New York puts me at the center of a world on the move. I am placed out in the open—for better or for worse—and my relative solitude enables me to search for ideas and words adequate to this open state.

The upheaval of rationalist and humanist assumptions carried out by the recent French thought we were discussing earlier was understood first and most thoroughly in the United States—without preconceived notions, without a totalizing conservatism, and with the help of the federalist spirit that characterizes the political and academic scene in your country. Today, new ideas have a better chance of being heard in New York than at the Sorbonne or in the Parisian newspapers. The penchant for structuralism and poststructuralism of which Paris is often accused never would have existed had it not been cultivated in America, for "Parisianism" has been crystallizing for almost half a century thanks to exchanges between Paris and American universities.

The drawbacks of this warm welcome Americans give to new experiences lie in partisan simplification and technical excess. I find that the reasoning ability of American students has taken a dangerous turn for the worse during the past twenty years or so. They have abandoned argumentation, answering instead in a yes-or-no format as if they were computers or were trained to select the correct answer from a list of possibilities.[3] So they have some knowledge and can sort through information, but they do not think—they do not allow the painstaking work of doubt, style, and argumentation to make its way into their language. I am obviously overstating the nature of a threatening tendency, but it is nonetheless quite real. In a similar vein, the social, political, and psychological pain experienced by young people and by sexual, ethnic, and religious minorities has materialized in dogmatic attitudes: I am obviously referring to the phenomenon of "political correctness." Many proponents of this movement believe in good faith that they are assimilating and adapting to American life the essential ingredients of what they call, a bit simplistically, "French theory." In truth, however, their analyses are often reductive, ignoring the classical authors who provided a foundation for our work and neglecting the nuanced meanings of our writings. These proponents retreat into a devotion to purity (speaking about the providential worth of "women," "blacks," "gays and lesbians," etc.) or into the anarchy of ultrasubjective thinking (the refusal of meaning, a grossly exaggerated "deconstructivism").

Still, my hostility toward these extremes is not akin to the bitterly ironic view held by some self-righteous French circles. I am aware of the conservatism that characterizes certain circles of the American academy and of the provincial puritanism of political circles that use the "American retreat" to denounce all acts of free thought. In that sense, it is true that there is little room for a nonconformist, and there will be even less in the future since the atmosphere in America is spreading, particularly in Western democracies. I see no other solution than to resist on both fronts: to oppose a critical discourse to the defenders of the academic and political establishment by continuing to pay attention to corrosive movements in society and culture and by developing ideas able to forestall these processes, on the one hand, and to fight all forms of reductiveness with the pride and necessity of taking upon oneself the memory of the tradition, on the other. At a time when nations and continents tend to withdraw into themselves when they are not directly involved in conflicts, intellectuals have a responsibility to adopt the cosmopolitan dream of the ancient Stoics: in the megalopolis of today, we are the inheritors of all traditions; Europe and America are our common ground; let us rebuild the bridges that we have been too quick to destroy; let us avoid falling into the trap of Europhobia or Ameriphobia. If we are to improve the way we welcome those who come knocking at our doors, we must not act like depressed cultures, for only cultures filled with pride can enhance and transcend their identity cards.

Your work has had an extraordinary impact on many humanistic disciplines. What do you consider to be your most substantial contribution to contemporary intellectual inquiry?

If there is something original about me, I believe it lies in the totality of my existence: the existence of a female intellectual. Born in the Balkans during World War II, having learned French as a second language at a fairly young age, passionately interested in mathematics and astronomy, and then attracted to the human enigma—medicine and literature, choosing literature in the end, exiled in France to carry out this investigation, adopted by a universalist intelligentsia at the height of structuralism and poststructuralism, a lover, a wife, a mother, trying to think about the joy and distress that did not spare me during these states, trying to write about them . . . Roland Barthes defined this adventure very early on as that of a "foreigner," and he was right.[4] To discourage people from focusing on the nationalist sense of the word "foreigner," I would say that I am a *migrant*. I like to think that since humanity speaks, it is in a state of transit: between biology and meaning, the past and the future, pleasure and the absurd. A woman is perhaps closer to this basic transitivity because of motherhood, her bond with childhood, and her ambiguous feelings toward the social bond and toward the sacrifice it imposes (we seek a social stability rooted in sacrifice even though we turn away from it in favor of an immeasurable sensibility).

One could submit my theoretical writings to this migrant position by searching for the points of opening and crisis that make each "system" into a "living system." When I looked at the text as a "structure" to suggest that we read an "intertextuality" into it, when I proposed that we interpret "meaning" as a process and a "significance" brought into play by the two modalities of the "semiotic" (the drive representative contingent on biology and on the archaic bond with the maternal object" and the "symbolic" (the linguistic representative contingent on the oedipal stage, castration, and the paternal function), or when I suggested that we stop enclosing literature merely in the text (even though that approach is more beneficial than reductive psychological or sociological readings), discerning instead an *experience* that considers the sensations close to Being, I believe I was pursuing the same unconscious project: contemplating instability, movement, and rebirth. Melancholia and love are two paroxystic states of this transitivity, and I wrote a book about each of them. Becoming a psychoanalyst is perhaps akin to this project, though in the form of a wager: although limits and horror are what constitute the speaking being, psychoanalysis offers the possibility of rebirth.

In New Maladies of the Soul, *you state that Madame de Staël was the first female intellectual. How do you see yourself with respect to her legacy? Are you a female intellectual?*

I have an enormous amount of admiration for Madame de Staël. Her uneasiness, her need for movement, her passionate interest in men, and especially her emphasis on the unbearable nature of the feminine condition (women writers incited hatred and ridicule during the first modern republic that was revolutionary France—a republic that Necker's daughter nevertheless embraced) draw her particularly close to me. More important, though, is her extraordinarily intelligent view of literature (*De la littérature considérée dans ses rapports avec les institutions sociales* [The Influence of Literature upon Society]), of national customs, of history (I think of *Circonstances* and *Considérations*, which contain brilliant passages about modern democracies and about the standardization of the individual, as it occurs, for example, in the reign we now call the media).[5] I am even more impressed by her extraordinary conviction that despite all obstacles, the only way for a woman to remedy the incompatibility between happiness and glory is to write. Was Madame de Staël fearful, too concerned about security, marriage, and recognition? Not really. She was an enthusiast who believed that the female situation is perfectible through education, that the republic should benefit from the wit and spirit of women, and that writing is the only passion that can be cultivated to counteract internal emptiness and the abandonment of other people—to "exist beyond the self." Of course, I do not follow her sentimental forays into love, happiness, or glory. And in truth, I belong to an entirely different family of thinkers.

Madame de Staël's life and work are an excellent example of how much the world has changed since Freud, even as compared with minds as lively and rigorous as her own. As this mistress rejected by Benjamin Constant often emoted, women need support before they can hunt for other prey. The cruel mind I inherited from psychoanalysis would ask: the support of which Superego, of which father? "Glory is the radiant mourning of unhappiness," said Germaine. I should like to add that "happiness is the mourning of unhappiness."

I now feel ready to begin a study that has always fascinated me but that I have hesitated to undertake because of its difficulty: the study of contemporary "female genius." I would no doubt begin with Madame de Staël. But I would like to look at work that is more radical, less encyclopedic, and more compact: Colette and her version of freedom as a sensuality put into French words, Melanie Klein and her awareness of the psychosis endemic to the human being, Hannah Arendt at the crossroads of life (bios/zoon) and history. As you can see, they are not really "female intellectuals," since I target a woman writer as well as specialists (a psychoanalyst, a philosopher–political scientist). In the end, I love the peasantlike libertine ingénue that is Colette, but I am a member of the austere German Jewish family of Klein and Arendt. I would say that all these women think and write within the-being-of-language and that their femininity leaves a decisive mark on these thoughts. I share that ambition.

Some of your work has been controversial, such as your distinction between the semiotic and the symbolic and your skepticism about the existence of "women's writing." Have any of your ideas been misconstrued or misunderstood by the English-speaking public?

French feminists are often criticized for their lack of zeal, virulence, and even militantism. People forget about the specificity of the French tradition, which I was exposed to and so absorbed. Although all past and present societies are fundamentally misogynous (which should be considered alongside Freud's belief that the feminine is more difficult to recognize for "both sexes"), each country manifests this misogyny in its own way. And because modern French society has neither a representative government nor a collective male participation in the State, it is the first society to "combine" the two sexes in public life such that "opinion," endowed with a strong feminine component, offsets the arbitrariness of the sovereign. This aspect of French society is reflected in the art of conversation, in the role women play in the administration of wealth, and in the freeing-up of morality as well as the eminent status of libertines. In contrast, English puritanism and the liberal institutions that

America inherited establish the separation of the sexes: women are clearly set aside because of their "difference," but this difference is limited to sensibility or motherhood and does not strive for shared social participation. To put it briefly, the French side offers a "universalism" that endorses women but sacrifices their difference (the Republic that distrusts feminine singularity is therefore regressive as compared with the status of women in the eighteenth century—it will continue to propagate the universal virtues to which both men and women lay claim and is a direct descendant of this French universalism), and the Anglo-Saxon side professes a "difference" that culminates in a segregation and exclusion that will be counteracted by more logically rigorous forms of feminism developed in these countries. One could criticize the unilateral nature of these two options and speak at length about their respective benefits and advantages, yet in the end these two emancipating movements, on opposite sides of the Atlantic, are inherently incompatible.

I believe that this "universalism," of which the French are accused and to which French women are said to be too quick to "submit" with "affectation" and without regard for their best "interests," is not simply an ideological artifact. Universalism is innately contingent on the way the social contract and social restraint are inscribed in the *existence of a language*. Insofar as men and women speak, they obey the *same logic*. A major part of "values" and "rights" as well as thinking patterns and psychosexual behavior has to do with language, or the social contract, or castration, or the "universal."

Yet the process of signification is more than just a language. A complex array of nonlinguistic representations fosters the very practice of language: drive, sensation, prelanguage, rhythm, melody, and so on. These other elements go to the heart of the contemporary debate incited by cognitivism: can the complex workings of the signifying process be assimilated into a single logical system, or should we accept the idea that many logics exist, and so create models for sensation without assimilating sensation into the syntax and logic that articulate the signs of language?

I'll finish my digression there and return to the "universal" and the "different." Thinking about the feminine, but also about other cultural experiences of difference (such as poetic language and contemporary art and poetry, which are in no way mere "deviations" from the norm) led me to articulate my notion of the semiotic and symbolic. For every speaking being, the symbolic is the horizon of the "universal" bond with other members of his group and is rooted in the signs and syntax of his national language. The semiotic is transverbal: it is made up of archaic representatives of drives and the senses that depend on the mother and biology. Both men and women, in different ways according to their psychic structures and their histories, combine these components to become "different" and "universal," singular and compatible.

I have just told you how my conception of signification allows me to participate in the debate between the "universalists" and the "differentialists," and, I believe, to show that such debates are ultimately unnecessary. I want to propose a differentialist conception of the speaking subject that includes female subjects, but that considers the universal constraint *as well as* concrete ways to mark it with the exceptional nature of each subject. In this conception, women's difference is manifested inside this constraint as a difference from a group that is the other sex, but it resists the self-enclosed category of the "feminine" because I am particularly aware of what characterizes each woman. Yet this difference is also inscribed inside the universal symbolic bond, from which it would be absurd to try to exclude women.

I believe that much of what has been written in the United States about my conception has been inaccurate. People have either defined and glorified the "semiotic" as if it were a female essence or else claimed that I do not grant enough autonomy to this "essence," this "difference."[6] I hear in such reductive statements traces of the age-old debate between the "universalists" and the "differentialists." I have the impression that American feminists cling to differentialism and fan the flame of a war between the sexes that is no doubt quite real. My goal is to inscribe difference at the heart of the universal and to contribute to what is much more difficult than war: the possibility, with a little bit of luck, that men and women, two human species with sometimes conflicting desires, will find a way to understand each other.

You have spoken in the past about the way your psychoanalytic practice and novel writing have complemented your scholarly work. What projects are you planning for the next stage of your career?

Our century is at once a technical apotheosis and a time of great human distress. Through the vagaries of history, but also because I have been a woman, a lover, a wife, and a mother, this distress has had repercussions for me and will continue to do so. What is at stake here is not female masochism or what is known as such. Yet it is true that if a woman manages to overcome disarray, she gains a disillusioned ability to understand the critical states of beings and the world. The thoughts her energy unfolds convey an intense pleasure to her soul and mean more to her than happiness does.

I would thus like to continue my psychoanalytic studies on the borderline states of what can be represented psychically and on the conflicts between soma and the psyche. At the same time, fiction has become an indispensable way for me to keep my unconscious open, which is necessary for liberty and vitality—not only because I am a psychoanalyst but so that "death will not live a human life." My next novel, *Possessions,* is a metaphysical detective story in which the cadaver of a decapitated female translator is found in Santa Barbara. Like all novels, it is an autobiographical work.

EDITOR'S INTRODUCTION

1. In the introduction to her recent book-length study on Kristeva, Kelly Oliver notes astutely that Kristeva's critics have often taken "extreme" positions that reduce Kristeva's work to mutually exclusive categories. Oliver points out that Kristeva's work has been described as both "essentialist" and antiessentialist, as promoting "anarchy" and as "conservative or even fascist," as "open[ing] up the possibility of change" and as "clos[ing] off the possibility of change," as "ahistorical" and as "fundamentally concerned with [. . .] history," as "useful for feminism" and as "not [useful]," and so on. See Kelly Oliver, *Reading Kristeva*, pp. 1–2.

2. Several important essays from these two books have been translated into English in *Desire in Language: A Semiotic Approach to Literature and Art*.

3. *Remembrance of Things Past* 3:944.

4. See "Julia Kristeva Speaks Out."

Profiles

I. JULIA KRISTEVA IN PERSON

1. *Ed.: Strangers to Ourselves.*

2. *Ed.:* Kristeva wrote a moving tribute to Sofia for a *Le Nouvel observateur* piece on European cultural capitals. See "Memories of Sofia."

3. *Ed.:* This presentation became Kristeva's first published article. It appeared as "Bakhtine, le mot, le dialogue et le roman" in an April 1967 issue of *Critique*. The article was reprinted in *Séméiotiké* and subsequently translated as "Word, Dialogue, and Novel" in *Desire in Language* and in *The Kristeva Reader*.

4. *Ed.:* Kristeva eventually wrote a thesis on this topic that was published as *Le Texte du roman*. An essay from this work entitled "From Symbol to Sign" is included in *The Kristeva Reader*.

5. *Ed.:* Kriseva and Tzvétan Todorov introduced Bakhtin to the West.

6. *Ed.:* In the spring of 1974, Kristeva went with Roland Barthes, Philippe Sollers, Marcelin Pleynet, and François Wahl on a much-publicized trip to China. She discusses some of her observations in "Women Is Never What We Say" and, more extensively, in *About Chinese Women.*

7. *Ed.:* Included in the present book.

8. *Ed.:* See "Remarques sur la fonction du langage dans la découverte freudienne," in *Problèmes de la linguistique générale* 1:75–87.

9. *Ed.:* In the end, Lacan did not join the Tel Quel members on their trip to China.

10. *Ed.:* See "Stabat Mater" in *Tales of Love* and *The Kristeva Reader.*

11. *Ed.:* See *New Maladies of the Soul.*

2. INTELLECTUAL ROOTS

1. *Ed.:* Borrowing from Nietzsche by way of Philippe Sollers, Kristeva contrasts "monumental history" with teleological, linear, and "cursive" history. See "Semiotics: A Critical Science and/or a Critique of Science," in *The Kristeva Reader,* and "Women's Time," in *The Kristeva Reader* and in *New Maladies of the Soul.*

3. A CONVERSATION WITH JULIA KRISTEVA

1. *Ed.:* On Kristeva's notion of intertextuality, see "Intertextuality and Literary Interpretation," and n. 3 of that interview.

2. *Ed.:* See, for example, *Powers of Horror, Tales of Love,* and *Black Sun.*

3. *Ed.:* Kristeva is referring here to Freud's discussion of word-presentations and thing-presentations in appendix C of the metapsychology papers in *Standard Edition* 14:209–16.

4. Special issue, "The Politics of Interpretation," *Critical Inquiry,* p. 278. *Ed.:* Kristeva has a piece in the same issue entitled "Psychoanalysis and the Polis." It is reprinted in *The Kristeva Reader.*

5. *Ed.:* This article was published as "The Ethics of Linguistics" in *Desire in Language.*

6. *Ed.:* Kristeva's notion of *le sujet-en-procès* plays on both meanings of *procès.* The Kristevean subject, then, is both a subject-in-process and a subject-on-trial.

7. *Ed.:* Kristeva analyzes the Don Juan myth in *Tales of Love,* in a chapter entitled "Don Juan, or Loving to Be Able To."

8. *Ed.:* More specifically, Culler claims that Kristeva's notion of the genotext can be linked to Derrida's remarks on the absence of an ultimate meaning and the free play of signification: "In the absence of any primitive notion of the meanings or effects of a text (any judgment of this kind would repre-

sent, in [Kristeva's] view, an insidious foreclosure which tried to establish a norm), there is nothing to limit the play of meaning" (p. 247). Culler's criticism seems off base, however, for just as the "semiotic" is always already inscribed in the "symbolic," the "genotext" is inseparable from the "phenotext," that is, from the signifying process that "obeys the rules of communication and presupposes a subject of enunciation and an addressee" (*Revolution*, p. 84). The genotext, moreover, is a process of signification comparable to Freud's primary processes; it is not a method of interpretation. See chap. 10 of *Revolution in Poetic Language* ("Genotext and Phenotext") as well as "L'Engendrement de la formule" in *Séméiotiké*.

9. *Ed.:* The article from *Séméiotiké* to which the interviewer is referring was published as "Semiotics: A Critical Science and/or a Critique of Science" in *The Kristeva Reader*. Kristeva says the following: "Literature does not exist for semiotics. It does not exist as an utterance [parole] like others and even less as an aesthetic object. It is a *particular semiotic practice* which has the advantage of making more accessible than others the problematics of the production of meaning posed by a new semiotics, and consequently it is of interest only to the extent that it ('literature') is envisaged as irreducible to the level of an object for normative linguistics" (p. 86).

10. *Ed.:* This interview has been translated as "Woman Is Never What We Say" and included in the present volume.

4. CULTURAL STRANGENESS AND THE SUBJECT IN CRISIS

1. *Ed.:* See n. 6 in "A Conversation with Julia Kristeva."

2. *Ed.:* Included in the present book.

3. *Ed.:* See "A Society on the Move: Intellectuals in America" in the present book.

4. *Ed.:* See n. 7 in "A Conversation with Julia Kristeva."

5. *Ed.:* See "The Ethics and Practice of Love."

6. *Ed.:* See n. 3 in "Julia Kristeva in Person."

7. *Ed.:* See "Intertextuality and Literary Interpretation," and n. 3 of that interview.

8. *Ed.:* "Stabat Mater," in *Tales of Love* and *The Kristeva Reader*.

Psychoanalysis

5. THE ETHICS AND PRACTICE OF LOVE

1. *Ed.:* See D. A. Winnicott, "Transitional Objects and Transitional Phenomena."

2. *Ed.: Standard Edition* 21:1–56.

6. MELANCHOLIA AND CREATION

1. *Ed.: Standard Edition* 14:237–58.
2. *Ed.:* Ibid., 18:1–64.

7. NEW MALADIES OF THE SOUL

1. *Ed.: Standard Edition* 19:1–66.
2. *Ed.:* Marcel Proust, *Remembrance of Things Past* 3:944.

Women

8. WOMAN IS NEVER WHAT WE SAY

1. *Ed.:* This interview was partly translated by Marilyn August as "Woman Can Never Be Defined" and published in Elaine Marks and Isabelle de Courtivron, *New French Feminisms.*

2. *Ed.:* Kristeva's resistance to posit a female subject has been a contentious point for some Anglo-Saxon feminists. For a hostile account, see Nancy Fraser, "The Uses and Abuses of French Discourse Theories for Feminist Politics." For a reasoned and thoughtful approach, see Alice Jardine, "Opaque Texts and Transparent Contexts: The Political Difference of Julia Kristeva," and Martha Reineke, "Life Sentences: Kristeva and the Limits of Modernism." For a more extensive discussion, see Toril Moi, *Sexual/Textual Politics.*

3. *Ed.:* See n. 6 in "Julia Kristeva in Person."

4. *Ed.: Des Chinoises,* translated into English as *About Chinese Women.*

5. *Ed.:* Kristeva's best-known discussion of feminism is an essay entitled "Women's Time" that has been published in a translation by Alice Jardine and Harry Blake in *The Kristeva Reader* and in a translation by Ross Guberman in *New Maladies of the Soul.* For an excellent overview, see Alice Jardine, "Introduction to Julia Kristeva's 'Women's Time.' "

9. "UNES FEMMES": THE WOMAN EFFECT

1. On the "semiotic" and the "symbolic" and problems of modern art as they relate to the crisis of the State, the family, and religion in the West, see J. Kristeva, *La révolution du langage poétique. Ed.:* The crisis of the State, the family, and religion is discussed in the untranslated portion of *La révolution du langage poétique.*

2. *Ed.:* Kristeva uses the term *negativity* in its Hegelian and Freudian sense, calling it a process that functions as the fourth term in the Hegelian dialectic. See the section entitled "Negativity: Rejection" in *Revolution in Poetic Language.* See also Philip Lewis, "Revolutionary Semiotics."

3. See Michéle Mattelart, "Le Coup d'Etat au féminin."

4. *Ed.:* See Jacques Lacan, "Le complexe, facteur concret de la psych-

analyse familiale" and "Les complexes familiaux en pathologie," in
Encyclopédie française 8.40.5–16 and 8.42.1–8.

10. FEMINISM AND PSYCHOANALYSIS

1. *Ed.:* The interview was reprinted with some minor changes in E. H. Baruch and L. Serrano, *Women Analyze Women in France, England, and the United States.*

2. *Ed.:* See "Women Is Never What We Say."

3. *Ed.:* Most likely *pulsions* in the original, or "drives."

4. *Ed.:* In addition to *Powers of Horror*, see J. Kristeva, "Approaching Abjection."

11. WOMEN AND LITERARY INSTITUTIONS

1. *Revolution in Poetic Language.*

2. The woman in question is Patricia Goldman-Rakic. See P. S. Goldman and P. T. Rakic, "Impact of the Outside World upon the Developing Primate Brain," and P. S. Golman-Rakic et al., "The Neurobiology of Cognitive Development."

3. In French, the human sciences refer to a combination of the social sciences and humanities where there is a specific focus on "the human"—e.g., anthropology, psychology, linguistics, literature, etc.

4. In English in this interview.

Culture

12. MEMORIES OF SOFIA

1. *Ed.:* Kristeva is referring here to her father, who died in a Sofia hospital. See *The Old Man and the Wolves.*

13. AMERICA: A SOCIETY ON THE MOVE

1. *Ed.:* Kristeva uses Lacan's scandalous phrase here: "Il n'y a pas de rapport sexuel" (literally, "There is no sexual relationship").

14. PSYCHOANALYSIS AND POLITICS

1. *Ed.:* See *About Chinese Women.*

2. *Ed.:* See n. 3, "Julia Kristeva in Person."

3. *Ed.:* *Rabelais and His World* and *Problems of Dostoevsky's Poetics.*

4. *Ed.:* See, for example, Hannah Arendt, *Essays in Understanding, 1930–1954* and *The Human Condition.*

15. INTERVIEW: The Old Man and the Wolves

1. *Ed.:* See *Remembrance of Things Past* 3:924–25.

2. *Ed.:* See *Nations Without Nationalism.*

16. GENERAL PRINCIPLES IN SEMIOTICS

1. *Ed.:* See R. Thom, *Modèles mathématiques de la morphogenèse.*

2. *Ed.:* See L. A. Zadeh, *Fuzzy Sets and Decision Analysis.*

3. E. Benveniste, "Structuralisme et linguistique," in *Problèmes de la linguistique générale* 2:11–28.

4. "Le 'langage poétique' chinois," pp. 47–75.

5. *Ed.:* This is most likely an allusion to Jacques Derrida. As Toril Moi explains, "Kristeva's disparaging remark about philosophers who retain only the 'notion of analysis as *dissolution*, and write in a style similar to that of an outmoded *avant-garde* such as symbolism' ('A New Type of Intellectual: The Dissident' [*The Kristeva Reader*, p. 300]), alludes to [a] critique of Derrida, the implication being that if Derrida in the late 1970s writes like Mallarmé in 1890, his work is less subversive than some would have it" (introduction to *The Kristeva Reader*, p. 17).

6. *Ed.:* See chap. 5, "The Thetic: Rupture and/or Boundary," in Julia Kristeva, *Revolution in Poetic Language.*

7. *Polylogue*, p. 8.

8. Ibid., p. 7.

9. *Ed.:* For further readings on Kristeva's theoretical approach to semiotics and semiology, and a presentation of what she terms "semanalysis," see "The System and the Speaking Subject," "From Symbol to Sign," and "Semiotics: A Critical Science and/or a Critique of Science," in *The Kristeva Reader; Séméiotiké;* and Kristeva's three essays in *La Traversée des signes.* For "applied" semiological studies, see the untranslated portion of *Révolution du language poétique* as well as *Polylogue* and *Desire in Language.*

17. INTERTEXTUALITY AND LITERARY INTERPRETATION

1. *Ed.:* See n. 3, "Julia Kristeva in Person."

2. *Ed.:* See M. Bakhtin, *Rabelais and His World* and *Problems of Dostoevsky's Poetics.* Kristeva, along with Tzvétan Todorov, introduced Bakhtin's work to the West.

3. *Ed.:* On Kristeva's notion of intertextuality, see her "L'Intertextualité," in *Le Texte du roman;* "Poésie et négativité" and "L'Engendrement de la formule," in *Séméiotiké;* "Word, Dialogue, Novel," in *The Kristeva Reader;* and "Breaching the Thetic: Mimesis," in *Revolution in Poetic Language.* For an excellent overview, see C. M. Johnson, "Intertextuality and the Psychical Model."

4. *Ed.: Soleil Noir: Dépression et mélancholia,* translated as *Black Sun: Depression and Melancholia.*

5. *Ed.:* Most likely "Mémoire."

6. *Ed.:* Translated as "Stabat Mater" in *The Kristeva Reader*.

7. *Ed.:* See Julia Kristeva, "The Father, Love, and Banishment," in *Desire in Language*.

18. READING AND WRITING

1. *Ed.:* See Pascal, *Pensées*, fragments 135–39 in the Lafuma edition, or fragments 139–43 in the Brunschvicg edition.

19. AVANT-GARDE PRACTICE

1. *Ed.:* In "Metalanguage as a Linguistic Problem" (*Selected Writings* 7:113–21), the well-known essay in which Jakobson posits his six functions of language, Jakobson defines poetic language as the function that emphasizes the "message" for its own sake, and he maintains that poetry and poetic language are not one and the same.

2. *Revolution*, p. 103

3. Ibid., p. 191.

4. T. Adorno and M. Horkheimer, *Dialectic of Enlightenment*.

5. E. H. Baruch and P. Meisel, "Two Interviews with Julia Kristeva," in *Partisan Review. Ed.:* Both these interviews are included in the present book.

6. Julia Kristeva, "Le Sujet-en-procès," p. 108 (author's translation). *Ed.:* This article was reprinted in *Polylogue*.

7. *Dialectic of Enlightenment*, esp. "The Culture Industry: Enlightenment as Mass Deception," pp. 129–67.

8. "Making history now appears to me [. . .] a task that, if it has not become impossible, has not been displaced. Rather than compiling 'archives,' other questions make us stretch meaning into fiction. [. . .] What follows, then, will be an autobiography in the first person plural, a "we" of complicity, friendship, love." *My Memory's Hyperbole*, p. 262.

9. *Ed.:* See *Time and Sense: Proust and the Experience of Literature*.

10. Kristeva is referring here to the fact that the reception of her novel was to a large extent based on biographical information, the "spotting" of familiar names. Olga's and Hervé's relationship was thus identified as Kristeva's relationship with her husband, Philippe Sollers, the famous writer and theorist. Other famous—or notorious—characters include Roland Barthes as Bréhal, Claude Lévi-Strauss as Strich-Meyer, Jacques Lacan as Lauzun, Emile Benveniste as Benserade, Jacques Derrida as Saïda, and Michel Foucault as Scherner.

11. *Ed.:* See "Joyce 'The Gracehoper' or Orpheus's Return," in *New Maladies of the Soul*.

12. *Les Samouraïs*, pp. 171–72 (author's translation).

13. *Ed.:* See *Powers of Horror, Black Sun,* and *Strangers to Ourselves.*

14. *Ed.:* See *Tales of Love* and *In the Beginning Was Love: Psychoanalysis and Faith.*

15. "Two Interviews," p. 127.

16. "My Memory's Hyperbole," p. 263.

17. "Two Interviews," pp. 126–27.

18. *Ed.:* See J. Kristeva, *Nations Without Nationalism.*

19. *Ed.:* This biography was translated into English as *Roland Barthes: A Biography.*

Literature

20. ON CÉLINE: MUSIC AND THE "BLUNDER"

1. *Ed.:* See *Revolution in Poetic Language.*

2. *Ed.:* See Scholem, *On Jews and Judaism in Crisis: Selected Essays.*

3. *Ed.:* For further readings on Céline, see J. Kristeva, "Actualité de Céline;" *Powers of Horror;* and "Psychoanalysis and the Polis" in *The Kristeva Reader.*

21. PROUST: "A SEARCH FOR OUR TIME"

1. *Ed.: Remembrance of Things Past* 2:255.

22. ON *The Samurai*

1. *Ed.:* This interview has been previously translated by Léon Roudiez as "Concerning *The Samurai*" and published in *Nations Without Nationalism.*

2. *Ed.:* See *Time and Sense: Proust and the Experience of Literature.*

3. *Ed.:* See M. Blanchot, "The Gaze of Orpheus."

4. *Ed.:* For an English translation of Shalamov's work, see *Graphite.*

5. *Ed.:* See n. 10, "Avant-Garde Practice."

6. *Ed.:* See M. Bakhtin, *Rabelais and His World* and *Problems of Dostoevsky's Poetics.*

Perspectives

23. JULIA KRISTEVA SPEAKS OUT

1. *Ed.:* See n. 6, "Julia Kristeva in Person."

2. *Ed.: Strangers to Ourselves,* pp. 38–39.

3. *Ed.:* Kristeva appears to be referring here to a tendency reflected in an anecdote she has recounted to me. Invited to speak at a major American university, she proceeded to give a talk on Montesquieu's complex views on the individual and the community. Members of the audience immediately shot up their hands and exclaimed, "How can you speak of Montesquieu! He's a racist,

sexist, imperialist, homophobe . . ." As the discussion continued, it became clear that no one in the audience had ever read a word of Montesquieu. It is because of incidents such as these that several well-known members of the French intellegentsia have expressed publicly their extremely hostile (and perhaps one-sided) view of what they call American "political correctness."

4. *Ed.:* See Roland Barthes, "L'Etrangère" (translated as "Kristeva's *Séméiotiké*"). "History and form, the science of signs and the destruction of the sign: it is all these fine antitheses, comfortable, conformist, stubborn, and self-assured, which the work of Julia Kristeva cuts across, scarring our young semiotic science with a *foreign* mark, in accord with the first sentence of *Séméiotiké*: '*To make language into work*, to work in the materiality of what, for society, is a means of contact and of comprehension—is this not to make oneself, from the start, foreign to language?' " (p. 171).

5. *Ed.: Des Circonstances actuelles qui peuvent terminer la Révolution et des principes qui doivent fonder la République en France; Considérations sur les principaux événements de la révolution française.*

6. Ed. See, for example, Nancy Fraser, "The Uses and Abuses of French Discourse Theories for Feminist Politics"; and Ann Rosalind Jones, "Julia Kristeva on Femininity: The Limits of a Semiotic Politics." For a vituperative reading of the "semiotic," see Jennifer Stone, "The Horrors of Power: A Critique of Kristeva." For a discussion supporting Kristeva's claim, see Pam Morris, "Re-Routing Kristeva: From Pessimism to Parody."

INTERVIEWS WITH KRISTEVA

Baruch, E. H., and P. Meisel. "Two Interviews with Julia Kristeva." Trans. Brom Anderson and Margaret Waller. *Partisan Review* 51, no. 1 (1984): 120–32.

Bauer, C., and P. Oullet. "De la généralité sémiotique." *Etudes littéraires* 10, no. 3 (December 1977): 337–46.

Bélorgey, E. "A propos des *Samouraïs*." *L'Infini* 30 (Summer 1990): 56–66.

Boucquey, E. "unes femmes." *Les Cahiers du GRIF* 7 (1975): 22–27.

Clark, S., and K. Hulley. "An Interview with Julia Kristeva: Cultural Strangeness and the Subject in Crisis." *Discourse: Journal for Theoretical Studies in Media and Culture* 13, no. 1 (Fall–Winter 1990–91): 149–80.

Collin, F. "Entretien avec Julia Kristeva." *Les Cahiers du GRIF* 32 (1985): 7–23.

Francblin, C. "Deux témoinages sur la société en mouvement: les intellectuels divisés." *Art Press International* 1 (Summer 1976): 2–3.

———. "*Les nouvelles maladies de l'âme*." *Art Press International* 178 (March 1993): 58–60. Reprinted in *L'Infini* 42 (Summer 1993): 67–73.

Gavronsky, S. "Interview with Julia Kristeva." *Pequod: A Journal of Contemporary Literature and Literary Criticism* 35 (1993): 182–89.

Grisoni, D. "Les Abîmes de l'âme." *Magazine littéraire* 244 (July–August 1987): 16–18.

Henric, J. "La Musique et 'la gaffe.' " *Art Press International* 2 (November 1976): 10–11.

Jardine, A., and A. Menke. "Julia Kristeva." In A. Jardine and A. Menke, eds., *Shifting Scenes: Interviews on Women, Writing, and Politics in Post-68 France*, pp. 113–24. New York: Columbia University Press, 1993.

Kolocotroni, V. "Interview with Julia Kristeva." *Textual Practice* 5, no. 2 (Summer 1991): 157–70.

Kurzweil, E. "An Interview with Julia Kristeva." *Partisan Review* 53, no. 2 (1986): 216–29.

Lipkowitz, I., and A. Loselle. "Interview with Julia Kristeva." With an introduction by Martha Buskirk. *Critical Texts* 3, no. 3 (Spring–Summer 1986): 3–13.

Nicolas, A. "Kristeva: Proust 'une recherche pour notre temps.' " *L'Humanité* (May 27, 1994): 18–19.

"Psych et Po." "La femme, ce n'est jamais ça." *Tel Quel* 59 (1974): 19–24.

Sichère, B. "Roman noir et temps présent." *L'Infini* 37 (Spring 1992): 75–86.

"Sofia." *Le Nouvel observateur* 13, special issue on European cultural capitals (1992): 37–37.

Waller, M. "An Interview with Julia Kristeva." In P. O'Donnell and R. C. Davis, *Intertextuality and Contemporary American Fiction*, pp. 280–93. Baltimore: Johns Hopkins University Press, 1989.

BOOKS BY KRISTEVA

About Chinese Women. London: Marion Boyars, 1986.

Black Sun: Depression and Melancholia. Trans. Léon Roudiez. New York: Columbia University Press, 1989.

Desire in Language: A Semiotic Approach to Literature and Art. Trans. Thomas Gora, Alice Jardine, and Léon Roudiez. Ed. Léon Roudiez. New York: Columbia University Press, 1980.

In the Beginning Was Love: Psychoanalysis and Faith. Trans. Arthur Goldhammer. New York: Columbia University Press, 1988.

The Kristeva Reader. Ed. Toril Moi. New York: Columbia University Press, 1986.

Language: The Unknown. New York: Columbia University Press, 1992.

New Maladies of the Soul. Trans. Ross Guberman. New York: Columbia University Press, 1995.

The Old Man and the Wolves. Trans. Barbara Bray. New York: Columbia University Press, 1993.

Polylogue. Paris: Editions du Seuil, 1977.

Powers of Horror: An Essay on Abjection. Trans. Léon Roudiez. New York: Columbia University Press, 1982.

Revolution in Poetic Language. Trans. Margaret Waller. New York: Columbia University Press, 1984.

La Révolution du langage poétique: L'avant-garde à la fin du XIXème siècle: Lautréamont et Mallarmé. Paris: Editions du Seuil, 1974.

The Samurai. Trans. Barbara Bray. New York: Columbia University Press, 1992.

Séméiotiké: Recherches pour une sémanalyse. Paris: Editions du Seuil, 1974.

Strangers to Ourselves. Trans. Léon Roudiez. New York: Columbia University Press, 1991.

Tales of Love. New York: Columbia University Press, 1987.

Le Texte du roman: Approche sémiotique d'une structure discursive transforma-tionnelle. The Hague: Mouton, 1970.

Time and Sense: Proust and the Experience of Literature. Trans. Ross Guberman. New York: Columbia University Press, 1996.

La Traversée des signes. Ed. Julia Kristeva. Paris: Edition du Seuil, 1975.

ESSAYS AND ARTICLES BY KRISTEVA

"Actualité de Céline." *Tel Quel* 71/73 (Fall 1977): 45–52.

"Approaching Abjection." Trans. John Lechthe. *Oxford Literary Review* 5 (1982): 125–49.

"Bakhtine, le mot, le dialogue et le roman." *Critique* 21, no. 14 (April 1967).

"Le Sujet-en-procès." In P. Sollers, ed., *Artaud.* Paris: U.G.E., 10/18, 1973.

"Mémoire." *L'Infini* 1 (1983): 39–54.

"My Memory's Hyperbole." Trans. Athena Viscusi. In D. C. Stanton, ed. *The Female Autograph: Theory and Practice of Autobiography from the Tenth to the Twentieth Century.* Chicago: University of Chicago Press, 1984.

BOOKS AND ESSAYS ON KRISTEVA

Barthes, R. "L'Etrangère." *La Quinzaine Littéraire* 94 (May 1–15, 1970): 19–20. Trans. as "Kristeva's *Séméiotikè*" in R. Barthes, *The Rustle of Language,* trans. Richard Howard. New York: Hill and Wang, 1986.

Butler, J. "The Body Politics of Julia Kristeva." *Hypatia* 3, no. 3 (Winter 1989): 104–18.

Fraser, N. "The Uses and Abuses of French Discourse Theories for Feminist Politics." *Boundary 2: An International Journal of Literature and Culture* 17, no. 2 (Summer 1990): 82–101.

Jardine, A. "Introduction to Julia Kristeva's 'Women's Time.' " *Signs: Journal of Women in Culture and Society* 7, no. 1 (Autumn 1981): 5–12.

———. "Opaque Texts and Transparent Contexts: The Political Difference of Julia Kristeva." In *The Poetics of Gender,* ed. Nancy K. Miller. New York: Columbia University Press, 1986.

Johnson, C. M. "Intertextuality and the Psychical Model." *Paragraph: A Journal of Modern Critical Theory* 11, no. 1 (March 1988): 71–89.

Jones, A. R. "Julia Kristeva on Femininity: The Limits of a Semiotic Politics." *Feminist Review* 7, no. 1 (Spring 1981): 247–63.

Lewis, P. "Revolutionary Semiotics." *Diacritics* 4, no. 3 (Fall 1974): 28–32.

Millet, K. *Sexual Politics.* New York: Ballantine, 1978.

Moi, T. *Sexual/Textual Politics: Feminist Literary Theory.* London: Methuen, 1985.

Morris, P. "Re-Routing Kristeva: From Pessimism to Parody." *Textual Practice* 6, no. 1 (Spring 1992): 31–46.

Oliver, K. *Reading Kristeva: Unraveling the Double Bind.* Bloomington: Indiana University Press, 1993.

Reineke, M. "Life Sentences: Kristeva and the Limits of Modernism." *Soundings: An Interdisciplinary Journal* 71, no. 4 (Winter 1988): 439–61.

Stone, J. "The Horrors of Power: A Critique of Kristeva." In *The Politics of Theory: Proceedings of the Essex Conference on the Sociology of Literature, July 1982,* ed. Francis Barker et al., pp. 38–48. Colchester: University of Essex, 1983.

OTHER WORKS MENTIONED

Adorno, T., and M. Horkheimer. *Dialectic of Enlightenment.* Trans. John Cumming. London: Verso, 1986.

Arendt, H. *Essays in Understanding, 1930–1954.* Ed. Jerome Koh. New York: Harcourt, Brace, 1994.

———. *The Human Condition.* Garden City, N.Y.: Doubleday, 1959.

Armstrong, N. *Desire and Domestic Fiction: A Political History of the Novel.* New York: Oxford University Press, 1987.

Bakhtin, M. *Problems of Dostoevsky's Poetics.* Trans. Caryl Emerson, with an introduction by Wayne Booth. Minneapolis: University of Minnesota Press, 1984.

———. *Rabelais and His World.* Trans. Helene Iswolsky. Cambridge, Mass.: MIT Press, 1965.

Barthes, R. *A Lover's Discourse: Fragments.* Trans. Richard Howard. New York: Hill and Wang, 1978.

———. *Writing Degree Zero and Elements of Semiology.* Trans. Annette Lavers and Colin Smith. Boston: Beacon Press, 1970.

Baruch, E. H., and L. Serrano. *Women Analayze Women in France, England, and the United States.* New York: New York University Press, 1988.

Benveniste, E. *Problèmes de la linguistique générale.* 2 vols. Paris: Gallimard, 1974.

Blanchot, M. *The Gaze of Orpheus, and Other Literary Essays.* Trans. Lydia Davis. Ed. P. Adams Sitney, with a preface by Geoffrey Hartmann. Barrytown, N.Y.: Station Hill Press, 1981.

Calvet, J.-L. *Roland Barthes: A Biography.* Trans. Sarah Wykes. Bloomington: Indiana University Press, 1995.

Chodorow, N. *The Reproduction of Mothering: Psychoanalysis and the Sociology of Gender.* Berkeley and Los Angeles: University of California Press, 1978.

Critical Inquiry (issue entitled "The Politics of Interpretation"), vol. 9, no. 1 (September 1982).

Culler, J. *Structuralist Poetics: Structuralism, Linguistics, and the Study of Literature.* Ithaca: Cornell University Press, 1975.

Debord, G. *Comments on the Society of the Spectacle.* Trans. Malcolm Imrie. London: Verso, 1990.

Dinnerstein, D. *The Mermaid and the Minotaur: Sexual Arrangements and Human Malaise.* New York: Harper and Row, 1976.

Encyclopédie française. Ed. Henri Wallon. Vol. 8. Paris: Larousse, 1938.

Firestone, Shulamith. *The Dialectic of Sex: The Case for a Feminist Revolution.* New York: Quill, 1993.

Freud, S. *Standard Edition of the Complete Psychological Works of Sigmund Freud.* Ed. James Strachey. 24 vols. London: Hogarth Press, 1953–74.

Goldman, P. S., and P. T. Rakic. "Impact of the Outside World upon the Developing Primate Brain." *Bulletin of the Menninger Clinic,* special issue, 43, no. 1 (January 1979): 20–28.

Goldman-Rakic, P. S., et al. "The Neurobiology of Cognitive Development." In M. Haith and J. Campos, eds., *Infancy and Developmental Psychobiology,* pp. 281–344. Vol. 2 of *Handbook of Child Psychology.* New York: John Wiley and Sons, 1983.

Jakobson, R. *Selected Writings of Roman Jakobson.* The Hague: Mouton, 1985.

Marks, E., and I. de Courtivon, eds. *New French Feminisms.* New York: Schocken, 1981.

Mattelart, M. "Le Coup d'Etat au féminin." *Les Temps modernes* (January 1975).

Proust, M. *Remembrance of Things Past.* Trans. C. K. Scott Moncrieff and Terence Kilmartin. 3 vols. New York: Vintage, 1982.

Reiser, M. *Mind, Brain, Body: Toward a Convergence of Psychoanalysis and Neurobiology.* New York: Basic Books, 1984.

Scholem, G. *On Jews and Judaism in Crisis: Selected Essays.* Ed. W. J. Dannhauser. New York: Schocken, 1976.

Shalamov, V. *Graphite.* Trans. John Glad. New York: Norton, 1981.

Sichère, B. *Eloge du sujet: du retard de la pensée sur le corps.* Paris: Grasset, 1990.

Thom, R. *Modèles mathématiques de la morphogenèse. Receuil de textes sur la théorie des catastrophes et applications.* Paris: U.G.E., 1974.

Winnicott, D. A. "Transitional Objects and Transitional Phenomena." *International Journal of Psycho-Analysis* 34 (1953).

Zadeh, L. A. *Fuzzy Sets and Decision Analysis.* New York: Elsevier Science, 1984.

Psychosis: and the avant-garde, 16–17, 213, 231–232; existentialism and, 13

Religion, 11, 262–263; and contemporary life, 14–15; and dietary taboos, 90; in Eastern Europe, 223–224; and foreigners, 40–41; Judaism, 233; and psychoanalysis, 10–11; and sexual difference, 90; and the speaking subject, 96; anti-Semitism, 232–233
Reproduction, sexual: future of, 120–121, 126–128

Sartre, Jean-Paul, 13–15, 242–243; and depression, 196; *see also* Existentialism
Saussure, Ferdinand: contrasted with Freud, 22; critique of, 16
Semiotics: *see* Semiology
Semiotic and the symbolic, the, 20–23, 104–105, 185–186, 212–213, 268–269; the American academy and, 269; and Lacan, 22–23; in Nerval, 193; and universalism and difference, 268–269; and women, 66, 104–105, 109, 124
Semiology, 180–187; and the body, 182; and ethnography, 183–184; formal models in, 180–181; generalized theories in, 181, 185–186; history of, 180; and literary criticism, 182–183, 187; and neuroscience, 186; and non-Western practices, 182; personal experience with, 222
Shalamov, Varlam, 246
Socialism, 14; critique of, 45, 198; in France, 154–155; and the unconscious, 14; *see also* Marxism

Sollers, Philippe, 6–8
Soviet Union, former, 167–169
Spinoza, Baruch, 25
de Staël, Germaine (Mme), 90, 266–267
Stein, Gertrude, 67
Structuralism, 6, 14–15, 32, 50, 205–206; critique of, 19, 50, 205–206; and semiology, 180–181
Style, 55; personal writing, 33–34, 55–56, 205–206; poststructuralism and, 260
Subject-in-process, the, 26, 37–38, 190

Teaching, 38, 56–57; and the literary canon, 130–132
Tel Quel, 6–7

United States, 5, 44, 141–145, 160–161, 199–201, 263–265; art in, 143–144; and the avant-garde, 141–142; feminism in, 144–145, 160, 269; and French politics, 157–160, 264–265; Marxism in, 44–45, 116; political life in, 143–155, 155–156, 199–200; and the reception of French thought, 263; and women, 267–268; *see also* American academy

Weil, Simone, 252
Women, 45–46, 98, 104–112, 265–267, 270; and art, 109–110; and avant-garde practice, 98–99; and the body, 72; in Céline, 234; in China, 99–101; and contemporary upheavals, 72; and discourse, 209–210, 234; in the eighteenth century, 43, 210, 268; as foreigners, 45–47; French and American

Text: $^{11}/_{13.5}$ Adobe Garamond
Compositor: Columbia University Press
Printer: Edwards Brothers
Binder: Edwards Brothers